Best of the Best

QVC
Family
Cookbook

Favorite Family Recipes from
QVC Viewers, Guests and Friends

Best of the Best

QVC

Family
Cookbook

Favorite Family Recipes from
QVC Viewers, Guests, and Friends

EDITED BY
Gwen McKee
AND
Barbara Moseley

ILLUSTRATED BY Tupper England

QUAIL RIDGE PRESS
Preserving America's Food Heritage

ISBN-10: 1-893062-72-4
ISBN-13: 978-1-893062-72-6

Printed in Canada
Book design by Cynthia Clark • Cover photo by Greg Campbell
All other photos courtesy Gwen McKee and Barbara Moseley

First printing, July 2005 • Second, September 2005

Library of Congress Cataloging-in-Publication Data
Best of the best QVC family cookbook : favorite family recipes from QVC
    viewers, guests, and friends / edited by Gwen McKee and Barbara
    Moseley ; illustrated by Tupper England
        p. cm. —
    Includes index.
    ISBN 1-893062-72-4
        1. Cookery, American. I. McKee, Gwen. II. Moseley, Barbara.
    III. QVC (Firm)

TX715.B4856545 2005
641.5973—dc22   2005001588

On the cover: Garden Goodness Squash Sauté (p. 104),
Onion Ring Parmesan Chicken (p. 137)

QUAIL RIDGE PRESS
P. O. Box 123 • Brandon, MS 39043
e-mail: info@quailridge.com • www.quailridge.com

Table of Contents

Preface

*W*hat a privilege to hear from so many QVC viewers sending us their favorite recipes! Certainly from our perspective at Quail Ridge Press, we have learned that talking about food is a universal common language, and further, that sharing a favorite recipe with others is like being able to share one of your joys, so that they can enjoy it, too. And share they did!

Several years ago we invited QVC viewers to submit recipes to a special cookbook collection, *Best of the Best from QVC Cookbook.* It was such a resounding success that QVC and QRP—and popular demand from viewers wanting to share their favorite recipes—deemed it time to do it again. This time, we knew we wanted to make it the *QVC Family Cookbook,* because from hosts to guests to viewers, and lots of folks in between who work hard to bring the whole process and all the people together, QVC is one big, active, in-touch family. Viewers feel they are a part of the QVC family, and they are. And quite a few people in this family know how to cook!

What a tremendous response! We received thousands of recipes. It was quite an endeavor to select which ones would make the book, and then to choose from that list which recipes would be awarded prizes. Judging was a tasty, but formidable task. Our committee tested the recipes in their own homes, Barbara and I tested them in our home kitchens, and many were tested in our Quail Ridge Press kitchen. The contest committee voted on each recipe for taste, texture, originality, ease of cooking, how well the instructions and method worked, whether the ingredients were easy to find, and would you make it again. The fifty with the most stars (we used a five-star grading system) were awarded a QVC gift certificate. One of these was awarded the grand prize—an all-expense trip to QVC for two. We think that after trying any of these wonderful recipes, you will agree that every recipe in this book is a real winner. At our Quail Ridge Press lunch/judging sessions, there was a whole lot of yumming going on.

Besides excellent recipes, we have included on the chapter opening pages, photos of our families having fun together, plus some inside photos we have taken around QVC, sort of our viewpoint of what goes on behind the scenes. We wanted to give you additional information about Studio Park and some of the wonderful people who are instrumental in making all these live shows continuously come together. Since we included host recipes in the first book, this time we brought you some recipes from some of the guests you see often on QVC that we happen to know are pretty good cooks. In keeping with the family theme, we included "scrapbook entries" telling personal stories about good people having good times around good food.

There are so many people to thank for making this book happen. Stacey Parker was our buyer who started the ball rolling, and later Jonas Marusa, John Schrogie, Andrea Lanning, and Kenwal Verma all helped coordinate the effort. Darlene Daggett, who is now QVC's President of US Commerce, and who had the idea for the first contest cookbook, is a cookbook collector and avid cook herself. It was wonderful to get her support once again. Barbara Moseley, my co-editor and best friend, and I could not do all we do without the help of our wonderful staff at QRP: Terresa Ray, Sheila Simmons, Cyndi Clark, Annette Goode, Lisa Flynt, Holly Hardy, Karen Moseley, Leona Tennison, Trey Moseley, Dana Walker, and especially Melinda Burnham, who was so enthusiastic about testing and evaluating the recipes. Tupper England has once again sprinkled the text with her whimsical drawings. Beaucoups of thanks to you all.

But the ones who deserve the most thanks are all the people who sent in their recipes, whether they ended up being printed in this book or not . . . you are all winners. Thank you for sharing not only your recipes, but often your stories and family traditions that go along with them. Our motto at Quail Ridge Press is Preserving America's Food Heritage. These recipes are indeed doing just that.

Always my best,
Gwen McKee

Beverages and Appetizers

Anytime Low-Carb Coffee Chiller

½ cup cold strong coffee
1 ounce unsweetened chocolate
1–2 teaspoons artificial sweetener
  (to taste)

¾ cup low-carb ice cream
  (vanilla, chocolate, or coffee)
Whipped cream (optional)

In blender, place cold coffee, unsweetened chocolate, and artificial sweetener. Blend until chocolate is chopped into small pieces. Add ice cream; blend until smooth.

Top with whipped cream, if desired. Serve immediately. Makes one serving.

Tracy Gerber, Holtsville, NY

Easy Homemade Kahlúa

So good to have on hand. Great gift!

2 cups water
¼ cup instant coffee crystals
4 cups sugar

1 ounce vanilla
3⅓ cups vodka

Bring water to a boil. Add instant coffee and sugar. Boil and stir until dissolved. Cool completely. Add vanilla and vodka. Can be used immediately.

Melanie Pope, Trimont, MN

My mother made the best Kahlúa. She stored it in dark bottles and let it age awhile. She lovingly gave each bottle as a gift. Her Kahlúa was so treasured that people would not pour out the last drop until they got another bottle!

—Gwen

Banana Crush Punch

3 cups water
1½ cups sugar
2 cups orange juice
1 (46-ounce) can pineapple juice

⅓ cup lemon juice
3 ripe bananas
1½ (2-liter) bottles ginger ale

Mix water, sugar, and juices in a large bowl. Mash bananas in a small bowl, then put mashed bananas with a small amount of juice mixture in blender to liquefy. Mix banana and juice mixture with remaining juice mixture. Put punch mixture into 2 plastic containers and freeze completely.

Remove containers of punch from freezer 2–3 hours before serving. Remove frozen punch from containers and place into large bowl. Mash with potato masher to a crush consistency. Put crushed punch into punch bowl and add ginger ale. This punch should be slushy when served. Serves 35–50, depending on serving size.

Doris Flynn, Nashville, TN

Power Up Punch

Kids love this. We made it at vacation bible school and it was the hit of the week.

1 gallon orange sherbet
6 cups vanilla ice cream

3 large bottles lemon-lime soda

Evenly divide sherbet, ice cream, and soda between 2 large punch bowls. Be sure to put soda in last so that it will get really foamy. Let sit about 30 minutes to allow the sherbet and ice cream to melt.

Ilene Boman, Clinton Township, MI

Delicious Citrus Punch

1 (16-ounce) can frozen orange
  juice
2 (46-ounce) cans unsweetened
  pineapple juice
1 (12-ounce) can frozen
  lemonade
¼ cup lime juice

2½ cups sugar
8 cups water
4 (28-ounce) bottles ginger ale
2 (28-ounce) bottles carbonated
  water (seltzer)
Oranges and cherries for creating
  an ice ring

Mix all juices and sugar in a large pitcher. Fill an ice ring mold, then pour remainder into punch bowl; dilute with water, ginger ale, and seltzer. Add orange slices and cherries to the ice ring mold; freeze. Remove from mold; float in punch bowl.

Teresa Tieman, Dover, DE

Every year someone is assigned to make "the punch" for the McKee family Christmas party. It is made and frozen in milk cartons, then thawed the day before the party. The little kids love dipping and pouring their own punch with the ladle . . . something they consider a "cool" thing. They enjoy serving the grown-ups, too.

—Gwen

Summer Delight Fruit Dip

This looks so pretty on a large plate with cut-up fruit around the sides of the plate, and a smaller bowl in the center, filled with the dip. Delicious.

1 (8-ounce) bar cream cheese, softened
¼ teaspoon ginger
½ cup powdered sugar
2 tablespoons frozen orange juice concentrate
2 tablespoons grated orange zest

1 (13-ounce) jar marshmallow crème
Summer fruit (watermelon, cantaloupe, strawberries, grapes, honey dew melon, pineapple, bananas)

Blend cream cheese in blender until soft; add ginger and powdered sugar; blend. Blend in orange juice and orange zest. Add marshmallow crème last, and blend very well. Serve with fruits of choice.

June Houghton, Spanish Fork, UT

Kahlúa Fruit Dip

A wonderful and easy dip.

1 (8-ounce) package cream cheese, softened
1 (8-ounce) carton sour cream
¾ cup brown sugar
¼ cup Kahlúa

1 (8-ounce) container whipped topping, thawed
3 ounces chopped salted peanuts
Strawberries, kiwis, bananas, melons, etc.

Combine cream cheese, sour cream, brown sugar, and Kahlúa. Mix until fluffy. Fold in whipped topping and nuts. Refrigerate overnight. Serve with sliced fruit.

Julie Hamric, Mount Airy, MD

Editor's Extra: It's hard to get enough fruit in our diets, and my family is not prone to pick up a piece of fruit and eat it whole. But if I peel it and cut it, then offer it with a yummy dip, they love it! Me, too!

Crunchy Apple Dip

2 (8-ounce) packages cream
  cheese, softened
1¼ cups brown sugar
½ cup granulated sugar
2 teaspoons vanilla
1 (12-ounce) can pineapple juice

4–6 Granny Smith apples,
  washed and sliced, peel them if
  you like
1 (8-ounce) package toffee bits,
  crushed

In a mixing bowl, thoroughly mix cream cheese, brown sugar, granulated sugar, and vanilla. Cover and refrigerate. In a bowl, cover apple slices with pineapple juice and place in refrigerator overnight.

   When ready to serve, blend toffee bits into cream cheese mixture with mixer. Take apples out of juice and serve with dip.

Billie Burns, Union Grove, AL

Dilly Tuna Dip

The longer it sits, the dillier it gets.

1 (5-ounce) package sweet and
  spicy tuna (vacuum-packed)
½ cup mayonnaise
½ cup sour cream
¼ cup horseradish sauce

Squirt of hot sauce
Squirt of lemon juice
2–3 teaspoons dill weed
Chopped onion to taste

Combine all ingredients and chill. Serve with crackers, celery sticks, or cucumber rounds.

Christy Campbell, Brandon, MS

Last Minute Shrimp Dip

2 (8-ounce) packages cream
  cheese, softened
1 cup sour cream
2 envelopes dry Italian dressing
  mix

2 (4-ounce) cans tiny shrimp,
  drained and rinsed
1 teaspoon lemon juice

With electric mixer on medium speed, blend softened cream cheese and sour cream. Add Italian dressing mix and blend thoroughly. Fold in shrimp with large wooden spoon (rather than mixer) to avoid breaking up shrimp. Add lemon juice and chill. Serve with chips, crackers, or fresh-cut celery.

Karen Ford, Eagle, ID

Shrimp Dip Supreme

1 (8-ounce) package cream
  cheese, softened
1 (7-ounce) can medium shrimp,
  chopped
1/2 cup finely chopped green
  olives
3–4 green onions, chopped
1 1/2 tablespoons dill pickle
  relish, or 2 dill pickles, grated

3 slices jalapeño, chopped
2 tablespoons good quality
  mayonnaise
1/4 teaspoon garlic powder
1/4 teaspoon cracked black
  pepper
1/4 teaspoon creole seasoning

Blend all ingredients together. Refrigerate for flavors to blend. Serve with crackers or make tea sandwiches.

Note: If using for tea sandwiches, you may need more mayonnaise.

Paula Fondren, Clinton, MS

Confetti Crab Dip

2 (8-ounce) packages cream
  cheese
3/4 pound fresh crabmeat, flaked
  and drained
1/4 cup minced green onions
3 tablespoons mayonnaise
2 tablespoons sour cream
1/4 teaspoon salt

1/4 teaspoon dry mustard
1/8 teaspoon garlic powder
1/8 teaspoon sweet red pepper
  flakes
1 (2-ounce) jar diced pimento
1 tablespoon Sauterne wine
1 tablespoon chopped fresh
  chives

Place cream cheese in a 1-quart casserole. Microwave uncovered on HIGH for 1–1 1/2 minutes, until softened. Stir well. Stir in crab-meat, green onions, mayonnaise, sour cream, and seasonings. Cover with heavy-duty plastic wrap and microwave on HIGH for 2–3 minutes or until thoroughly heated. Stir after one minute. Stir in pimento and wine. Sprinkle with chopped chives. Serve warm dip with assorted crackers. Yields 3 1/2 cups.

Alberta Lee Kaiser, New Port Richey, FL

Disappearing Crab Dip

This will quickly disappear!

2 (8-ounce) packages cream
  cheese, softened
1 tablespoon lemon juice
1 tablespoon grated sweet onion
2 tablespoons Worcestershire

2 tablespoons mayonnaise
1 (16- to 20-ounce) jar cocktail
  sauce
2 or 3 (8-ounce) cans crabmeat,
  or 1–1 1/2 pounds fresh

Mix softened cream cheese, lemon juice, grated onion, Worcestershire, and mayonnaise. Mix well and spread evenly over platter. Then place crabmeat (I always check well for any missed shells) over entire top. Serve with any type of crackers or chips to your liking.

Debbie Robertson, Coffeyville, KS

RoRo's Reuben Dip

1 (8-ounce) package cream
  cheese, softened
1 cup sour cream
1 cup thick and chunky salsa
8 ounces finely chopped corn
  beef

1 cup shredded Swiss cheese
$\frac{1}{2}$ cup sauerkraut, rinsed,
  drained, and chopped
2 cloves garlic, minced
Salt and pepper to taste

Combine cream cheese, sour cream, and salsa in a bowl. Beat with hand mixer on low speed until well blended. Add remaining ingredients and mix well. Place in a baking dish and bake for 20–30 minutes at 350°. Great with chips, crackers, or rye bread crisps.

James Lamb, Jackson, MS

When I was little, I couldn't pronounce my sister Rosemary's name, so I called her "RoRo." The name stuck and soon the entire neighborhood was calling her RoRo. To this day, friends my age think that is her real name. This is my version of her recipe. (It's another thing I changed without her permission.) You won't believe how delicious this is . . . it's a WOW!

—James Lamb

No-Wing Chicken Wing Dip

Easier to eat, and lots more meat!

**4 chicken breast halves, boiled
    and shredded**
⅓–½ jar chicken wing sauce
**2 cups shredded mozzarella
    cheese, divided**

**1 (8-ounce) package cream
    cheese, softened**
1 cup blue cheese dressing

Heat chicken and wing sauce; add ½ cup mozzarella cheese.
Spread cream cheese in 9x13-inch baking dish. Spread chicken
mixture over cream cheese. Spread blue cheese dressing over
chicken mixture. Sprinkle with remaining mozzarella cheese.
Bake at 375° for 20 minutes.

Serve with tortilla chips or celery sticks for dipping.

Rosanne Baxter, Rochester, NY

Oh! So Good Chicken Spread

**1 (8-ounce) package cream
    cheese, softened**
½ cup sour cream
1 teaspoon dried minced onion
½ teaspoon onion salt

½ teaspoon Worcestershire
¼ teaspoon cayenne pepper
**2 (10-ounce) cans chunk white
    chicken, drained**

In a mixing bowl, combine first 6 ingredients. Fold in chicken.
Cover and refrigerate for at least 1 hour. Serve with crackers, raw
vegetables, or on party bread rounds. Makes about 3 cups.

Ruthann Dulovich, Monongahela, PA

Editor's Extra: It takes two minutes to put frozen chicken and a little
seasoning in a crockpot before you go to bed. Next morning, have ready
a container for the chicken, and tin foil to wrap the bones and skin for
discarding. This will take maybe 10 minutes. Now you have delicious,
fresh-cooked chicken to make all kinds of wonderful dishes.

Mexican Fiesta Dip

This is so easy and people love it!

1 (16-ounce) container sour cream
1 (16-ounce) container cottage cheese
1 package taco seasoning mix

8 ounces Cheddar cheese, shredded
1 bunch green onions, chopped
1 tomato, chopped

Mix sour cream, cottage cheese, and taco seasoning together in bowl. Spread on serving plate or shallow dish. Sprinkle with Cheddar cheese. Sprinkle green onions over cheese layer, then sprinkle tomatoes over top. Serve with corn tortilla snack chips. Enjoy!

Lisa Lemieur, Greensboro, NC

Best Ever Taco Dip

This dip is always a favorite, and everyone asks me for the recipe!

LAYER ONE:
1 cup sour cream
1 (8 ounce) package cream cheese, softened

1 can bean dip (located in the chip aisle)

Mix and spread in bottom of 9x13-inch baking pan.

LAYER TWO:
1 pound ground beef
1 package taco seasoning

1 tablespoon dark steak sauce

Cook beef and taco seasoning like you would to make tacos. When done, add steak sauce; stir and spread over Layer One.

LAYER THREE:
3 green onions, sliced
Shredded Cheddar

Chopped tomatoes (optional)

Sprinkle onions and cheese on top of Layer Two. Microwave or bake till hot and cheese melts. Doesn't take long. Garnish with chopped tomatoes, if desired. Serve with your favorite tortilla chips.

Kimberly Dodge, Kansasville, WI

Baked Super Nacho Dip

1 (4-ounce) can chopped green
  chiles, drained
1 (8-ounce) tub soft cream
  cheese, regular or light
1 pound ground beef
½ cup tomato sauce
¼ cup water
½–1 package taco seasoning
  to taste
1 (4-ounce) can sliced black
  olives, drained
2 cups shredded cheese
  (Mexican blend or colby Jack)
Sour cream, at room temperature
1 small tomato, diced
2 tablespoons chopped green
  onions

Drain green chiles and mix with cream cheese; spread in a 9x9-inch (2-quart) glass baking dish. In skillet, brown, drain, and crumble ground beef. Add tomato sauce, water, and taco seasoning. Cook thoroughly until mixture is thick. Spread hamburger mixture on top of cream cheese layer in baking dish. Next, layer olives and cheese. Bake in 325° oven, uncovered, for 20 minutes, or until cheese is bubbly. Garnish the top center with a large dollop of sour cream, diced tomato, and green onions. Serve with tortilla chips.

Charlene Olson, Minot, ND

Enchilada Dip

1½ pounds ground beef
1 onion, diced
2 (10-ounce) cans enchilada
  sauce
1 (10¾-ounce) can cream of
  chicken soup
2 (15-ounce) cans kidney
  beans, drained
1 bag tortilla chips, divided
2 cups shredded Cheddar cheese

Brown beef and onion in skillet. Drain. Add enchilada sauce, cream of chicken soup, and kidney beans; mix.

Lightly grease a 9x13-inch baking dish. Cover bottom with some crushed tortilla chips. Add beef mixture and top with shredded Cheddar. Bake at 400° for 30 minutes or until cheese bubbles. Serve with remaining tortilla chips.

Theresa Granthum, Liverpool, NY

Prairie Fire Dip

1¼ pounds ground beef sirloin
2 teaspoons minced garlic
1 (10-ounce) can diced tomatoes
  with green chiles

1 (15-ounce) can chili with beans
1 (16-ounce) loaf processed
  cheese, cut up

Preheat oven to 350°. Brown ground sirloin in pan with minced garlic. Drain grease. Add diced tomatoes and chili with beans. Stir in cheese and continue stirring until all cheese is melted. Pour into a casserole dish and place in preheated oven, uncovered; cook for 50–60 minutes. Serve with nacho chips for dipping.

Note: For a spicier dip, use hot chili and beans and Mexican processed cheese loaf.

Cheryl Kitterman, Fort Lauderdale, FL

Hot Texas Dip

DIP:
1 pound lean ground beef
1 large onion, chopped
2 cloves garlic, crushed
1 cup hot or spicy ketchup
2 tablespoons chili powder

2 (15-ounce) cans kidney beans
  (1 can puréed with juice, 1 can
  drained and coarsely smashed)
Salt and pepper to taste

Brown ground beef in large skillet; add onion and continue to cook until onion is tender. Add remaining Dip ingredients and simmer about 10 minutes, until good and bubbly. Put into a chafing dish.

TOPPING:
1 large onion, chopped
1 (4-ounce) can chopped ripe
  olives

2 cups grated sharp Cheddar
  cheese

Mix onion, olives, and cheese, and sprinkle over Dip ingredients. Cover chafing dish until cheese has melted. Serve with freshly made corn tortilla chips or favorite packaged tortilla chips. Enjoy!

Sally Marsh, Fremont, CA

Quick and Easy Party Salsa

This is a very quick and easy recipe for salsa. You can prepare it for a party dip, use it in tacos, serve it over grilled chicken, and—for those low-carb lovers—eat it with celery sticks.

1 white onion	2 tablespoons garlic powder
2 jalapeño peppers	2 teaspoons salt
8 Roma tomatoes	1 lime, juiced
1 bunch fresh cilantro	Tortilla chips
2 tablespoons white vinegar	

Peel white onion and cut in half. Cut stems off jalapeño peppers, then cut them in half. For a mild salsa, de-seed the peppers; otherwise include the seeds. Place items in food processor and chop. Cut tops off tomatoes, then cut tomatoes in half. Place tomato halves in food processor with previous mixture. Cut stems off cilantro and add to food processor. Blend until salsa is at the consistency you like.

Place salsa in a large bowl and mix in the following: white vinegar, garlic powder, salt, and lime juice. Serve with tortilla chips.

Note: You can cut up the vegetables by hand, but using a food processor makes it much quicker!

Lisa Marcotte, Yuba City, CA

Editor's Extra: I use an old-fashioned, metal vegetable peeler to easily remove the seeds from jalapeños. Just cut them in half lengthwise, and use the pointed end of the peeler to remove the seeds.

Sometimes when I have prepared a dish to take somewhere, I realize way down the road that I have forgotten it in the refrigerator! So when I put the dish in, I put my car keys on top of it! Works every time.

—Gwen

Fabulous Bean and Pea Salsa

1 (15-ounce) can black-eyed peas
1 (15-ounce) can black beans
1 (11-ounce) can shoe peg corn
1 (7-ounce) can green chiles
1 (14-ounce) can Mexican
  tomatoes with lime and
  cilantro

1 (8-ounce) bottle Italian
  dressing (your favorite)
1 tomato, chopped
1 cup chopped red onion
Salt, pepper, and garlic to taste

Drain peas, beans, and corn. Mix all ingredients together in medium bowl with lid; let marinate in refrigerator for an hour. Serve with big scoop corn chips.

Marietta Shigekawa, Santa Ana, CA

Creamy Artichoke Spread

12 ounces cream cheese, softened
1 cup mayonnaise
3–5 large cloves garlic, minced
2 green onions, minced
$\frac{1}{2}$ teaspoon garlic salt
$\frac{1}{8}$ teaspoon dill weed
1 (14-ounce) can water-packed
  artichoke hearts, drained and
  chopped

1 cup grated Monterey Jack
  cheese
$\frac{1}{2}$ cup grated Swiss cheese
Assorted crackers or tortilla
  chips

Mix together cream cheese, mayonnaise, garlic, green onions, and spices till smooth. Add artichoke hearts and grated cheeses and mix well. Chill. Serve with assorted crackers. Also good with tortilla chips.

Note: Use only fresh garlic; four cloves give a good bite!

Debbie Pettee, Grass Valley, CA

Editor's Extra: For a smoother consistency, mix all except grated cheeses in food processor, then add cheeses.

Chick Dip

. . . a blender breeze.

1 large clove garlic, sliced
1 can chickpeas, drained,
   reserve juice
$^1/_4$ cup lemon juice

$^1/_4$ cup vegetable oil
1 tablespoon tahini paste
$^1/_2$ teaspoon salt, or to taste

Place all ingredients in a blender, placing the garlic at the bottom. Blend until all ingredients are mixed and consistency is smooth. If mixture is too thick, add a bit of the reserved juice from the chickpeas. Serve with pita bread wedges and/or sliced vegetables.

Note: If you want to use this as a salad dressing, thin with reserved juice from chickpeas and/or water.

Paula Wobby, Sterling, VA

Pecan Crusted Spinach Dip

1 (16-ounce) bag frozen spinach
2 (8-ounce) packages cream
   cheese, softened
$^1/_2$ cup mayonnaise
1 (10$^3/_4$-ounce) can cream of
   mushroom soup
1 cup grated fresh Parmesan
   cheese

1 (14-ounce) jar artichokes,
   drained and chopped
$^1/_3$ cup chopped onion
1$^1/_2$ cups herb stuffing, crushed
$^1/_2$ cup chopped pecans
White corn chips

Preheat oven to 400°. Thaw spinach and squeeze thoroughly dry. Combine cream cheese, mayonnaise, and soup. Stir in spinach, Parmesan cheese, artichokes, and onion. Place in greased 2-quart oblong baking dish. Combine stuffing and pecans and sprinkle over top. Bake 20–25 minutes until hot and lightly browned on top. Serve with white corn chips.

Susan L. Anderson, Fort Madison, IA

Classically Delicious Broccoli Dip

1 stick butter	1 (10¾-ounce) can cream of
1 small onion, finely chopped	mushroom soup
2 cloves garlic, finely chopped	3 cups shredded Cheddar cheese
1½ cups finely chopped	2 crowns broccoli florets,
mushrooms	steamed, chopped

In a medium saucepan over low heat, melt butter. Sauté onion, garlic, and mushrooms in butter until tender. Add soup and cheese. Stir constantly until cheese is melted. Add broccoli florets; stir and mix well. Serve hot with chips (scoopable corn chips are best).

Christina Mendoza, Ann Arbor, MI

QVC's entrance foyer welcomes you with huge photographs of their broadcast expansions around the world.

Hot Onion Soufflé Dip

12–16 ounces chopped onions
  (2 medium)
3 (8-ounce) packages cream
  cheese, softened

2 cups grated fresh Parmesan
  cheese
½ cup mayonnaise

Combine all ingredients; place in baking dish or soufflé pan. Bake in preheated 425° oven 10–15 minutes until heated thoroughly. Serve with large corn chips.

Note: This makes a lot, so you may want to halve or third it to serve fewer guests.

Sherry Naron, Memphis, TN

Greek Theatre Dip

¾ pound butter, softened
1 (8-ounce) package cream
  cheese, softened
1 clove garlic, smashed or
  chopped
1 (4-ounce) package feta cheese

1 teaspoon dried oregano
10 Roma tomatoes
1 bunch green onions
2 tablespoons chopped or
  sliced black olives

In a food processor, combine butter, cream cheese, garlic, feta cheese, and oregano. Process until smooth. Spread in a pie pan or quiche dish.

Chop Roma tomatoes in ¼-inch dice. Spread in 2-inch wide circle around rimmed edge of dish. Chop green onions and spread inside tomato ring, leaving small circle open in center. Fill center circle with black olives. Serve with pita bread triangles or assorted crackers. Can make ahead and refrigerate.

Donna Kasle, Shaker Heights, OH

Best Ever Garlic Cheese Spread

1 (8-ounce) package cream
  cheese
4 ounces grated sharp Cheddar
  cheese

²/₃ cup evaporated milk
1 clove garlic, chopped fine,
  or ¹/₂ teaspoon garlic powder

Allow both cheeses to soften to room temperature. Blend all ingredients with mixer or food processor until smooth. Serve with warm French bread. Also excellent as a dip for chips.

Note: Grating your own cheese makes for a smoother spread.

Terri Varnell, Brooklet, GA

Cheese in a Bread Bowl

1 (3- to 5-pound) round
  pumpernickel rye bread
1¹/₂ pounds sharp Cheddar
  cheese, grated
¹/₄ pound crumbled blue cheese
1 teaspoon dry mustard

2 tablespoons soft butter
1 teaspoon Worcestershire
2 tablespoons grated onion or
  chives
1 (12-ounce) can beer
Paprika and parsley for garnish

Hollow out bread, reserving as much a possible to serve with the dip. Put all ingredients, except beer, in a bowl to soften, about 30 minutes. Add beer slowly and beat until smooth and fluffy. Fill bread bowl with cheese mixture. Garnish with paprika and parsley and refrigerate. Serve on a big bread board with reserved rye or party rye bread.

Debbie Dean, Cross Lanes, WV

Brie Cheese Appetizer

This recipe is so easy and so good, it will become an entertaining favorite.

¼ cup (or more) chopped
  fresh basil
2 large cloves garlic, chopped
2 tablespoons chopped parsley
1 small jar sun-dried tomatoes
  in oil (reserve oil, chop
  tomatoes)

¼ cup chopped toasted
  pine nuts
¼ cup grated Parmesan cheese
2 tablespoons olive oil
1–1½ pounds Brie cheese,
  brought to room temperature

Mix first 6 ingredients together. Moisten with reserved tomato oil and olive oil, a little of each at a time, until mixture is of spreading consistency. Remove top rind from cheese. Spread mixture over Brie cheese, patting it as necessary to adhere to cheese. Serve with crackers, bread, or toast points.

Note: Can be made a day ahead and chilled until ready to use. Bring back to room temperature to serve.

Beverly Porter, Albuquerque, NM

Cheese Wheel Basket

So simple . . . so impressive.

1 (8-count) can crescent rolls

1 wheel Edam or Gouda cheese,
  peeled

Spread crescent roll dough out on wax paper and "seal" all the seams using fingers dipped in water. Place cheese wheel in the center and wrap dough around it evenly. Bake at 350° for 30 minutes or until brown all over (the cheese needs time to soften and partially melt inside).

Kathy Harrison, Franklin, TN

Bacon Cheese Ball

Deli cheese balls can be costly . . . this one just tastes rich.

**2 (8-ounce) packages cream
  cheese, softened**
**½ cup salad-dressing-type
  mayonnaise**

⅓ cup Parmesan cheese
**10 slices bacon, cooked and
  crumbled**
¼ cup sliced green onions

Mix all ingredients together, then form into a ball and refrigerate.
Serve with crackers of your choice.

Debbie Dean, Cross Lanes, WV

Cheddar Cheese Fingers

So good, so quick, and so easy—you'll make them again and again!

**1 (8-ounce) package grated
  Cheddar cheese**
**6 slices bacon, fried crisp,
  crumbled**
**1 (4-ounce) package slivered
  almonds**

1 small onion, chopped
1 cup mayonnaise
**1 loaf thin-sliced bread, crusts
  removed**

Mix all ingredients, except bread. Spread onto bread slices. Cut
each slice into 3 strips and freeze on cookie sheet. Remove frozen
from sheet and store in plastic freezer bags, in freezer, until needed. To prepare, bake in 400° oven for 10 minutes. A delicious
appetizer in a pinch.

Mary Ellen Ignatius, Jacksonville, FL

Editor's Extra: Easy to use packaged, fully-cooked bacon slices and
throw everything in food processor. Yum!

What Am I? Chopped Liver?

This is a wonderful vegetarian pâté that everybody loves. Delicious!

1/2–3/4 pound fresh green beans
  (will not work with frozen . . .
  too watery)
4 medium to large onions, peeled
2–3 tablespoons vegetable oil

3/4 cup walnuts
2 hard-boiled eggs, peeled and
  chopped
Salt and pepper to taste

Trim and steam green beans till cooked. Slice onions and sauté in oil till dark brown. Grind walnuts in food processor till fine, but not a paste. Add remaining ingredients and process till of appropriate consistency. It will seem loose, but will solidify in the refrigerator.

Helen Kasman, New York, NY

Editor's Extra: Barbara was so sure she wouldn't like this . . . till she tasted the first bite. It's a winner.

Buttery Asparagus Roll-Ups

1 loaf white bread
1 (8-ounce) package cream
  cheese, softened
3 ounces crumbled blue cheese

1 egg
1 bunch fresh asparagus
1 stick butter

Cut crust off 25 slices of white bread. Flatten bread with rolling pin. Mix cream cheese, blue cheese, and egg until smooth, and spread on bread. Place an asparagus spear on one end of each slice of flattened bread and roll tightly. Melt butter; dip rolled asparagus into melted butter, and place on a cookie sheet. Freeze for 1 hour (can be frozen up to 6 months). Rolls can be cut in half for petite appetizers. Bake in preheated 350° oven for 20 minutes.

Marie Umbriac, Hometown, PA

Wow Deviled Eggs

1 dozen large eggs
3 heaping tablespoons creamy
   horseradish sauce
3 heaping tablespoons
   mayonnaise
Dash salt

Dash white pepper
1 small shallot, chopped fine
Dash garlic powder
Chopped pimento, bacon bits, or
   chopped dill for garnish

Hard-boil eggs; cut in half lengthwise. Separate yolks and whites. Mash yolks. Add equal amounts of horseradish sauce and mayonnaise into yolks. (You want a firm consistency.) Add salt, white pepper, chopped shallot, and garlic powder; mix well. Refill egg whites with yolk mixture. Sprinkle chopped pimento on top of each egg.

Joni Sliwoski, Honolulu, HI

The Best Cocktail Kielbasa

1 cup ketchup
1–2 tablespoons horseradish

1 pound Polish kielbasa
Clear carbonated soda

Prepare cocktail sauce by mixing ketchup and horseradish; chill. Peel film from kielbasa; cut into ¼-inch diagonal slices. In a single layer, place kielbasa into frying pan and pour soda over just enough to cover. Bring to a simmer. As soda begins to evaporate, lower heat, and continuously turn kielbasa to prevent burning. Cook until liquid is gone and kielbasa is candied and browned. Serve with cocktail sauce.

Jennifer Eby, Dillsburg, PA

Buttermilk Sausage Balls

The secret is in the buttermilk—it makes it so moist!

2½ cups all-purpose baking
  mix
4–5 ounces sharp New York
  cheese, grated

1 pound hot sausage,
  room temperature
¼ cup buttermilk

Mix baking mix and cheese together. Add sausage and buttermilk and mix well. Roll into small balls and bake at 425° for 10–12 minutes.

Becki Richardson, Auburn, AL

Editor's Extra: Freeze balls on a baking sheet, then put into freezer bag. Bake at 400° for 12–15 minutes.

Crab Wontons

1 pound imitation crab,
  flake-style
1 (8-ounce) package cream
  cheese, softened

Salt and pepper to taste
1 (12-ounce) package wonton
  wrappers

Coarsely chop crab. Mix with cream cheese; season with salt and pepper. Put approximately 1 tablespoon of crab mixture into center of each wonton wrapper. Fold over to form a triangle; seal edges with water. Deep-fry in hot oil until crisp and light golden brown. Makes approximately 40 wontons.

Note: May be frozen before frying.

Michele Ortiguerra, Oxnard, CA

Crowd Pleasing Crabmeat Appetizer

2 sticks butter
2 (8-ounce) packages cream
  cheese
2 (7½-ounce) cans crabmeat

Party rolls in package
  (small size)
Paprika

Melt butter and cream cheese together over medium heat. Add crabmeat; mix well. Spoon on party rolls that are split in half. Sprinkle with paprika and bake in 350° oven until bubbly. Break apart and serve. May add additional seasoning, if desired.

Karen Haywood, San Mateo, CA

Editor's Extra: Fun to add different seasonings, if desired.

Alaskan Salmon Pinwheels

1 (15-ounce) can salmon, or
  2 cups cooked/flaked
1 (8-ounce) package cream
  cheese, softened
4 tablespoons salsa or picante
  sauce

2 tablespoons chopped parsley
1 teaspoon dried cilantro
1/4 teaspoon ground cumin
  (optional)
Flour tortillas

Drain salmon (smoked or regular) and remove any bones or skin. In a small bowl, combine salmon, cream cheese, salsa, parsley, cilantro, and cumin, if desired. Spread 4–5 tablespoons of the mixture (or as much as you want) over each tortilla. Roll each tortilla up tightly and wrap individually with plastic wrap (or you can put on a plate and cover). Refrigerate 2–3 hours. Slice each rolled tortilla into bite-size pieces, about 1 inch. Serve.

Barbara Sherman, Cordova, AK

Spicy Shrimp Appetizer

1/2 cup margarine
2 tablespoons Dijon mustard
1 teaspoon chili powder
3 cloves garlic, crushed
1 teaspoon black pepper
1/2 teaspoon pepper sauce
2 tablespoons hot sauce

2 tablespoons seafood seasoning
1/4 teaspoon basil
1/4 teaspoon thyme
1/4 teaspoon oregano
1 1/2–2 pounds large shrimp,
  peeled and deveined

Put everything except shrimp into a saucepan and simmer 5–7 minutes. Pour over shrimp in deep-dish pie plate, and broil till shrimp are pink and curled, about 7 minutes.

Laura Keating, Chalfont, PA

Mrs. Cavuoti's Mushrooms

These are unbelievably delicious!

12 large mushroom caps
  (save stems)
2 cups Italian bread crumbs
2 cloves garlic, minced

$^2/_3$ cup olive oil, divided
Juice of 2 lemons, divided
$^1/_2$ cup grated Parmigiano

Finely chop mushroom stems. In a bowl, mix stems, bread crumbs, and garlic. Gradually add about $^1/_2$ cup olive oil until mixture sticks together and is moist. Squeeze in juice of one lemon. Stuff caps with mixture. Sprinkle with grated Parmigiano.

  Bake at 350° until crumbs are golden, about 30 minutes. Drizzle remaining olive oil on mushrooms about halfway into baking to prevent mushrooms from drying out. Squeeze remaining lemon juice over caps before serving.

Tab Morgan, Carrollton, TX

East-West Snackers

$^1/_3$ cup canola oil, divided
40 wonton wrappers
1 (15-ounce) can chili, no beans
1 (10-ounce) can tomatoes
  and green chiles, well drained

1 cup finely shredded colby
  Jack cheese
1 cup chow mein noodles

Preheat oven to 350°. Lightly oil mini-muffin pans. Place a wonton wrapper in each cup. Lightly brush oil on each wrapper. Bake 5 minutes. Mix chili with tomatoes and green chiles. Place a teaspoon of the filling in each wrapper. Sprinkle cheese on top, dividing evenly among tarts. Bake 8–10 minutes or until cheese is melted. Remove from oven and from pans. Sprinkle chow mein noodles on top of each tart. Makes 40 appetizers.

Patricia Harmon, Baden, PA

Editor's Extra: Wonton wrappers add fun shapes and new life to old flavor combinations.

Scott's Duck D'Oeuvres

This is fabulous! Even those who say they don't like duck, love this recipe.

5 deboned duck breasts
1 pound sliced bacon
1 onion, rough chopped

1 (3-ounce) package cream
cheese
1 small jar sliced jalapeños

Cut duck breasts into bite-size pieces (about 8–10 per breast). Cut entire package of bacon into thirds. Assemble as follows: piece of duck breast, dab of cream cheese, piece of onion, slice of jalapeño (or $1/2$ slice, according to taste); wrap in slice of bacon, then skewer with toothpick. Grill on medium heat until bacon just begins to crisp. Remove and brush with Harry's Miracle Finishing Sauce.

HARRY'S MIRACLE FINISHING SAUCE:
1 stick butter
$1/2$ cup lemon juice
$1/2$ cup Worcestershire
$1/4$ cup soy sauce
$1/4$ cup steak sauce

2 chicken bouillon cubes
1 teaspoon black pepper
$1/4$ teaspoon garlic salt
3–4 tablespoons brown sugar

Mix all ingredients together in saucepan over medium heat and stir until melted. Will keep in refrigerator for up to 2 months, but you will use it up before then. This sauce is delicious brushed on all grilled meats: steak, burgers, pork chops, chicken, duck, dove, etc.

Scott Anderton, Collierville, TN

Bread
and Breakfast

No-Knead-to-Rise Beer Bread

2 cups self-rising flour
3 tablespoons sugar

1 (12- to 14-ounce) can beer
1 stick butter, melted

Combine flour, sugar, and beer in mixing bowl with a spoon. Mix for about 2 minutes. Pour into greased loaf pan and bake at 350° for 30 minutes. Remove from oven and pour melted butter over bread; return to oven and cook for 30 additional minutes.

Rosemary Morrow, Raymond, MS

The Simplest and Best Spoon Bread

Great with barbecued ribs or ham.

1 stick butter or margarine
2 eggs, beaten
1 cup sour cream

1 (8½-ounce) box corn muffin
mix
1 cup milk

Melt butter or margarine in microwave in medium-size bowl. Add beaten eggs and remaining ingredients. Mix well. Pour into greased 8x11-inch casserole dish. Bake at 350° for 45 minutes or until golden brown. Cut into squares and serve hot. No need to butter—it's already in there.

Nicole Segneri, Atlanta, GA

People-Pleasing Polenta Cakes

6 strips bacon
1½ cups boiling water
2 tablespoons corn syrup
⅔ cup cornmeal

1 egg, well beaten
½ cup flour
1 teaspoon salt
1 teaspoon baking powder

Cook bacon till crisp. Reserve drippings. Place water and corn syrup in saucepan. Whisk in cornmeal and cook till thick as mush. Cool. Add crumbled bacon and egg, then flour, salt, and baking powder, sifted together. This will be thick. Form into patties or sausage shapes. Roll in flour and cook till brown in reserved bacon drippings. Drain and serve with maple syrup.

Jane F. Clapp, Berwick, ME

Mexican Corn Cake Casserole

Great with soup or a crockpot meal, or all by itself!

1 cup yellow cornmeal
1 teaspoon baking powder
½ teaspoon salt
¼ cup sugar
4–5 whole California mild
  green chiles, canned
8 ounces cottage cheese

8 ounces sour cream
1 (16-ounce) can creamed corn
1 (16-ounce) can whole-kernel
  corn, drained
½ cup oil
2 eggs, beaten
1 cup shredded Jack cheese

Preheat oven to 400°. Spray or grease a 9x13-inch pan. Set aside. Mix dry ingredients together and set aside. Slice chiles into large-dice pieces. Mix wet ingredients together. Add dry ingredients to wet ingredients. Stir in cheese and chiles. Pour mixture into pan. Bake at 400° for 25 minutes, then reduce heat to 350° for 20 minutes or until top is golden brown. Can be served hot or at room temperature. Freezes well, too.

Gloria Orr, San Diego, CA

Cheesy Garlic Bread

4 tablespoons margarine,
  softened
2 tablespoons mayonnaise
1 teaspoon garlic salt
$\frac{1}{2}$ cup shredded mozzarella
  cheese

$\frac{1}{2}$ cup shredded Cheddar
  cheese
$\frac{1}{4}$ cup shredded Monterey Jack
  cheese
$\frac{1}{4}$ cup grated Parmesan cheese
1 loaf French bread

Mix all ingredients, except bread. Slice French bread loaf down the middle; spread cheese mixture onto bread, and leave open-face. Bake in 375° oven until golden brown, about 14 minutes.

Jan McAlvey, Chelan, WA

Debberino's Bisclets

2 sticks butter, softened
2 cups self-rising flour
1 cup sour cream

1 cup grated Cheddar cheese
1 teaspoon garlic powder
  (optional)

Mix butter and flour; stir in sour cream and Cheddar cheese. Spoon into ungreased tiny muffin tins. Bake in 450° degree oven 8–10 minutes.

Debbie Wedgeworth, Pass Christian, MS

Libba's Comfort Food

1 clove garlic, cut
4 slices French bread
2–3 tablespoons butter, softened
1 (14½-ounce) can Italian
   stewed tomatoes
½ teaspoon minced garlic

Pinch baking soda
½ teaspoon sugar
2 tablespoons Italian bread
   crumbs
3 tablespoons Parmesan

Rub cut side of garlic over bread, then butter each bread slice. Put on baking sheet and bake in 250° oven 45 minutes or till dry.

   While bread is baking, bring tomatoes, garlic, baking soda, and sugar to a boil, then let them stew (simmer over low heat for a long time) in a covered pot till bread is ready. Put bread in sprayed casserole. Pour tomatoes over. Top with mixture of bread crumbs and Parmesan. Bake 15 minutes at 350°. Yum! Comfort food!

Diane Mitchell, Baton Rouge, LA

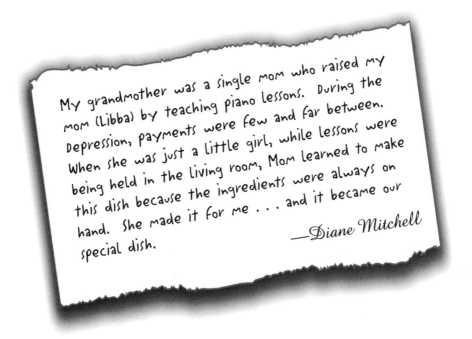

My grandmother was a single mom who raised my mom (Libba) by teaching piano lessons. During the Depression, payments were few and far between. When she was just a little girl, while lessons were being held in the living room, Mom learned to make this dish because the ingredients were always on hand. She made it for me . . . and it became our special dish.

—Diane Mitchell

N'awlins' Muffulettas

OLIVE SALAD:

1 cup pimento-stuffed green olives, crushed

½ cup drained kalamata olives, crushed

2 cloves garlic, minced

¼ cup roughly chopped pickled cauliflower florets

2 tablespoons drained capers

1 tablespoon chopped celery

1 tablespoon chopped carrot

½ cup pepperoncini, drained

¼ cup marinated cocktail onions

½ teaspoon celery seed

1 teaspoon dried oregano

1 teaspoon dried basil

¾ teaspoon ground black pepper

¼ cup red wine vinegar

½ cup olive oil

¼ cup canola oil

In a medium bowl, combine all ingredients. Mix well and transfer mixture into a glass jar (or other non-reactive container). If needed, pour in more oil to cover. Cover jar or container and refrigerate at least overnight.

(continued)

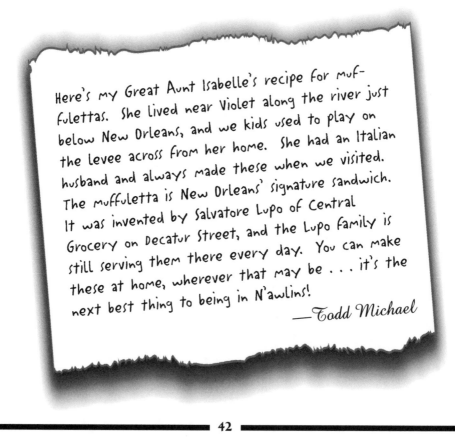

Here's my Great Aunt Isabelle's recipe for muffulettas. She lived near Violet along the river just below New Orleans, and we kids used to play on the levee across from her home. She had an Italian husband and always made these when we visited. The muffuletta is New Orleans' signature sandwich. It was invented by Salvatore Lupo of Central Grocery on Decatur Street, and the Lupo family is still serving them there every day. You can make these at home, wherever that may be . . . it's the next best thing to being in N'awlins!

—Todd Michael

(N'awlins' Muffulettas continued)

MUFFULETTA:

2 (1-pound) loaves Italian
  bread
8 ounces thinly sliced Genoa
  salami
8 ounces thinly sliced cooked
  ham

8 ounces sliced mortadella
  (bologna)
8 ounces sliced mozzarella cheese
8 ounces sliced provolone cheese

Cut bread loaves in half horizontally (use round loaves for an authentic muffuletta experience). Hollow out some of the excess bread to make room for filling. Spread each piece of bread with equal amounts Olive Salad, including oil. Layer bottom half of each loaf with ½ the salami, ham, mortadella, mozzarella, and provolone. Replace top half on each loaf and cut sandwich into quarters.

    Serve immediately, or wrap tightly and refrigerate for a few hours; this will allow the flavors to mingle and the Olive Salad to soak into the bread. Serve cold. One sandwich serves one ravenous person or two hungry people. Great to rewrap, and take along—you'll be the hit of the party!

Todd Michael, Baton Rouge, LA

Stuff the "V" French Bread

1 loaf French bread, halved
  lengthwise
1 (8-ounce) package cream
  cheese, softened
1 cup mayonnaise
1 jar dried beef, chopped

1 bunch green onions, chopped
1 (4-ounce) can chopped black
  olives
1 package dry Italian dressing
  mix

Cut a shallow V-trough down center of each loaf half. Mix remaining ingredients and spread over entire surface of bread, filling "V" with extra mixture. Slice and serve cold, or heat until warm.

Rosemary Morrow, Raymond, MS

Sausage Stuffed French Loaf

1 loaf French bread
½ cup chopped celery
½ cup chopped onion
1 pound ground sausage
  (hot or mild)

1 egg, beaten
¼ cup milk
1 cup grated cheese
1 tablespoon butter or margarine

Split the French loaf horizontally with sharp bread knife, creating a large bun. Remove center soft portion and place bread crumbs in large bowl, leaving a shell of crust. Sauté celery and onion in butter; set aside. Brown sausage and drain; mix with bread crumbs. Add celery and onion, egg, and milk. Mix thoroughly. Place mixture on bottom portion of French loaf shell. Cover with cheese, and place top of French loaf shell over the mixture. Spread small amount of butter or margarine over the top and wrap in aluminum foil. Bake in 350° oven for ½ hour. Remove from oven and let stand for 10 minutes to cool. Cut loaf in slices. Makes about 16–20 portions.

Cindy Daniel, Midlothian, VA

Through sun, rain, sleet, and snow, the show must go on. Food stylists Holli and Bobbi Cappelli help Gwen no matter the weather. QVC broadcasts twenty-four hours a day and only closes one and a half days a year.

Yummy Sausage Bread

2 loaves frozen bread dough
1 pound plain bulk sausage
1 pound hot bulk sausage
1 (4-ounce) can mushrooms,
  drained (optional)

16–24 ounces shredded
  mozzarella cheese

Raise 2 loaves of frozen bread dough overnight. Brown sausages together; crumble. If desired, add mushrooms. Drain and rinse with hot water; blot between paper towels to remove moisture. Roll each roll of dough out. Spread half of sausage on each. Cover with shredded mozzarella cheese. Fold; use toothpicks to hold together. Bake at 350° for 15–25 minutes. Take out when just starting to brown.

Connie Early, Rantoul, IL

Pizza Pepperoni Bread

1 loaf frozen bread dough,
  thawed
$1/4$ teaspoon oregano
$1/4$ teaspoon seasoned salt
$1/2$ teaspoon parsley flakes
$1/4$ teaspoon garlic powder
1 (8-ounce) jar pizza sauce

1 ($3^1/2$-ounce) package
  pepperoni slices
Sliced onions, mushrooms, olives
  (optional)
2 cups grated mozzarella cheese
$1/4$ cup butter, melted

Roll out dough to a 9x13-inch rectangle. Combine seasonings. Brush pizza sauce over bread dough and sprinkle with seasonings, reserving a small amount for topping. Arrange pepperoni on dough with onions, mushrooms, and olives, if desired, and cover with cheese. Roll dough up lightly to look like French bread. Seal it and place on a greased jellyroll pan, sealed-side-down; pinch ends closed. Brush top with melted butter and sprinkle with some of the combined seasonings. Let rise 1 hour. Bake at 350° for 30 minutes, until golden brown. Cool 10 minutes and slice. Yields 10–12 slices.

Bev Moe, Gwinn, MI

Cafe-Style Hawaiian Wrap

Tastes even better than it looks . . . and it's beautiful.

1 (8-ounce) package cream
  cheese, softened
⅓–½ cup coconut syrup or
  cream of coconut (if syrup not
  available)
1 (20-ounce) can crushed
  pineapple, drained, save juice
1 red bell pepper, diced
1 green bell pepper, diced
1 small sweet onion, diced

2 cups diced ham
2 cups cooked instant white rice
1 cup shredded mild Cheddar
  cheese
½ teaspoon salt (optional)
½ teaspoon ground white
  pepper (optional)
8 veggie wraps or (10-inch) flour
  tortillas, room temperature

Mix cream cheese with coconut syrup and ⅓ cup pineapple juice
(reserve remaining ⅓ cup) until smooth. In sauté pan, cook diced
red pepper, green pepper, and onion in remaining ⅓ cup pineapple juice on medium-high heat until tender-crisp. Add ham and
cook 2 minutes more. Mix cooked rice with vegetables and ham.
Fold in drained crushed pineapple. Add cheese, salt, and white
pepper.

Spread 2–3 tablespoons cream cheese mixture on a 10-inch
wrap to cover. Put ¾ cup rice and veggie-ham mixture in the middle of wrap (more or less, depending on how big you like your
wraps). Turn outside edges of the wrap in and roll up. Place seam-side-down on plate to serve. You may cut wrap in half diagonally
if you wish. You can prepare this in advance; just wrap in plastic
wrap and refrigerate. Then just microwave 2–2½ minutes. Serve
with extra coconut cream cheese.

Merilee Kenning, North Chili, NY

Hamaroonies

2 (8-count) cans crescent rolls
1 pound deli ham, shaved
1 pound sharp Cheddar cheese, finely grated

½ stick butter, melted
Shredded lettuce, olives, and pickles for garnish (optional)

Unroll crescent rolls and cut each individual crescent roll in half so that you have 2 triangles per section. Place about 2 tablespoons ham in the middle of the dough. Top with about 1 tablespoon shredded cheese. Fold crescent in half and seal edges with a fork so that it is in a triangle shape. Brush top with melted butter. Place on a cookie sheet and bake at 400° about 8 minutes or until golden brown. Remove from oven and let sit on cookie sheet for about a minute. Remove with spatula to a platter. Garnish with shredded lettuce, olives, and pickles, if desired.

Hayden Markowitz, Saint Simons Island, GA

Banana Pecan Bread

This is very quick and easy to make and super delicious!

1 cup sugar
1 (8-ounce) package cream cheese, softened
2 medium-size ripe bananas, mashed

2 eggs
2 cups baking mix
1 teaspoon vanilla
½ cup chopped pecans

Cream sugar and cream cheese in bowl until fluffy. Beat in bananas and eggs. Stir in baking mix, vanilla, and pecans until moist. Pour into greased 5x9-inch loaf pan. Bake at 350° for one hour. Cool on baking rack before removing from pan.

Doris M. Lloyd, Lattimore, NC

Orchard Fresh Apple Muffins

A dozen terrific muffins!

1½ cups all-purpose flour
½ cup instant nonfat dry milk
⅓ cup granulated sugar
2 teaspoons baking powder
1 teaspoon cinnamon, divided
½ teaspoon salt
1 egg

½ cup water
1 medium apple, peeled, finely chopped
¼ cup butter, melted
⅓ cup chopped nuts
¼ cup firmly packed brown sugar

Combine flour, nonfat dry milk, granulated sugar, baking powder, ½ teaspoon cinnamon, and salt in a large bowl. Beat egg with water. Stir in apple and butter. Add all at once to flour mixture; stir just until moistened (batter will be very stiff). Fill 12 buttered 2½-inch muffin cups ⅔ full. Combine nuts, brown sugar, and remaining ½ teaspoon of cinnamon. Sprinkle over each muffin. Bake at 375° for 15–20 minutes. Remove from pan immediately. Serve warm.

Tammy Maldonado, Millbrae, CA

Top o' the Mornin' Breakfast Muffins

¼ cup vegetable oil
¾ cup sugar
3 eggs, lightly beaten
1 cup mashed ripe bananas (2 medium)
¾ cup chunky applesauce

1 teaspoon vanilla
2⅓ cups all-purpose baking mix
¾ cup natural wheat and barley cereal
½ teaspoon cinnamon

Preheat oven to 350°. Mix ingredients, by hand with wooden spoon, in order given. Mix each ingredient well before adding next one. Then, beat all ingredients vigorously by hand for 30 seconds. Fill muffin tins (½ cup size) ¾ full and bake 25–35 minutes or until toothpick comes out clean. Makes about 18.

Note: If using mini-muffin pans, bake only 15–17 minutes.

Irene Marano, Portsmouth, RI

Red, White, and Blue Coffee Cake

BATTER:

4 cups all-purpose flour
3 teaspoons baking powder
1 teaspoon baking soda
1 teaspoon salt
½ cup butter, softened
1⅔ cups sugar
2 eggs

1 teaspoon vanilla extract
1 teaspoon almond extract
2 cups buttermilk
1 (21-ounce) can blueberry
  pie filling
1 (21-ounce) can cherry filling

Preheat oven to 350°. Grease and flour a 13x18-inch baking pan. Sift flour, baking powder, soda, and salt. Set aside.

Beat butter and sugar until light and fluffy. Beat in eggs one at a time. Add flavorings. Beat in flour mixture alternately with buttermilk. Pour batter in pan.

Spoon golf ball-size portions of pie fillings onto cake. Alternate flavors so you can have a slice of blueberry and cherry at the same time. Pre-bake for 25 minutes at 350°, then remove from oven.

CRUMBS:

1 cup sugar
1¼ cups flour

½ cup butter, softened
3 tablespoons cinnamon

Combine all ingredients, and mix until it resembles coarse crumbs. Sprinkle on top of pre-baked cake with filling. Return to oven and bake an additional 15–20 minutes or until a toothpick inserted comes out clean.

Karin Molczyk, Ellicott City, MD

As young parents, we once drove all the way to Picayune for our kids to see a "big fireworks show" on the 4th of July. We sat in a grocery store parking lot and watched a handful of fireworks light up the sky. We laugh now, but it was special to us then.
—Gwen

Crème Brûlée French Toast

A delicious new taste for a breakfast favorite.

1 stick lightly salted butter
1 cup packed dark brown sugar
1 tablespoon corn syrup
1 (16-inch) loaf pre-sliced
   French bread
5 large eggs

1½ cups half-and-half
   (can use fat free)
1 teaspoon vanilla
1 tablespoon amaretto
Maple syrup
Pecan pieces (optional)

In a small saucepan, melt butter with brown sugar and corn syrup over medium heat, stirring until smooth. Pour into a greased 9x13x2-inch baking dish. Arrange bread slices in one layer in baking dish, squeezing to fit, if necessary. In a bowl, whisk together eggs, half-and-half, vanilla, and amaretto. Pour mixture over bread. Cover and refrigerate overnight.

The next morning, preheat oven to 350°. Place baking dish of bread, uncovered, on middle rack, and bake until edges of bread are lightly golden, about 35–40 minutes. Serve with warmed maple syrup and pecan pieces, if desired.

Stephanie Hixon, Birmingham, AL

Fried Banana-Stuffed French Toast

2 bananas
4 (1½-inch) slices sourdough
  bread
4 eggs, beaten
½ teaspoon vanilla extract

Canola oil
3 teaspoons cinnamon
5 tablespoons sugar
Syrup (optional)

Peel and slice each banana lengthwise, then crosswise into 4 pieces. Cut a small pocket into one side of each slice of bread. Stuff 2 pieces of banana into each pocket, being careful not to poke any holes in the bread. Mix eggs and vanilla. Dip each slice of bread into egg mixture until bread is thoroughly wet. Heat 2 inches of oil to 365°. Fry each slice for one minute or until golden brown on all sides. Drain on paper towels. Mix cinnamon and sugar on a plate, and dip each fried slice of bread in the mixture. Serve immediately with syrup, if desired.

Lisa Harden, Chesterfield, MI

Holiday Morning French Toast

1 cup brown sugar
½ cup butter, melted
3 teaspoons cinnamon, divided
3 apples, cored and thinly sliced
½ cup dried cranberries
  or raisins

1 loaf French bread, cut into
  1-inch slices
6 eggs
1½ cups milk
1 teaspoon vanilla

Combine brown sugar, butter, and 1 teaspoon cinnamon. Toss with apples and cranberries or raisins, and spread evenly over bottom of greased 9x13-inch pan. Arrange slices of bread on top. Mix eggs, milk, vanilla, and remaining cinnamon until well blended. Pour mixture over bread, soaking bread completely. Cover and refrigerate 4–24 hours.

Cover with foil and bake in preheated 375° oven 40 minutes. Uncover and bake 5 minutes more. Remove from oven and let stand 5 minutes before serving. Serves 12.

Melanie Pope, Trimont, MN

Caramel Apple French Toast

½ cup caramel topping
12 (½-inch-thick) slices
French bread
3 eggs
⅔ cup milk

2 tablespoons frozen apple
juice concentrate
1 teaspoon vanilla flavoring
¼ cup chopped pecans
⅛ teaspoon cinnamon

Spread caramel on 6 slices French bread. Make a sandwich with other slices. Place in 9-inch greased baking dish. Combine eggs, milk, apple juice concentrate, and vanilla. Pour over bread. Cover and refrigerate overnight.

Remove from refrigerator 30 minutes before baking. Bake at 350° for 30–35 minutes or until edges are brown.

HOT CARAMEL SYRUP:
2 cups sugar
1 cup water

1 teaspoon caramel flavoring
1 teaspoon maple flavoring

Combine ingredients in saucepan, and bring to a boil for one minute. Serve over French toast.

Susan L. Anderson, Fort Madison, IA

Cheese 'n' Chile Grits

1½ cups quick grits
(not instant)
1½ teaspoons salt
6 cups boiling water
1 stick margarine

1 pound processed cheese,
cubed
3 eggs, beaten
1 (4-ounce) can chopped
green chiles, drained

Cook grits in salted water until thickened, about 5 minutes. Keep pot covered (or your stove will be a mess!). Add margarine and cheese; stir until melted. Add eggs and chiles; mix well and pour into a buttered 9x13x2-inch baking dish. Bake 1½ hours at 275°.

Brenda Clark, Fort Worth, TX

Editor's Extra: For an extra "kick," use Mexican processed cheese.

Fast and Fabulous Chile Relleno Casserole

4 eggs, separated
1 (12-ounce) can evaporated
  milk
3 tablespoons flour
Salt and pepper to taste

1 pound Jack cheese
1 pound Cheddar cheese
3 or 4 (4-ounce) cans diced
  green chiles
Salsa (optional)

Preheat oven to 325°. Beat egg whites till stiff. Beat egg yolks; add evaporated milk, flour, and seasonings. Fold in whites. Layer in greased casserole starting with egg mixture, then cheeses, next chiles. Keep layering until all the egg mixture is gone; finish with cheeses. Bake uncovered for one hour. Top with salsa, if desired.

Note: Leftovers are good sliced and fried for breakfast.

Bob Brewster, Fritch, TX

Eggs Newport

An excellent brunch dish served with fruit.

1 (10³/₄-ounce) can cream of
  mushroom soup
¹/₂ cup milk
1 (4-ounce) can chopped
  mushrooms, drained
1 small onion, chopped
¹/₂ cup mayonnaise

8 hard-cooked eggs, sliced,
  divided
2 cups shredded sharp Cheddar
  cheese, divided
8 slices bacon, fried crisp,
  crumbled, divided

In a medium bowl, combine soup, milk, mushrooms, onion, and mayonnaise to make sauce. In 1¹/₂-quart greased baking dish, layer ¹/₂ of eggs, ¹/₃ of cheese, ¹/₃ of bacon, and ¹/₂ of sauce; repeat layers, ending with remaining ¹/₃ cheese and bacon on top. Bake 20 minutes at 350°. Serve over toast or English muffins.

Jan Diehl, Green Camp, OH

Easy Omelet for Eight

2 (16-ounce) cartons liquid egg
  substitute, divided
4 cups fresh baby spinach
2 cups sliced mushrooms

1 cup chopped onions
1 cup grape or cherry tomatoes
1 cup crumbled feta cheese
Salt and pepper to taste

Preheat oven to 350°. Spray a 9x13-inch pan with nonstick spray.
Pour one container egg substitute into greased pan. Add fresh
baby spinach, mushrooms, onions, tomatoes, feta, salt and pepper.
Pour in remaining egg substitute. Mix together all ingredients.
Bake at 350° for 45 minutes. Serves 8.

Moira Jablon, St. Louis, MO

Since I enjoy the taste of feta cheese, spinach,
mushrooms, and tomatoes, I mixed up some of
my favorite ingredients to create this delicious
dish. Even my children devour it!

—Moira Jablon

Quiche Muffins

1 (4-ounce) can sliced mushrooms, drained	6 ounces Swiss cheese, shredded
½ onion, chopped	6 ounces colby cheese, crumbled
1 package bran muffin mix	¾ cup half-and-half
6 eggs	1 (10-ounce) package frozen spinach, thawed and drained

Combine all ingredients in a large bowl. Pour into individual muffin cups and bake at 400° for 25 minutes or until done. Makes 18–24.

Linda Casto, Millwood, WV

Best Do-Ahead Breakfast Quiche

This recipe will never fail to win compliments!

10 slices white bread, crusts removed	½ teaspoon dry mustard
6 eggs (or equivalent amount of egg substitute)	½ teaspoon salt
2 cups milk	1 pound smoked ham, diced
½ cup (1 stick) butter or margarine, melted	1 pound Cheddar cheese, grated

Tear bread into small pieces; put in 9x13-inch baking pan that has been sprayed with nonstick cooking spray. Beat eggs, milk, melted butter, dry mustard, and salt. Pour over bread and add ham and cheese. Put in refrigerator for at least 3 hours or overnight. Bake at 350° for about 45 minutes until crusty and puffy.

For vegetarian version: Omit ham and add 1 (10-ounce) box chopped broccoli, thawed and fully drained, and ½ cup each finely chopped onion and red pepper.

For low-carb version: Use low-carb (wheat-type) bread with crusts removed in lieu of white bread.

Natalie Leon Golankiewicz, Pittsburgh, PA

Colorful Crustless Quiche

On special occasions, I bake this in my heart-shaped quiche dish. My diabetic husband loves this flavorful dish!

1 pound regular pork sausage
1 large yellow onion, diced
2 tablespoons olive oil
1 package dry buttermilk ranch dressing mix, divided
1 teaspoon garlic powder, divided
3 medium zucchini, shredded

Kosher salt and ground black pepper to taste
6–7 eggs
⅓ cup evaporated milk
1½ cups Cheddar Jack cheese, grated
Sliced tomato for garnish

Brown and crumble sausage in a medium skillet. Remove from skillet; drain on paper towels. In the same skillet, sauté onion in olive oil; season with dry buttermilk ranch dressing mix (reserve ½ teaspoon), and ½ teaspoon garlic powder. Remove to separate dish. In same skillet, sauté the zucchini; season with a dash of kosher salt and ground black pepper.

In a bowl, with a hand beater, whip eggs, evaporated milk, remaining ½ teaspoon ranch dressing mix, remaining ½ teaspoon garlic powder, kosher salt, and ground black pepper to taste. Stir in grated cheese.

Spray a deep-dish pie pan with nonstick spray and layer as follows: browned sausage, seasoned onions, and seasoned zucchini. Pour egg/cheese mixture over all. Bake at 350° for 25–30 minutes. Serve in wedges; garnish with sliced tomato.

Susan Cathey, Grapevine, TX

When the saying "real men don't eat quiche" came out in the eighties, I wondered about all the guys I knew who bragged about making the best omelets. I figure a quiche is somewhat like an omelet in a crust. Nowadays it seems men are a lot more open-minded.
—Gwen

Soups, Chilies, and Stews

Mother Hubbard Soup

2 pieces bacon
1 boneless pork chop
3 boneless chicken thighs
2 sweet Italian sausage links
1 stick celery
1 carrot
1 large onion
3 cloves garlic

1 (15-ounce) can chicken broth
1 (15-ounce) can great Northern
   beans
1 (14½-ounce) can garlic
   and onion diced tomatoes
¼ teaspoon thyme
¼ teaspoon basil

Fry bacon till crisp, then chop next 7 ingredients in order and add to large stockpot. Sauté till vegetables are soft and meat is no longer pink. Add remaining ingredients and simmer 45 minutes. Serves 4–6.

Marlene Svasek, Columbus, NE

Editor's Extra: At other times when cooking pork, chicken, or sausage, put aside a few pieces and freeze in a "Mother Hubbard" container for this yummy soup!

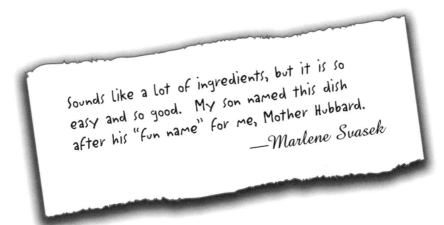

Sounds like a lot of ingredients, but it is so easy and so good. My son named this dish after his "fun name" for me, Mother Hubbard.
—Marlene Svasek

Easy Crockpot Lentil Soup

1 package dried lentils
3 stalks celery
1 large onion
1 large potato
1½ cups prewashed, prepackaged cole slaw mix (cabbage and carrots)
1 teaspoon garlic powder
½ teaspoon dried thyme
1 tablespoon dried parsley
Salt and pepper to taste
1 (14½-ounce) can chicken broth
1 (10¾-ounce) can condensed chicken soup (any kind)
1 (28-ounce) can diced tomatoes
Water

Spray crockpot with cooking spray. Wash dried lentils and place in crockpot. Wash and coarsely chop vegetables, then add to crockpot. Add cole slaw mix directly from package.

Sprinkle all spices over ingredients in crockpot. Pour broth, soup, and tomatoes into crockpot; fill crockpot within one inch of top with water. Cook on HIGH 2 hours. Then turn crockpot to LOW and cook at least 6 more hours.

Interesting Variations: Vary the flavor of the canned soup (such as creamed soup, chicken and rice, chicken noodle, ramen noodle soup, etc.). Add additional vegetables (such as mushrooms, broccoli, squash, or cauliflower). Vary the type of dried beans (such as split peas, black-eye peas, or navy beans).

Note: Bigger beans such as navy or black-eyed must be soaked in water overnight before using in a crockpot.

Gail Bradshaw, Chesapeake, VA

Flavorful White Bean Soup

3 cups peeled, cut-up sausage
  (kielbasa is good)
1 tablespoon cooking oil
1 medium onion, finely chopped
6 cups chicken broth
2 cups water
1 bay leaf
½ teaspoon black pepper
¼ teaspoon thyme

¼ teaspoon poultry seasoning
Dash red pepper flakes
Salt to taste
½ teaspoon basil
1–2 cups frozen cauliflower
1 (15-ounce) can Northern
  white beans
1 (15-ounce) can garbanzo beans

In large saucepot, cook sausage and onion in cooking oil until meat is browned and onion is transparent. Add rest of ingredients, except cauliflower and beans. Bring to a boil, then simmer covered 6–8 minutes. Add cauliflower, and bring to boil; add beans, and simmer 5 minutes. Enjoy!

Peggy Smith, Holland, MI

Cheesy Hash Brown Potato Soup

4 stalks celery, chopped
1 large yellow onion, diced
1 large leek, thinly sliced
3–4 tablespoons butter
1 (50-ounce) can chicken broth
1 (2-pound) bag frozen hash
  browns

1 tablespoon flour
½ cup milk
1 quart half-and-half
1 (16-ounce) jar processed cheese
Crumbled cooked bacon
Sliced green onions

In a large stockpot (6 quart or larger), sauté celery, onion, and leek in butter until softened. Add chicken broth and hash browns; bring to a boil. In small bowl, mix together flour and milk. When soup is boiling, quickly stir milk/flour mixture into soup to thicken to a consistency of stew. (Might have to repeat flour/milk step to get desired consistency.) Once soup is thickened, reduce heat; add half-and-half and processed cheese. Continue stirring until cheese is thoroughly blended. DO NOT BOIL after adding half-and-half and cheese. Ladle into crocks and top with crumbled bacon and green onions.

Gina Graville, Madison, WI

Garden Cheese Soup

1 cup sliced celery
1 cup chopped onion
2 tablespoons margarine
²/₃ cup flour
4 cups water
2 tablespoons instant chicken
    bouillon
¹/₄ teaspoon pepper

2 cups frozen broccoli-
    cauliflower-carrot combination
1 cup frozen hash brown
    potatoes
3 cups milk
2¹/₂ cups shredded Cheddar
    cheese

In large kettle or Dutch oven, cook celery and onion in margarine until tender; stir in flour until smooth. Gradually add water, then bouillon, pepper, and vegetables; bring to a boil. Reduce heat; cover and simmer 15 minutes. Add milk and cheese. Cook and stir until cheese melts and soup is hot (do not boil). Serve immediately.

Amy Teraberry, Scottsdale, AZ

Cauliflower, Potato, and Cheese Soup

6 cups water
4 potatoes, diced
2 cubes chicken bouillon
1 head cauliflower florets
¹/₂ teaspoon onion powder
Salt and pepper to taste
2 tablespoons dried parsley flakes

¹/₂ teaspoon nutmeg
1 (10³/₄-ounce) can cream of
    celery soup
1¹/₂ cups diced American cheese,
    or 1 (10³/₄-ounce) can
    Cheddar cheese soup

Bring water and potatoes to a boil, then simmer, adding bouillon cubes, cauliflower, onion powder, salt, pepper, parsley, and nutmeg. Cook until vegetables are tender, approximately 30 minutes, then add soup and cheese, stirring until blended. Serve with a pinch of nutmeg on top.

Allison "Judy" Gaskill, Toms River, NJ

Editor's Extra: Add more cheese for a cheesier flavor and thicker consistency.

Thanksgiving Butternut Squash Soup

I concocted this tasty soup to serve to dear friends on a cold Thanksgiving Day as a first course . . . and everyone who was there is still talking about it! Here it is!

2 medium-size butternut squash
6 tablespoons butter, divided
1 tablespoon honey
2½ cups finely chopped yellow onions
2 carrots, peeled and chopped (optional)
3 teaspoons curry powder (optional)

2 apples, peeled, cored, and chopped
1 (16-ounce) can pumpkin
4 cups chicken stock
1½ cups apple cider
Salt and freshly ground pepper to taste
Crème Fraîche or sour cream for garnish

Slice squash lengthwise into halves; scrape out seeds. Baste interior of squash with 1 tablespoon butter and honey; wrap in foil, then bake at 375° for one hour or until soft. Melt remaining butter in large pot; add chopped onions, carrots, and curry powder. Cook, covered, over low heat until tender, 15–20 minutes. With a spoon, scrape out baked squash from shell and add to pot with apples, pumpkin, and stock; bring to a boil. Reduce heat immediately, and simmer partially covered until apples and squash are tender, about 20 minutes.

Either purée in pot with a hand-held mixer after cooling somewhat, or strain, reserving liquid, and process the solids separately in a food processor. Then add 1 cup stock and process until smooth. Return soup to pot; add apple cider until soup is of desired consistency.

Season with salt and pepper to taste. Reheat briefly and serve garnished with Crème Fraîche or sour cream. Shredded apples with a dash of cinnamon is also a nice garnish if you prefer. Makes 4–6 large servings.

Note: To make your own Crème Fraîche, combine 1 cup whipping cream with 2 tablespoons buttermilk in a glass container. Cover and allow to stand at room temperature 8–24 hours, or until very thick. Stir well, cover, and keep refrigerated; will keep up to 10 days.

Bruce Kolb, New York, NY

Creamy Tomato Soup

My mother, Jackie Cisterino, passed this family favorite down to me . . . and I am so pleased to be able to share it with my "QVC family."

3 garlic cloves, minced
1 sweet onion, finely diced
1 carrot, finely diced
1 stalk celery, finely diced
¼ cup extra virgin olive oil
1 (28-ounce) can crushed
  tomatoes (fire roasted, if
  available)
1 (15-ounce) can diced tomatoes
½ (6-ounce) can tomato paste

1 (32-ounce) box chicken broth
3 chicken or vegetable bouillon
  cubes
½ pint heavy cream
½ pint half-and-half
½ pint buttermilk
1 bunch fresh basil, cut into
  thin ribbons
Salt and pepper to taste

In large Dutch oven, sauté vegetables in oil until soft. Add tomatoes, paste, broth, and bouillon cubes. Simmer 20 minutes on low heat. Stir in liquids. Add basil and salt and pepper to taste. Simmer another 20 minutes. For a chunky soup, serve as is. For a creamy soup, purée in batches in a food processor or blender. Makes 8 servings.

Marie Louise Kier, QVC Guest, Chester Springs, PA

In the QVC kitchen, Marie Louise Kier preps food for one of the many products she demonstrates on QVC.

Red Pepper Pasta Soup

Unbelievably delicious!

¹/₄ cup olive oil
1 red onion, thinly sliced
2 cups sliced mushrooms
  (optional)
3 red bell peppers, seeded,
  thinly sliced
¹/₂ teaspoon red pepper flakes
Pepper to taste
4 cloves garlic, crushed
1 teaspoon sugar

2 (14¹/₂-ounce) cans diced
  tomatoes with garlic and onion
8 cups chicken stock
12 ounces uncooked mini-penne
  pasta
3 chicken breast halves, cooked
  and cut into bite-size pieces
1 cup heavy cream
1 cup grated Parmesan cheese

Heat oil over medium-high heat. Add onion, mushrooms, peppers, red pepper flakes, and pepper. Reduce to medium, and cook 3–4 minutes. Add garlic; cook another minute. Add sugar and tomatoes, and simmer uncovered 15 minutes.

Add stock and pasta; bring to a boil and cook until pasta is tender, about 10 minutes. Add chicken, cream, and Parmesan; heat through. Pepper again to taste.

Note: You may need to add more stock, water, or white wine if the soup is too thick.

Janet DeFeo, FPO, AE

Editor's Extra: Regular penne is fine, if you can't find mini.

Creamy Corn Chowder

1 large onion, chopped fine
1 stick margarine
2 (10¾-ounce) cans cream of
   chicken soup
3 (16-ounce) cans cream-style
   corn
2 (16-ounce) cans whole-kernel
   corn, drained

1 quart half-and-half
Milk, enough to make desired
   thickness
4–5 medium to large potatoes,
   peeled and diced
1 pound processed American
   cheese, cut up
Salt and pepper to taste

In a large stockpot, sauté chopped onion in melted margarine. Add soup, corn, half-and-half, and enough milk to make the soup as thick as you want. Cook this mixture slowly 20–30 minutes, stirring to keep from sticking.

In a separate pot, boil potatoes until tender; drain and add to corn mixture. Add chopped cheese and salt and pepper to taste. Continue cooking until cheese is melted. Serve hot with corn bread.

Brenda Bailey, Gentry, AR

Crawfish Corn Chowder

1 pound crawfish tails
½ cup chopped green onions
½ tablespoon real butter
½ teaspoon red pepper
½ teaspoon minced garlic
2 (10¾-ounce) cans cream of
   potato soup

1 (16-ounce) can cream-style
   corn
1 (16-ounce) can whole-kernel
   corn, drained
1 (8-ounce) package cream
   cheese
1 soup can milk

Sauté crawfish and green onions in butter. Add remaining ingredients, stirring constantly, and bring to a boil; reduce heat to medium low and cook about 45 minutes. Serves 6–8.

Melanie Gibson, Madison, MS

Really Creamy Cream of Broccoli Soup

³⁄₄ (16-ounce) bag frozen chopped broccoli	¹⁄₄ cup margarine
¹⁄₄ cup chopped onion	¹⁄₄ cup flour
1 quart chicken broth (3 cups)	³⁄₄ cup evaporated milk
	Salt and pepper to taste

Bring broccoli, onion, and broth to a boil. Simmer until broccoli softens, 30–45 minutes. Melt margarine and add flour. Stir to make a thick paste; let cook 5 minutes on low heat. Add paste to broccoli mixture and blend well. Add evaporated milk and continue to simmer another 30 minutes. Season with salt and pepper to taste.

Donna Zonio, Endicott, NY

Easy Shrimp Bisque

This is a simple recipe, yet it tastes like a gourmet specialty!

2 cups sliced fresh mushrooms	1 (26-ounce) can cream of mushroom soup
¹⁄₄ cup finely chopped onion	
3 tablespoons butter	1 cup milk
1 (8-ounce) package frozen tiny shrimp, thawed (or fresh shrimp)	1 (8-ounce) can tomato sauce
	¹⁄₂ cup sour cream
	Freshly ground pepper

Sauté mushrooms and onion in butter in a large saucepan. Add thawed shrimp, and sauté for 5 minutes. Add mushroom soup and milk; heat slowly to a simmer. Stir in tomato sauce and sour cream. Be sure to heat slowly to prevent scorching. Heat thoroughly until creamy. Add ground pepper to taste. Crabmeat may be substituted for the shrimp for variation.

Tammy Calkins, Centralia, WA

Chicken Wild Rice Soup

You will want to sop the bottom of your bowl for sure.

1 small onion, diced
1 pound bacon, diced
2 chicken breasts, cooked,
   shredded
1 (10¾-ounce) can cream of
   chicken soup
1 (10¾-ounce) can cream of
   potato soup

1 pint half-and-half
2 cups milk
1 (8-ounce) can sliced
   mushrooms, sliced, undrained
2 cups grated American cheese
2 cups cooked wild rice

Fry onion and bacon in large soup pot. Bacon should be crisp and onion clear. Drain fat from bacon (using your locking lid colander if you have one). Add shredded chicken to soup pot. Add both cans of soup, half-and-half, milk, mushrooms, and cheese to soup pot, and start to simmer over low heat. Allow to simmer about 45 minutes, stirring frequently to blend flavors. Add wild rice to soup mixture. Continue to stir frequently to blend the flavors, and simmer until cheese is completely melted. When soup appears well mixed and all ingredients melted and hot, serve with a nice French bread or hard dinner rolls of your choice.

Nedra Sheeley, Adel, IA

Editor's Extra: Cooking ⅓ cup real wild rice (not a blend) according to package directions will yield 2 cups cooked rice, but remember it will take about 50 minutes. A mixture of brown and wild rice will cook a little quicker, and is good, too.

My grandmother was a great believer in chicken soup when you were feeling bad. It seemed to work miracles . . . or maybe I just liked chicken soup.

—Barbara

Chicken-Tortilla Soup

3–4 cooked chicken breasts,
  shredded
2 cloves garlic, pressed
1 (28-ounce) can diced tomatoes
1 (10¾-ounce) can tomato soup
4 cups chicken stock

1 teaspoon cumin
1 teaspoon chili powder
2 tablespoons Worcestershire
1 (10-ounce) package frozen
  white shoe peg corn

Add all ingredients together in a Dutch oven or stockpot. Cook on low heat until thoroughly heated.

TOPPINGS:
Tortilla chips, broken
Shredded Monterey Jack cheese

Sour cream

Serve with broken tortilla chips in bowl, with Monterey Jack cheese and a dollop of sour cream on top.

Kristin Stewart, Cary, NC

Best Ever Cheesy Chicken Soup

The addition of the Mexican-flavored cheese is what really makes this a different chicken soup.

1 package chicken noodle flavor
  soup starter
1 whole chicken, cut up, or
  4 or 5 breasts

1 (1-pound) loaf Mexican-style
  processed cheese (hot or mild,
  or ½ of each)

Prepare soup starter as directed on package; add chicken and cook till done. Remove chicken and cut into bite-size pieces, then add back to soup mixture. Cut cheese loaf into cubes and add to soup mixture; simmer till creamy. Serve with a skillet of hot corn bread.

Kay Williams, Clinton, MS

Pressure Cooker-Slow Cooker Mexican Soup

1½ pounds beef shanks (or stew meat)
Garlic powder
1 (15-ounce) can chicken broth
1–2 garlic cloves, crushed
1 (10-ounce) can beef broth
1 cup chopped cabbage
½ cup chopped onion
½ cup chopped celery
½ cup chopped carrots
½ cup chopped potato
½ cup corn
½ cup chopped jícama
½ cup chopped cilantro
1 cup Bloody Mary mix
1 (14.5-ounce) can stewed tomatoes, crushed or chopped smaller
Salt, pepper, and a little sugar to taste
1 tablespoon cumin
½ cup frozen peas (optional)

Sprinkle meat with garlic powder and let stand a few minutes. Pressure cook meat in chicken broth with crushed garlic cloves about one hour. Meanwhile, heat beef broth in slow cooker on HIGH.

Remove beef from pressure cooker and chop into bite-size pieces, then add to slow cooker with liquid from pressure cooker. Add vegetables, cilantro, Bloody Mary mix, stewed tomatoes, salt, pepper, and a little sugar to taste. Simmer on LOW at least 3–4 hours. Add cumin towards end of cooking time. Correct seasonings, if necessary. Add peas, if desired. Serve with additional chopped cilantro, jalapeño slices, or hot sauce.

Wilma Yanagisako, Hemet, CA

When I started school, my first lunch box was the old dome type that had a place for my Thermos, which was held in by a curved wire that snapped in the top of the box. Mother always had a surprise in there to make lunch more interesting. Sometimes in winter she filled the Thermos with soup as a treat.

— Barbara

Chilled Strawberry Soup

Makes a pretty presentation. Cool and delicious.

1/3 cup orange juice
2 (10-ounce) packages frozen
  strawberries, or 2 pints fresh
  strawberries, cleaned
1 pint whipping cream or light
  cream
1 (11-ounce) can Mandarin
  oranges

Dash of nutmeg
Orange zest
1 teaspoon whipped cream or
  nondairy frozen dessert topping
Fresh mint leaves

Combine orange juice and thawed or fresh strawberries in a blender. Purée for 1–1½ minutes. Add whipping cream and blend until thoroughly mixed. Do not over blend. Pour immediately into bowls. Garnish with nutmeg and orange zest.

Place a teaspoon of dessert topping in the middle of the soup, add 3–4 Mandarin orange segments to form a flower, then add mint leaves. Serves 4–6.

Sharon Voorhees, Longwood, FL

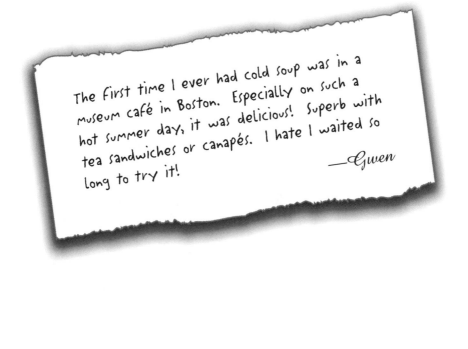

The first time I ever had cold soup was in a museum café in Boston. Especially on such a hot summer day, it was delicious! Superb with tea sandwiches or canapés. I hate I waited so long to try it!

—Gwen

Southwest Taco Chili

1 pound ground beef
1 cup diced onion
2 (16-ounce) cans stewed sliced
  tomatoes
1 (16-ounce) can navy beans,
  drained and rinsed
1 (16-ounce) can pinto beans,
  drained and rinsed
1 (16-ounce) can black beans,
  drained and rinsed

1 (16-ounce) can kidney beans,
  drained and rinsed
2 envelopes taco seasoning
1 (17-ounce) can corn
¼ cup chopped cilantro
Tortilla chips
Grated cheese for garnish
Sour cream and chives for
  garnish

In a large stockpot, brown ground beef. Drain. Add onion and cook until transparent. Add tomatoes, beans, and taco seasoning. Simmer for 20 minutes, then add corn and cilantro. Simmer for 20 more minutes or longer. The longer it simmers, the better it gets! Serve over chips, and garnish with cheese, sour cream, and chives. Freezes well.

Jennifer Harbour, Cypress, TX

Chili Dog Chili

I make this with five pounds of ground beef for cookouts for around twenty people—and never have any left over!

1 pound ground beef
¼ teaspoon salt
1 tablespoon chili powder

1 teaspoon yellow mustard
½ cup ketchup
Water

Mix all ingredients with uncooked beef in a heavy pot. Use small amounts of water (a total of about 4 tablespoons) to get this thoroughly mixed. Cook on medium-low heat for about 45 minutes, stirring often. DO NOT DRAIN. Refrigerate until all of the grease is solid. Spoon grease off top. It tastes best if it sits for around 12 hours. This will serve 4 people.

Bethany Martin, Clayton, GA

Editor's Extra: By using lean ground beef, you can serve this right away. Delish!

My Chili for Dad

3 pounds ground beef
2 large onions, chopped large
8 cloves garlic, crushed
4 tablespoons olive oil
5 medium stalks celery, chopped large
2 large green bell peppers, chopped large
2 large red bell peppers, chopped large
3 habanero peppers, seeded, chopped
3 jalapeño peppers, seeded, chopped
2 (16-ounce) cans whole Italian tomatoes

2 (6-ounce) cans tomato paste
6 tablespoons chili powder
2 tablespoons Worcestershire
3 tablespoons pepper sauce
4 teaspoons salt
Pepper to taste
4 (16-ounce) cans kidney beans, drained
¼ cup brown sugar
Shredded Cheddar cheese for garnish
Tortilla chips, crushed for garnish
Sour cream for garnish

In large saucepan, brown ground beef with onions and garlic in olive oil. Add celery, green and red peppers, and habanero and jalapeño peppers; stir frequently until slightly soft. Drain. Stir in undrained tomatoes, tomato paste, chili powder, Worcestershire, pepper sauce, salt, pepper, kidney beans, and brown sugar. Bring to a boil, then reduce heat. Simmer 2 hours, covered. Serve with shredded cheese, broken tortilla chips, and sour cream. Delicious.

Diane L. Knowles, Hampton, NH

Lip Smackin' Chili

1 large sweet onion, diced small	1–2 tablespoons chili powder
1 large green pepper, diced small	1 teaspoon cinnamon
1 pound lean ground beef	1/2 teaspoon cumin
2 (15½-ounce) can chili beans	Salt and pepper to taste
2–3 cloves garlic, pressed	1/4 cup uncooked elbow
1 (46-ounce) can tomato juice	macaroni
1 (4-ounce) can diced green chiles	Water, if needed

In a large soup pot or stockpot, add onion, pepper, and meat, and cook, stirring often, until meat is completely cooked. Drain all fat and return meat mixture to pot. Add beans, garlic, tomato juice, and green chiles. Season with chili powder, cinnamon, and cumin. Add salt and pepper to taste. Bring to a boil, then allow to simmer one hour, stirring often.

Taste after one hour and adjust seasonings. Add macaroni and water, as needed. Allow to simmer for one more hour. Taste again and adjust seasoning, if needed.

TOPPINGS:

Sour cream	Diced green onion
Shredded cheese	Oyster crackers

Serve with sour cream, shredded cheese, diced green onion, and oyster crackers.

Linda Heckman, Alexandria, VA

Proper manners were taught and expected when I was growing up. Lip smackin' was a no-no— but sometimes you just couldn't help it!
—Barbara

Chicken Licken' Chili

6 chicken breast halves, skinned
  and boned
1 medium onion, chopped
1 medium green pepper, chopped
2 cloves garlic, minced
1 tablespoon vegetable oil
2 (14.5-ounce) cans stewed
  tomatoes, undrained and
  chopped

2 (15-ounce) cans pinto beans,
  drained
⅔ cup medium picante sauce
⅓ cup mild picante sauce
2 teaspoons chili powder, or
  to taste
1 teaspoon ground cumin, or
  to taste
½ teaspoon salt

Cut chicken into 1-inch pieces. Cook chicken, onion, green pepper, and garlic in hot oil in a Dutch oven until lightly browned. Add tomatoes and remaining ingredients, except Toppings; cover, reduce heat, and simmer 20 minutes.

TOPPINGS:
Shredded Cheddar cheese
Sour cream

Diced avocado
Sliced green onions

Top individual servings with Toppings of your choice.

Dean Schneider, Naples, FL

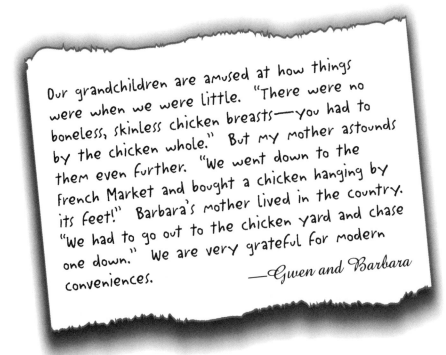

Our grandchildren are amused at how things were when we were little. "There were no boneless, skinless chicken breasts—you had to by the chicken whole." But my mother astounds them even further. "We went down to the French Market and bought a chicken hanging by its feet!" Barbara's mother lived in the country. "We had to go out to the chicken yard and chase one down." We are very grateful for modern conveniences.

—*Gwen and Barbara*

Simple, Simply Wonderful Beef Stew

2 pounds stew meat
1 medium onion, sliced
2 carrots, sliced
2 stalks celery, sliced
2 potatoes, peeled and cubed

1 (8-ounce) can tomato sauce
8 ounces water
1 teaspoon white sugar
1 envelope onion soup mix
2 tablespoons tapioca (dry)

Arrange meat in Dutch oven; top with vegetables. Mix together tomato sauce, water, and white sugar. Pour over meat and vegetables, and sprinkle with onion soup mix and tapioca. Cover and bake in 350° oven 2½ hours.

Cynthia Dafoe, Marquette, MI

Sour Cream Meatball Stew

2 pounds ground chuck
¼ cup grated Romano cheese
1 egg
¾ cup Italian bread crumbs
1 medium onion, diced
Salt and pepper to taste
1 (14½-ounce) can diced
tomatoes, not drained
2 tablespoons paprika
6 stalks celery, cut into
bite-size pieces

6 carrots, cut into bite-size
pieces
4 medium onions, quartered
½ pound string beans, sliced
1 (10-ounce) box frozen
whole-kernel corn
Fresh garlic to taste
Water
1 pint sour cream
½ pound elbow macaroni

Combine first 6 ingredients; form into medium-size meatballs. Brown meatballs in olive oil or corn oil. When browned, add tomatoes, paprika, vegetables, and garlic. Add enough water to cover. Simmer until vegetables are tender. Add sour cream and elbow macaroni; simmer until macaroni is tender. Serves 6–8.

Alberta Lee Kaiser, New Port Richey, FL

Hammy Mac Stew

1 small green pepper, chopped
1 small onion, chopped
$1/4$ cup cooking oil (or less)
1 pound ground chuck
2 (15-ounce) cans diced tomatoes
with basil and oregano (or
plain, if you prefer)

$1\frac{1}{2}$ cups uncooked elbow
macaroni

Sauté green pepper and onion in cooking oil, then add ground chuck and cook until browned. Add tomatoes and stew on medium heat about 45 minutes. Cook macaroni as directed on package. Combine cooked macaroni with the tomato-hamburger mixture. Serve with garlic toast for a delicious, quick, and easy meal!

Sharon Parsons, Follansbee, WV

I give this recipe to co-workers when they are looking for something quick to fix when they get home from work. My 9-year-old stepson loves it so much, he takes home the leftovers after he has spent the weekend with us.

—Sharon Parsons

Cowboy Stew

Simple and good!

2 pounds stew meat
2 tablespoons olive oil
1 teaspoon garlic powder
1½ cups salsa
1 (15-ounce) can peas, drained

1 (15-ounce) can corn, drained
1 (15-ounce) can green beans,
  drained
Salt and pepper to taste
2 cups cooked rice

Brown stew meat in olive oil. Add all other ingredients, except rice, and simmer for 2–3 hours, till meat is tender. Season to taste. Serve over rice.

Marie Mitchell, Hilliard, OH

Soup-er Simple Beef Stew

2 large onions, coarsely chopped
1 pound peeled baby carrots
1 pound red potatoes, peeled and
  cut into eighths
2 (10¾-ounce) cans golden
  mushroom soup, undiluted,
  divided

1½ tablespoons Cajun-type
  seasoning
2 pounds stew beef, cubed
2 tablespoons oil
1 envelope beef stew mix
1 tablespoon teriyaki sauce

Place onions, carrots, potatoes, one can of soup, and seasoning into a crockpot/slow cooker. Using a nonmetallic spoon, mix thoroughly. Cook on HIGH for one hour.

In the meantime, in a large skillet, lightly brown stew beef in oil. Drain, and store covered in the refrigerator if not ready to add to vegetables.

After vegetables have cooked for one hour, add stew beef, beef stew mix, and teriyaki sauce, and mix thoroughly with a non-metallic spoon. Pour second can of golden mushroom soup over top of stew, but do not mix. Turn pot down to LOW and cook 10–11 hours.

Refrigerate any leftovers immediately. May be stored up to 3 days in refrigerator in an air-tight container.

Janet Lariscy, Douglasville, GA

Curried Stew with Lamb

1 cup yogurt
1 tablespoon minced garlic
2 pounds lamb cubes
2 cups water
1 cup uncooked rice
1 tablespoon olive oil
1 large onion, grated
1/2 teaspoon ground cloves
1/2 teaspoon ground ginger
1/2 teaspoon ground cumin
3/4 teaspoon ground cayenne
   pepper
3 tablespoons good quality
   curry powder
2/3 cup slivered almonds,
   toasted
1 cup currants
8 cups rich vegetable broth

In a medium bowl, combine yogurt and garlic. Stir in the lamb cubes until coated. Cover, and refrigerate overnight.

In a saucepan, bring water to a boil. Add rice and stir. Reduce heat, cover, and simmer 20 minutes until all water is absorbed. Remove from heat and set aside.

Heat oil in a large skillet over medium-high heat. Sauté onion until tender. Stir in marinated lamb mixture. Season with cloves, ginger, cumin, cayenne and curry powder. Stir in almonds and currants, then reduce heat and simmer 2 hours. Stir in cooked rice and vegetable broth. Return to a simmer and cook 5 more minutes.

Chris Moretzsohn, Downingtown, PA

Editor's Extra: Raisins may be substituted for currants.

Salads

Hurry Curry Chicken Salad

3 cups diced cooked chicken
1 cup halved seedless red grapes
½ cup sweet pickle relish
½ cup chopped celery
¼ cup chopped onion
1 cup mayonnaise

1 tablespoon vinegar
½ tablespoon mustard
1 tablespoon sugar
Salt and pepper to taste
Dash of curry powder (about
    ½ teaspoon)

Combine diced chicken and halved grapes in large bowl. Add pickle relish, celery, and onion, and mix well. In a separate bowl, combine mayonnaise, vinegar, mustard, sugar, salt, pepper, and curry. Pour over chicken mixture and toss to mix. Chill. Serve on lettuce leaves.

Note: Pineapple tidbits may be added, if desired.

Dannie Anderton, Collierville, TN

Chicken Salad Supreme

Best if made a day ahead.

4 boneless, skinless chicken
    breasts
8 medium potatoes
¼ cup mayonnaise
¾ cup poppy seed salad
    dressing

2 apples, peeled and cored
4 hard-boiled eggs, chopped
4 stalks celery, diced
Salt and pepper to taste

Poach chicken 20 minutes or until juices run clear. Cool and cut into bite-size pieces. Boil potatoes until tender; peel and cut into bite-size pieces. Mix mayonnaise and poppy seed dressing. Chop apples into bite-size pieces. Gently combine all ingredients. Salt and pepper to taste.

Pat Johnson, Pembroke Pines, FL

Editor's Extra: Poach simply means to cook your food in liquid just below the boiling point, till it's just beginning to show some quivering.

Polka Dot Chicken Salad

1 (3-ounce) package lemon
  gelatin
1½ cups boiling water
2½ cups cut-up chicken (white
  meat), cooked
1 small onion, grated

½ cup chopped green pepper
½ cup chopped celery
1 cup mayonnaise-type salad
  dressing
½ teaspoon salt
1 cup English peas, drained

Mix gelatin with hot water until dissolved. Add to remaining ingredients, except peas, and mix well. When gelatin is cool, add peas and pour into mold.

Carol Kvetkosky, Tonawanda, NY

Dallas Summer Chicken Salad

½ cup thinly sliced celery
½ cup halved seedless red or
  white grapes
¾ cup cantaloupe balls
1 large banana, cubed
1 (8-ounce) can pineapple
  chunks, drained

2 cups cooked, cubed chicken
½ cup mayonnaise
Romaine lettuce leaves
¼ cup real bacon bits for
  garnish

In a large salad serving bowl, toss celery, grapes, melon balls, banana, pineapple, and chicken. Add mayonnaise and mix well. Arrange on lettuce leaves and garnish with bacon bits.

Pamela Weiner, Arlington, TX

Italian Cream Asparagus Chicken Salad

ASPARAGUS CHICKEN SALAD:

1 pound fresh asparagus
1½ cups chopped, cooked
  chicken
3 cups iceberg lettuce, torn into
  bite-size pieces

¼ cup slivered almonds, toasted
¼ cup chopped fresh parsley
1½ tablespoons raisins
1 red apple, unpeeled
Lettuce leaves (optional)

Snap off tough ends of asparagus. Remove scales with a vegetable peeler, if desired. Cook asparagus, covered, in a small amount of boiling water about 3 minutes. Plunge into ice water. Drain well. Cut asparagus into 1½-inch pieces. Reserve 8 pieces for garnish. Combine remaining asparagus and next 5 ingredients in a large bowl. Cut half of apple into ½-inch cubes and stir into chicken mixture. Reserve remaining apple for garnish.

ITALIAN CREAM DRESSING:

¾ cup sour cream
¼ cup crumbled blue cheese
  or Gorgonzola

1 tablespoon lemon juice
¼ teaspoon garlic powder
Freshly ground pepper

Combine all Italian Cream Dressing ingredients. Arrange salad in a lettuce-lined bowl, if desired. Garnish with asparagus and apple slices, then pour Italian Cream Dressing over salad. Or, if you prefer, toss salad with dressing in bowl, then garnish. Yields 4 servings.

Rebecca A. Rogers, Lexington, KY

Picnic Chicken Pasta Salad

This is great for a covered-dish gathering or picnic.

2 chicken breasts
2 cups chicken broth
4 cups water
1 pound bow-tie pasta
1 bunch broccoli, florets only
1/2 cup chopped purple onion
1/2 cup mayonnaise

1/2 cup sour cream
1/4 cup Dijon mustard
1 1/2 teaspoons white vinegar
3/4 teaspoon salt
1/2 teaspoon ground pepper
Parsley for garnish

Place chicken in a 4-quart pot. Add broth and water. Bring to a boil. Turn chicken over, and reduce heat to a simmer. Cook until done, about 40 minutes. Cool. Pull into small pieces. Place into a large bowl. Cook pasta in broth for 10 minutes, until al dente. During last 7 minutes of cook time, add broccoli and cook until fork-tender. Rinse broccoli and pasta under cold water; drain well. Add chicken and onion.

Mix mayonnaise, sour cream, mustard, vinegar, salt, and pepper in a bowl. Fold into pasta mixture. Garnish with parsley. Refrigerate until serving.

Brenda Harrison, Chattanooga, TN

Chicken Macaroni Salad

2 cups cooked chopped chicken
  breast
2 cups cooked macaroni
1 1/2 cups mayonnaise
1/2 cup mustard
1 bunch green onions, chopped
3 celery stalks, chopped

1 cup sliced black olives
3 large dill pickles, chopped
1 1/2 teaspoons seasoned salt
8 boiled eggs, divided (4 chopped
  and 4 sliced)
Paprika for garnish

Add all ingredients into large bowl, adding only chopped eggs; mix all together. Garnish with remaining egg slices on top. Sprinkle with paprika. Chill and serve.

Carol Grant, West Valley, UT

Tasty Tortellini Salad

1 (16-ounce) package frozen
  cheese tortellini
½ green pepper, diced
1 cup shredded Monterey Jack
  cheese
2 cups fresh broccoli florets,
  blanched
1 (8-ounce) bottle Italian salad
  dressing

Cook tortellini as directed and cool. Mix tortellini with remaining ingredients and refrigerate 2–3 hours to blend flavors. Use a container with a tight seal so you can flip the container over a few times while refrigerating to keep the salad dressing mixed through the tortellini.

Debbie Morreale, Forked River, NJ

Sandie's Spaghetti Salad

1 pound vermicelli pasta, broken
½ bell pepper, chopped
5 stalks celery, chopped
12 green onions, chopped
4 hard-boiled eggs, chopped
1 (5¾-ounce) jar stuffed green
  olives, sliced
1 quart mayonnaise
1 pound small fresh shrimp,
  cooked

Cook vermicelli as directed on package; drain. While pasta is still hot, add remaining ingredients, except shrimp. Just before serving, add shrimp. Serves 18–20.

Sandie Pidgeon, Vacaville, CA

Editor's Extra: Also good to use half salad-dressing-type mayonnaise for a sweeter salad. I used frozen cooked salad shrimp, and put them right in the hot spaghetti. Delicious!

Truly American Potato Salad

5 or 6 large potatoes, peeled, cooked, and diced
6–8 eggs, hard-cooked and diced
1 large onion, diced
½ cup sour cream
1 cup mayonnaise
1 tablespoon vinegar
2 tablespoons milk
2 teaspoons sugar
Salt and pepper to taste
½ green or red pepper, diced
6 stalks celery, chopped

Combine warm potatoes, hard-cooked eggs, and diced onion; mix well and set aside. Mix sour cream, mayonnaise, vinegar, milk, and sugar. Add salt and pepper to taste. Fold mayonnaise mixture, diced pepper, and celery into potato mixture. Chill 2–3 hours. Serves 12.

Linda Lehman, Belvidere, IL

John Rizzo, one of QVC's producers, points a situation out to Chris Clay at the Studio Operations desk. Just as the kitchen is the heart of the home, the "Ops Desk" is the heart of the studio. They can always tell who's supposed to be where and when.

Hot Potato! Salad

8 potatoes, baked, peeled, diced
¾ (1-pound) block pasteurized
  cheese, cubed
1 cup mayonnaise
½ cup chopped onion
Salt and pepper
½ pound bacon, cooked and
  crumbled
Sliced green olives

Combine first 5 ingredients and place in a greased 9x13-inch baking dish. Sprinkle with bacon and olives. Bake for one hour at 325°.

Elizabeth Williams, Sebring, OH

Potluck Pasta Salad

Makes a lot and is always in demand at picnics and church gatherings.

1 (16-ounce) package spiral
  pasta
5 cucumbers, chopped
3 cups grape tomatoes, halved
1 large sweet onion, chopped
1 yellow bell pepper, chopped
1 dozen eggs, hard-boiled and
  chopped

Fix pasta according to package directions and drain. Mix cucumbers, tomatoes, onion, and bell pepper. Add in pasta and eggs.

DRESSING:
2½ cups mayonnaise
¾ cup cider vinegar
¾ cup sugar
Salt and pepper to taste

Whisk all Dressing ingredients together.   Fold into pasta. Refrigerate 4 or more hours.

Dana Kelly, High Point, NC

When I was growing up, we lived on a farm. Mama went to the grocery store "in town" only once a week. When she ran out of choice food items, we would have pot luck. She could (and still can) make the most delicious meal out of practically nothing.

—Barbara

Southern Mashed Potato Salad

2–2½ pounds potatoes, peeled,
    cubed, and boiled until
    fork-tender
3 eggs, hard-boiled
1 stalk celery
½ small onion
½ green pepper
3 green onions

1 teaspoon seasoned salt
½ teaspoon garlic powder
2 teaspoons white vinegar
1 tablespoon plain mustard
½ cup mayonnaise
¾ cup pickle relish
1 tablespoon plus 1 teaspoon
    sweet pickle juice

After cooking potatoes and eggs, chill slightly. Finely chop celery, onion, green pepper, and green onions. Combine all ingredients in large bowl and mash well. Chill.

Cynthia Jordan and Jim Brady, Battle Ground, IN

Curried Shrimp Salad

Great alone, or as a side dish.

1 pound shrimp, cleaned,
    deveined, and cooked
1 tablespoon lemon juice
1 (6- to 8-ounce) package frozen
    petite peas

2 green onions, chopped
½–¾ cup mayonnaise
¼–½ teaspoon curry powder
    (depending on your taste)
Salt and pepper

Put shrimp into bowl; add lemon juice. Stir. Add all other ingredients, and mix well. Chill at least 2 hours before serving, so the flavors of the curry mix well. Serves 4–6.

Cheryl McRae, West Valley, UT

Sweet and Sour Broccoli Salad

**2 packages beef ramen noodles
   (save seasoning packets)
1 package broccoli slaw**

**1 (4-ounce) package slivered
   almonds, toasted
1 bunch green onion tops**

Pulse ramen noodles in food processor until broken; combine with broccoli slaw, toasted almonds, and green onion tops, and set aside.

DRESSING:
**½ cup sugar or sugar substitute
1 cup canola oil
¾ cup red wine vinegar**

**2 seasoning packets from
   ramen noodles**

Whisk together Dressing and toss with salad. Serve immediately.

Misty Organ, Marion, OH

Summer Broccoli Salad

This salad is even better the second day!

**8 cups fresh broccoli crowns,
   chopped
3 cups red grapes, halved**

**½ cup diced purple onion
1 cup grated Cheddar cheese
1 cup golden raisins**

Toss all salad ingredients together.

DRESSING:
**⅔ cup mayonnaise
3 tablespoons sugar**

**1½ tablespoons red wine
   vinegar**

Whisk together all Dressing ingredients until smooth. Pour over salad and toss until coated. Keep chilled until serving.

Jennifer Harbour, Cypress, TX

Artichoke and Rice Salad

A little bit different . . . a whole lot enjoyable.

1 (6-ounce) box chicken-flavored
  rice
4 green onions, thinly sliced
1/2 red or green pepper, seeded
  and chopped
1/4 cup finely chopped celery
12 pimento-stuffed green olives,
  sliced

2 (6-ounce) jars marinated
  artichoke hearts, diced
3/4 teaspoon curry powder
  (or more, if desired)
1/3 cup mayonnaise

Cook rice according to directions on box. Add onions, pepper, celery, and olives. Drain artichoke hearts (save marinade). Combine reserved marinade, curry, and mayonnaise.

Add diced artichoke hearts to rice, and toss with mayonnaise mixture. Chill or serve hot.

Norma Smith, Tucson, AZ

Awesome Cucumber Slices

3–4 large cucumbers, sliced
2 medium onions, sliced
1 tablespoon dill weed
1 cup sugar

1/2 cup vinegar
1/2 cup water
1 teaspoon salt

In a medium bowl, combine cucumbers, onions, and dill weed. In a saucepan, combine sugar, vinegar, water, and salt; bring to a boil. Pour over cucumber mixture; cover and chill for 3 hours or overnight. Yields 6 cups.

Dianne Krolikowski, Bella Vista, AR

Asparagus and Tomato Salad

¼ cup mayonnaise
1 tablespoon Dijon-style mustard
1 teaspoon salad vinegar
1 dash hot pepper sauce
Boston or Bibb lettuce leaves

1 (15-ounce) can asparagus
  spears, drained
2 eggs, hard-boiled, sliced
2 medium plum tomatoes, diced
1 cup watercress (optional)

For dressing, stir together mayonnaise, mustard, vinegar, and hot pepper sauce. Cover; chill up to 24 hours. Line 4 salad plates with lettuce. Top each with asparagus, eggs, tomatoes, and watercress, if desired. Serve with Dressing. Makes 4 servings.

Nita Caylor, Brandon, MS

Garlicky Good Tomato Cheese Salad

Can be served alone as a salad, or on top of warmed garlic toast as bruschetta.

½ cup quality balsamic vinegar
¼ cup quality light olive oil
8 large garlic cloves, minced
Salt and pepper to taste
1 (1-pound) block mozzarella
  cheese

2½–3 pounds ripe tomatoes
10 large basil leaves, slivered
  for garnish

Make marinade for salad by combining balsamic vinegar, olive oil, minced garlic, and salt and pepper to taste in a large glass bowl. Cut mozzarella cheese into approximately ¾-inch cubes, and add to marinade mixture. Toss gently to combine. Next, core and cube the tomatoes into ¾-inch square pieces. Add tomatoes to marinade and cheese mixture, and again toss gently to combine. Finally, cut fresh basil leaves into chiffonade, and again, mix this through. You can allow this mixture to stand at room temperature for 1–2 hours while periodically gently folding together all ingredients. The longer this salad marinates, the better the taste. Refrigerate any leftovers. Tastes best at room temperature.

Deborah Yablon, Niskayuna, NY

Sesame Cabbage Salad

SALAD:

1/2 cup slivered almonds
1 medium head cabbage,
    coarsely shredded
6 green onions, chopped

2 packs ramen noodles,
    uncooked and crushed
    (seasoning packets reserved)
4 tablespoons sesame seeds

Toast almonds at 350° for about 5 minutes. In a large bowl, mix together almonds with remaining Salad ingredients.

DRESSING:

6 tablespoons seasoned rice
    wine vinegar
1/2–1 cup vegetable oil or olive
    oil, according to taste
4 tablespoons sugar

1 teaspoon black pepper
1/2 teaspoon salt
1/2 teaspoon sesame oil
2 flavor packs from ramen
    noodles

Mix ingredients for Dressing, then pour over Salad ingredients. Stir thoroughly to mix. If you prefer the ramen noodles crunchy, serve right away. If you prefer the ramen noodles softer, refrigerate 2–3 hours so they can absorb the liquid.

Wendy Bell, Billings, MT

Summertime Pea Salad

1 (15-ounce) can peas
1 (16-ounce) can white corn
1 cup chopped onion
1/2 cup chopped green pepper
1/2 cup chopped red pepper
1 cup chopped celery

1/2 cup vegetable oil
1/2 cup vinegar
1/2 cup sugar
1 teaspoon salt
1/2 teaspoon pepper
1/2 teaspoon celery seed

Drain peas and corn, then combine with other ingredients. Chill thoroughly before serving.

June Morris, Afton, VA

Layer by Layer of Goodness

1 head lettuce, washed and torn
4 bunches green onions, chopped
4 stalks celery, chopped
1 (16-ounce) package frozen
    petite peas
Mayonnaise to taste (about 2 cups)
1 cup freshly grated Parmesan
    cheese
$^1/_2$ teaspoon garlic powder
2 teaspoons seasoning salt
3 teaspoons sugar
$^1/_2$ pound bacon, cooked,
    crumbled
1 cup grape tomatoes, if desired

Layer first 3 ingredients in a 9x13-inch glass dish. Spread with frozen peas, then mayonnaise over top. Mix Parmesan cheese, garlic powder, seasoning salt, and sugar together. Sprinkle over top of salad. Cover and refrigerate overnight.

Just before serving, top with crumbled bacon and tomatoes, if desired.

Kathy Compton, Sumner, WA

Spinach and Strawberry Salad

So pretty . . . so delicious!

1 bag baby spinach

1 quart strawberries

Rinse spinach and remove leaf stems. Cut strawberries into quarters.

DRESSING:
$^1/_2$ cup sugar
1 teaspoon minced onion
2 teaspoons poppy seeds
$^1/_4$ teaspoon Worcestershire
$^1/_4$ cup extra virgin olive oil
$^1/_2$ cup vinegar
$^1/_4$ teaspoon paprika

Combine ingredients. Shake and refrigerate. Combine Dressing with spinach and strawberries when ready to serve.

Variation: Instead of spinach, spring mix is a great alternative.

Diane Reed, Levittown, PA, and Diane Barndt, Silverdale, PA

Fruitfully Delicious Balsamic Dressing

Unbelievably good on mixed greens with strawberries and toasted nuts.

1¼ cups balsamic vinegar
  with maple syrup or sherry
2–3 teaspoons honey
1 teaspoon Dijon mustard
1 teaspoon grated lemon rind
2 teaspoons grated orange rind
½ orange, sectioned, seeded,
  chopped
6–8 dried apricots, chopped

½ teaspoon crushed fresh
  oregano
½ teaspoon grated fresh ginger
3–4 cloves garlic, chopped
Several sprigs parsley
½ cup olive oil
⅓ cup flax seed oil
Salt and pepper to taste

Combine all ingredients in blender or food processor, or shake in a jar. Refrigerate. Even better after it sits awhile.

Marilyn Oestreicher, Fairfield, CT

Pineapple Apple Salad

2 (8-ounce) cans pineapple
  tidbits, drained, reserve juice
2 Red Delicious apples, peeled
  and chopped (or grated)
½ cup finely chopped celery
¼ cup lightly toasted and
  chopped pecans

3 tablespoons reserved pineapple
  juice
3 tablespoons mayonnaise-style
  light salad dressing

Combine drained pineapple with apples, celery, and pecans. Set aside. Stir pineapple juice into salad dressing until smooth. Pour over apple mixture and toss well. Serves 6–8.

Anita Adcock, Iowa Park, TX

Penny's Peanutty Apple Salad

1 (16-ounce) can crushed
   pineapple, drained, reserve
   juice
2 cups mini-marshmallows
$\frac{1}{2}$ cup sugar
1 teaspoon flour

$1\frac{1}{2}$ teaspoons vinegar
1 egg, well beaten
$1\frac{1}{2}$ cups salted peanuts
2 cups diced apples
1 (8-ounce) carton whipped
   topping

Combine pineapple and marshmallows; refrigerate until ready to use, preferably next day. Combine sugar, flour, vinegar, egg, and reserved pineapple juice in saucepan. Cook till thick over medium heat for about one minute or more. Refrigerate overnight.

Next day, combine pineapple-marshmallow mixture with cooked sauce. Add salted nuts, chopped apples, and whipped topping. Mix together and serve.

Penny Wuestman, QVC Guest, West Dundee, IL

The green room provides a comfy setting for guests like Penny Wuestman and Gwen to chat and exchange ideas.

Frosty Grape Salad

Pretty in stemware or on lettuce leaves. These are to die for!

1 (8-ounce) carton sour cream
1 (8-ounce) package cream
  cheese, softened
½ cup white sugar

4 pounds seedless grapes, halved
1 cup chopped walnuts
¾ cup brown sugar

Mix sour cream, cream cheese, and white sugar, and pour over grapes. Just before serving, mix walnuts and brown sugar and sprinkle over top.

Cynthia Dafoe, Marquette, MI

Fluffy Fruit Salad

This is beautiful served in a pretty bowl. It is especially nice for the holiday table. The color is wonderful . . . just perfect for Thanksgiving!

1 (8-ounce) can crushed
  pineapple, undrained
1 (3-ounce) package orange
  gelatin
¾ cup sugar
1 (8-ounce) package cream
  cheese, softened

2 jars apricot baby food
1 (16-ounce) container
  whipped topping
½ cup chopped pecans

Combine undrained pineapple and gelatin. Heat over low heat until gelatin is completely dissolved. Remove from heat; add sugar and let cool to room temperature. Beat cream cheese and baby food together; add pineapple mixture. Stir in whipped topping and nuts. Chill overnight.

Donna Howell, Supply, NC

A Really Red Salad

Perfect for make-ahead company meals, especially for the holidays.

1 (3-ounce) box cherry gelatin
1 (3-ounce) box raspberry gelatin
1 cup boiling water
1 (8-ounce) can crushed
   pineapple, drained, save juice

1 (16-ounce) can whole berry
   cranberry sauce
1 (16.5-ounce) can bing cherries,
   drained, save juice
1 cup chopped pecans

Dissolve gelatin in boiling water. Cool gelatin with 1 cup reserved juices (use water if needed to make up 1 cup). Mix in remaining ingredients and pour into a 9x13-inch glass pan. Refrigerate overnight, or at least several hours before serving.

Faith Oakley, Randleman, NC

Cherry Cola Salad

1 (3-ounce) package cherry
   gelatin
½ cup boiling water
1 (8-ounce) package cream
   cheese, softened

1 (8-ounce) cola
1 (16-ounce) can dark sweet
   cherries, drained
½ cup broken pecans or
   walnuts

Dissolve gelatin in boiling water; add cream cheese and mix until smooth. Add cola and congeal slightly. Add well-drained cherries and pecans. Chill.

Marilyn Goodson, Bangs, TX

Light Lime Fluff

Excellent as a salad or dessert!

¹/₄ pound marshmallows
1 cup milk
1 (3-ounce) package lime-
  flavored gelatin
2 (3-ounce) packages cream
  cheese, softened

1 (20-ounce) can crushed
  pineapple, undrained
1 cup whipping cream, whipped

Melt marshmallows and milk in top of double boiler. When all marshmallows have melted, pour hot mixture over lime gelatin and stir until gelatin is dissolved into marshmallow mixture. Mix in cream cheese until fully dissolved. Add crushed pineapple. Let mixture come to room temperature. Fold in whipped cream. Pour into 9x13-inch pan. Chill until firm.

Note: To save a few calories, you can use a small container of whipped topping to replace the whipped cream.

Howard Schwartz, Belchertown, MA

It's funny how a particular dish can bring back memories. My aunt brought the most delicious congealed salad to us after our first baby was born. I remember the salad well and think about her when I read these recipes. —*Barbara*

Cran-Mallow Salad

1 bag fresh cranberries, washed
1 orange, quartered
1¼ cups sugar
4 cups mini-marshmallows
4 tart apples, diced
1 cup green grapes, halved
¾ cup pecan pieces
½ teaspoon salt
½ cup mayonnaise-type
   salad dressing
1½ cups frozen whipped
   topping, thawed

Grind cranberries and orange. Add sugar and marshmallows; chill overnight in covered bowl. Stir in apples, grapes, pecans, and salt. Fold in salad dressing and whipped topping. Chill.

Linda Casto, Millwood, WV

Wedding Salad

1 (8-ounce) package cream
   cheese, softened
½ (13-ounce) jar marshmallow
   crème
1 tablespoon orange juice
3 pounds Red Rome apples,
   peeled and chopped
1 cup green seedless grapes,
   sliced
½ cup raisins
½ cup slivered almonds
1 cup miniature marshmallows

With electric mixer, blend cream cheese, marshmallow crème, and orange juice. Blend fruit, almonds, and marshmallows with cream cheese mixture, then chill.

Lori Wagner, Oregon, OH

Vegetables

East Haven Eggplant Parmigiana

1 eggplant, peeled
Salt to taste
1 egg, beaten
½ cup cornmeal
1 (26-ounce) jar spaghetti sauce

⅓ cup Parmesan cheese
⅓ cup mozzarella cheese
1–1½ teaspoons garlic salt
1–1½ teaspoons oregano

Slice eggplant and salt lightly; dip in egg, then cornmeal. Fry in oil on both sides until golden brown. Layer eggplant with spaghetti sauce, Parmesan cheese, and mozzarella. Sprinkle with garlic salt and oregano. Bake at 350° for 30 minutes.

Dorothy Bock, Conyers, GA

When my husband, Frank was in graduate school at Yale, we rented an apartment in a large home. Our landlady took us under her wing, considering us part of her family, and taught me so much about cooking—especially Italian dishes like this wonderful Eggplant Parmigiana. Not long ago, we revisited the area, and when I knocked on the door, she and her daughter were excited to invite me in for lunch. As we sat around the same table eating her delicious food, the 35 years just seemed to disappear. I was once again that 20-year-old newlywed in East Haven, Connecticut.

—Dorothy Bock

Fried Eggplant Medallions

1 large eggplant
1 egg
3 cups seasoned bread crumbs
5 tablespoons grated cheese of
  choice

Pinches of oregano, basil leaves,
  and crushed red pepper
1 small garlic clove, minced
1 cup vegetable oil

Boil eggplant with skin on till very soft. Drain, then mash in large bowl. Add remaining ingredients except oil, and mix. Heat oil in frying pan. Shape eggplant mixture into patties and fry on both sides until brown. Serves 4–6 as a side dish, 8–10 as appetizers.

Anne Tredici, Staten Island, NY

Unbeatable Broccoli Casserole

1 large bunch broccoli
1½ sticks margarine
1 medium onion, chopped
1½ sleeves round butter-type
  crackers, crushed

2 (10¾-ounce) cans cream of
  mushroom soup
1 (8-ounce) package cream
  cheese
8 ounces shredded colby cheese

Cut florets from broccoli and soak in warm salted water for 15 minutes. Cook florets 15–20 minutes until tender. Drain well. Melt margarine in large skillet. Add onion and cook until tender and light brown. Remove onion from margarine and set aside. Add cracker crumbs to margarine and stir to coat. Heat soup until hot, then add cream cheese; stir until melted. In large casserole dish, layer broccoli, soup mixture, onion, and crackers. Repeat. Top with shredded colby cheese. Bake at 350 for 40–45 minutes.

Sonja Stringer, Ledbetter, KY

The Best Broccoli Fritters

2 broccoli stems, peeled
  (not the tops)
1/4 cup chopped onion
2 tablespoons butter
4 tablespoons flour

1 teaspoon baking powder
1 egg
2 tablespoons milk
Salt and pepper to taste
Oil for frying

Peel broccoli stems and chop finely (you should have about 1/2 cup). Sauté broccoli and onion in butter until soft and beginning to brown. Remove from heat and cool slightly.

Meanwhile, measure remaining ingredients except oil in a bowl and mix with a wire whisk. With a spoon, stir sautéed vegetables into batter mixture. Adjust consistency with extra milk or a little flour, if needed. You want to be able to spoon dollops of batter into oil.

Fry mounds of fritter batter a few at a time in about one inch of heated oil until they are golden brown. This browning occurs very quickly. Makes about 6 fritters.

Variation: Add 3/4 teaspoon chili powder to the batter mixture for Chili Broccoli Fritters.

Rita Swanson, Oxford, MS

E-Z Zucchini Fritters

1 cup zucchini, grated
1 small onion, chopped
2 eggs, beaten
1/2 cup flour

2 teaspoons baking powder
1/4 teaspoon salt
1 cup crushed cornflakes
Salt and pepper to taste

Mix together zucchini, onion, and eggs. In another bowl, sift together flour, baking powder, and salt. Add cornflakes and stir in zucchini mixture. Heat oil. Drop batter by tablespoon into hot oil, turning so they brown on both sides.

Thomasine Weber, Core, WV

Too-Easy Zucchini Casserole

4 medium zucchini
1 onion
4–8 ounces mushrooms
  (optional)
1 (6-ounce) box croutons

1 (26-ounce) jar spaghetti
  sauce with basil and garlic
1 (8-ounce) package grated
  mozzarella cheese, divided

Slice zucchini, onion, and mushrooms, if desired. Mix in large bowl with croutons. Add spaghetti sauce and pour half the mixture into a 9x13-inch baking dish. Cover with cheese and repeat layer, topping with remaining cheese. Cover and bake at 350° for 45 minutes.

Sharon DeMyer-Nemser, Cheshire, MA

Zucchini and Onion Grill

4 zucchini squash
2 onions

Olive oil (about ⅓ cup)
Salt and pepper to taste

Cut zucchini squash in half lengthwise, then crosswise. Cut onions in big chunks. Put zucchini and onions in bowl, with lid, with plenty of room. Drizzle with olive oil; add salt and pepper. Cover bowl and shake up. Put in refrigerator for at least an hour or overnight. Cook on a very hot indoor or outdoor grill, very fast, but not too long. You want the vegetables to be tender but firm. Enjoy!

Sandy Lamas, Vine Grove, KY

Zelicious Zucchini Quiche

3 small yellow squash, cut into
   medium-size pieces
3 small zucchini squash, cut
   into medium-size pieces
1 large onion, chopped
4 tablespoons olive oil
3 tablespoons dried crushed basil
3 tablespoons dried crushed
   oregano
Salt and pepper to taste

2 (8-count) cans refrigerated
   crescent rolls
1½ cups milk
5 eggs
2 (4-ounce) bags shredded
   mozzarella cheese
1 (4-ounce) bag shredded
   Cheddar or Monterey Jack
   cheese

Preheat oven to 350°. In large frying pan, sauté squash and onion in olive oil, adding basil, oregano, salt and pepper. Cook until tender. Let cool. Line a 12x17-inch baking pan with crescent rolls. Pat and stretch to fit bottom and sides. In large bowl, mix milk and eggs. Add cheeses and cooked squash and mix together. Pour over crescent rolls. Bake for 45–60 minutes or until firm and dark golden brown.

Note: To reduce fat in recipe, substitute low-fat or nonfat cheese and low-fat or nonfat milk. Omit olive oil for sautéing and use cooking spray. Also okay to use liquid egg substitute.

Noreen Reynolds, Torrington, CT

Garden Goodness Squash Sauté

When vegetables are abundant from my garden, this is one of my favorite, quick and easy—and oh! so delicious—ways to fix squash.

1 large onion, diced large
1 green pepper, seeded, diced large
2 medium zucchini squash,
   sliced ¼ inch
2 yellow squash, sliced ¼ inch

½ stick butter or margarine
½ teaspoon salt
¼ teaspoon pepper
¼ teaspoon Greek seasoning
1 teaspoon chopped basil

In large skillet or wok, sauté onion, pepper, and squash in butter until just tender. Add salt, pepper, seasoning, and basil. Cook on medium heat, tossing well, until cooked down somewhat (about 5 minutes). (Pictured on cover.)

Virginia Cantrell, Shelby, AL

Simply Squash Parmesan

**Equal amounts of yellow summer
  squash and zucchini
1 onion for every 2 squash
Salt and pepper to taste**

**1–2 (14½-ounce) cans crushed
  or diced tomatoes
1–2 teaspoons sugar (optional)
¼–½ cup Parmesan cheese**

Wash and slice squash, zucchini, and onions about ¼ inch thick.
Layer in large saucepan; lightly salt and pepper each layer to taste.
Cover with crushed or diced tomatoes. Add sugar, if desired.
Cook on medium heat until squash becomes translucent. Remove
from heat and add Parmesan cheese. Transfer to serving dish.
Mmmmm good.

Note: Amount of tomatoes will vary depending on amount of squash
and zucchini used.

Janet Trackey, Lake Luzerne, NY

Squash Pudding

**3 pounds yellow squash
½ cup chopped onions
½ cup bread crumbs, divided
2 eggs
4 tablespoons margarine or
  butter, melted, divided**

**1 tablespoon sugar
½ teaspoon pepper
Salt to taste
1 cup shredded Cheddar cheese**

Preheat oven to 350°. Slice squash into ¼-inch rounds. Cook
until soft but not mushy. Drain. Mash squash a little to break up
any large pieces, but mostly leave in large chunks. Mix squash and
remaining ingredients except cheese, using only half the margarine
and bread crumbs. Place in lightly greased 11x17-inch pan.
Sprinkle cheese on squash mix. Sprinkle with remaining ½ cup
bread crumbs. Drizzle remaining 2 tablespoons melted margarine
on top of crumbs. Bake one hour.

Howard Schwartz, Belchertown, MA

Squash Meal in a Dish

4–5 cups chopped yellow squash
(about 6 or 7)
1 small onion, diced
1 cup water
2 cups sour cream
1 (10¾-ounce) can cream of
chicken soup

2 (5-ounce) cans (or 1½ cups)
finely diced chicken meat
Salt and pepper to taste
1 bag (4 cups) bread crumbs
(corn bread works best)

In a covered 2-quart saucepan, place squash, onion, and enough water to cover. Slowly bring to a boil; simmer and steam till squash is very soft. Drain well in colander; put back in pan or bowl, and mix with a mixer on low speed till fairly smooth. Add remaining ingredients except bread crumbs, and mix all together (mixture will be lumpy).

Butter a 2- or 2½-quart deep baking dish; sprinkle bottom of dish with a small amount of bread crumbs. Add squash mixture to cover bread crumbs, then cover squash mixture with more bread crumbs; do this about 4 times, till you have a small amount of bread crumbs left. Sprinkle remaining bread crumbs on top and dot with butter or margarine. Bake in a 350° oven 35–40 minutes, till mixture is nicely browned and it looks like sides are pulling away from dish. Let cool about 10 minutes for it to set up. When done, a knife inserted in center should come out clean.

Note: If you prefer to use this as a side dish, just omit the meat. Also, you may substitute other types of poultry, if desired.

Dorothy Heck, Mifflin, PA

Four-Cheese Hash Brown Quiche

1 (24-ounce) package shredded
  hash brown potatoes, thawed
1/2 cup butter, melted
1 cup (4 ounces) shredded
  Cheddar cheese
1 1/2 cups (6 ounces) shredded
  mozzarella cheese
1/2 cup (3 ounces) shredded
  Parmesan cheese
1 (10-ounce) package frozen
  spinach, thawed

1 small sweet red bell pepper,
  chopped
1/2 medium-size sweet onion,
  diced
2 cups whipping cream
6 large eggs
1/2 teaspoon salt
1 teaspoon white pepper
1 cup crumbled feta cheese

Preheat oven to 425°. Grease an 11-inch deep-dish pie plate (bottom and sides) or use an ungreased 12-inch round stoneware dish. Press thawed hash browns between paper towels to remove excess moisture. Brush hash browns (bottom and edges) with melted butter. Fit hash browns into pie plate and press firmly (making a crust). Bake for 25 minutes. Remove from oven.

Lower oven temperature to 350°. Sprinkle Cheddar, mozzarella, and Parmesan cheeses evenly over bottom of crust. Spread well-drained spinach over cheeses. Sprinkle chopped red pepper and diced onion on top of spinach. Beat cream, eggs, salt, and pepper with whisk until fully incorporated. Pour on top of cheeses, spinach, onion and pepper. Sprinkle feta cheese on top. Bake for 40 minutes or until center is firmly set. Let stand for 15 minutes before serving.

Kari Hooker-Leep, Grand Island, NE

Easy Tomato Quiche

Delicious summer meal.

3 eggs, beaten
2 cups fat-free half-and-half
2 cups grated Cheddar cheese
1 (15-ounce) can diced tomatoes
   with garlic and onion, drained

$\frac{1}{2}$ teaspoon basil
2 deep-dish frozen pie crusts,
   thawed

Mix together eggs, half-and-half, cheese, tomatoes, and basil. Pour into pie crusts and bake at 375° for 45 minutes or until knife inserted near center comes out clean. Can be served hot or room temperature.

Mary Ellen Ignatius, Jacksonville, FL

Cheesy Broiled Tomatoes

A mighty tasty dish for most any meal.

Red ripe tomatoes (sliced
   $\frac{1}{4}$ inch)
Mayonnaise

Mozzarella cheese (shredded)
Bacon (fried crisply and
   broken into pieces)

Line a broiling pan with tin foil and spray with a nonstick cooking spray. Lay sliced tomatoes on the foil. Put a dollop of mayonnaise on each slice, then add mozzarella cheese, and top with bacon pieces. Broil until cheese melts and gets a little brown, about 1–2 minutes.

Kim Farrell, Ottawa, IL

A Whole Lot of Goodness in a Pot

2 pounds tender green beans, snapped
1/2 pound bacon, cut into pieces
4 large carrots, cut into bite-size pieces
2 or 3 large onions, cut into quarters
6 medium new potatoes, halved
Salt and pepper to taste

Wash and soak beans; let stand. Cook bacon in large skillet until translucent. Remove beans from water with hands, leaving some water on beans; add to bacon and stir well. Arrange carrots on top, cover with lid, and steam 30 minutes on low heat. Add onions and potatoes, cover, and cook until potatoes are done (about 20 minutes more). Just before everything is done (another 10 minutes), add salt and pepper, and cover to finish cooking. Makes 2–4 servings.

Marietta Shigekawa, Santa Ana, CA

Parmesan Green Beans

2 tablespoons butter
2 tablespoons all-purpose flour
1/2 teaspoon salt
1/2 teaspoon pepper
1/8 teaspoon garlic salt
1 cup 2% milk
3/4 teaspoon Worcestershire
4 tablespoons grated Parmesan cheese, divided
2 (14.5-ounce) cans cut green beans, drained

Melt butter in medium saucepan. Mix in flour, salt, pepper, and garlic salt. Stir in milk and heat until thickened. Add Worcestershire and 1/2 the Parmesan cheese. Add green beans and heat through. Add remaining Parmesan cheese and stir. Delicious!

Robin Boyd, Seaford, DE

Green Bean Toss About

6 slices bacon
½ (12-ounce) package frozen diced onion
½ (28-ounce) package frozen O'Brien potatoes

2 (15-ounce) cans Italian green beans, drained
Salt and pepper to taste
½ teaspoon Greek seasoning

In a large microwave-safe dish, cook bacon until crisp. Remove from microwave, crumble, and set aside; reserve drippings. Add onion and potatoes to drippings. Cook on HIGH 8–10 minutes, till potatoes are almost done. Add green beans and seasonings, mixing well. Cook an additional 8–10 minutes, stirring often. Add crumbled bacon and toss.

Meg Maulding, Brandon, MS

This is a wonderful alternative to regular green beans. My grandmother created this dish while trying to stretch a meal. It has become a family favorite.

—Meg Maulding

West Virginia Slow-Cooked Beans

**1–2 pounds fresh green beans,
  cut in half**

**1 pound salt pork (or bacon)
Salt and pepper to taste**

Wash beans. Cut salt pork into bite-size pieces and place in large saucepan; add beans. Cover beans with water. Add salt and pepper to taste. If using salt pork, use salt sparingly. Bring to a boil, then lower heat and simmer 4–6 hours, till beans are mushy. Add additional water, if needed. Serves 4–6.

Kelly Ann Branch, Marengo, IL

Almond Topped String Bean Casserole

This is a good, rich vegetable dish that tastes great served with barbecued chicken and sliced tomatoes in the summer.

**1 medium onion, sliced
2 (4-ounce) cans sliced
  mushrooms
$\frac{1}{2}$ cup butter
$\frac{1}{4}$ cup flour
1–1$\frac{1}{2}$ cups milk
$\frac{3}{4}$ pound medium-sharp
  Cheddar cheese
$\frac{1}{2}$ teaspoon salt**

**$\frac{1}{2}$ teaspoon hot sauce
2 teaspoons soy sauce
$\frac{1}{2}$ teaspoon pepper
1 teaspoon MSG (optional)
3 (16-ounce) packages frozen
  cut string beans, thawed,
  drained (may use canned)
Sliced almonds**

Sauté onion and mushrooms in butter until onion is transparent. Add flour, stirring until blended. Add milk and cook until smooth. Add cheese, salt, hot sauce, soy sauce, pepper, and MSG, if desired, and cook until cheese is melted. In a separate pan, cook string beans and drain well. Add to sauce mixture and pour into large casserole dish. Sprinkle with sliced almonds. Bake 20 minutes at 350°. Serves 8–10.

Paula Fondren, Clinton, MS

More Than Baked Beans

A great potluck take along.

1 pound ground beef
½ cup chopped onion
1 pound bacon, cooked and
   crumbled
½ cup molasses

1 tablespoon Worcestershire
½ cup ketchup
1 tablespoon dry mustard
1 (28-ounce) can pork and beans

Brown ground beef with chopped onion; drain. In a large bowl, combine ground beef and onion, crumbled bacon, and remaining ingredients. Pour into a 2- to 3-quart casserole dish that has been sprayed with cooking spray. Bake at 350° for about 30 minutes or until heated through.

Note: Instead of baking, can also go into a crockpot on LOW.

Mika Williams, Salisbury, NC

A Medley of Baked Beans

1 (1-pound) can green lima
   beans, drained
1 (1-pound) can red kidney
   beans, drained
2 (1-pound) cans navy beans,
   drained
½ pound bacon
½ tablespoon minced garlic

3 large Vidalia onions, cut in
   rings
½ cup cider vinegar
1 teaspoon salt
1 cup dark brown sugar
1 tablespoon mustard
1 (2-pound) can pork and beans

Rinse drained lima, kidney, and navy beans; set aside. Fry bacon and crumble; set aside. Save bacon drippings and add garlic, onions, vinegar, salt, brown sugar, mustard, and pork and beans. Cook covered about 20 minutes on simmer. Mix all ingredients in a lightly greased 3½-quart casserole, and bake at 350° one hour. Makes 3 quarts. Freezes well.

Queenie Campbell, Jasper, GA

Vegetable Cheesecake

Incredibly delicious! Great with a green salad and slices of ham.

3 cups grated zucchini (2–3 small ones)
3 tablespoons butter
1 medium onion, minced
2 cloves garlic, minced
$\frac{1}{2}$ teaspoon salt
1 medium carrot, grated
3 (8-ounce) packages cream cheese, softened
1 cup grated Swiss or Jack cheese
$\frac{1}{2}$ cup grated Parmesan cheese
4 large eggs
3 tablespoons flour
$\frac{1}{2}$ teaspoon each, basil and oregano
$\frac{1}{4}$ cup minced fresh parsley
1 tablespoon lemon juice
Pepper to taste
3–4 tablespoons fine dried bread crumbs, to line pan
2 medium tomatoes, thinly sliced

Lightly salt zucchini; let stand 15 minutes, then squeeze out excess water. Sauté first 6 ingredients in a large skillet, until onion is translucent. Remove from heat and set aside. In a mixing bowl, beat softened cream cheese on medium speed until smooth. Add mozzarella and Parmesan cheeses. Add eggs; beat one minute. On low speed, add remaining ingredients except bread crumbs and tomatoes. Add sautéed vegetables.

Butter a 9-inch springform pan and dust with fine bread crumbs. Pour cheese/vegetable mixture into prepared pan. Bake in preheated 375° oven for $\frac{1}{2}$ hour. Arrange thinly sliced tomatoes on top of cheesecake and bake for another $\frac{1}{2}$ hour. Cool on rack 10–15 minutes. Serve warm.

Krista Bendinelli, Hercules, CA

Roasted Vegetable Medley

1 potato, sliced	6–8 asparagus spears
2 carrots, sliced	Extra virgin olive oil
2 celery stalks, sliced	Garlic salt
1 zucchini, sliced	Old Bay Seasoning
1 summer squash, sliced	Basil
1 crookneck squash, sliced	Salt and pepper to taste
1 medium onion, sliced	Grated Parmesan cheese
6 mushrooms, sliced	Balsamic vinegar
2–3 tomatoes, sliced	

Place 2–3 layers of aluminum foil in a 9x13 baking dish. Make layers long enough to fold over and create a packet of foil. Layer vegetables. When about ½ way done, sprinkle with seasonings. Continue layering. Season vegetables once all have been added. Sprinkle with Parmesan cheese. Drizzle entire dish with both olive oil and balsamic vinegar to taste. Fold foil over vegetables to create a packet. Bake in 425° oven 45 minutes.

Note: This is a living recipe, a work in progress. Additional vegetables may be added as well as other spices. Greek seasoning works well.

Karen Doshier, Idyllwild, CA

Swiss Corn Bake

3 cups fresh corn, or 1 (9-ounce) package frozen, or 1 (16-ounce) can whole-kernel	½ teaspoon salt and pepper
	1 cup shredded Swiss cheese, divided
6 ounces evaporated milk	½ cup soft bread crumbs
1 egg, beaten	1 tablespoon butter, melted
2 tablespoons finely chopped onion	

Combine corn, milk, egg, onion, salt, and pepper, and ¾ cup cheese. Pour into greased casserole dish. Toss bread crumbs with butter and remaining Swiss cheese. Sprinkle over top of corn mixture, and bake at 350° for 25–30 minutes. Serve hot.

Judith Laino, Old Tappan, NJ

Corny Stuffed Peppers

8 medium green bell peppers,
  tops removed
¾ teaspoon salt, or to taste
1 pound ground beef
½ cup chopped onion
1 (12-ounce) can whole-kernel
  corn, drained
1 (8-ounce) can tomato sauce
1 teaspoon Worcestershire
2 cups shredded Cheddar cheese
Buttered bread crumbs

Precook peppers in boiling, salted water 5 minutes. Drain; sprinkle insides with salt, then set aside. Brown meat and onion in skillet; add corn, tomato sauce, and Worcestershire. Simmer until heated. Add cheese and stir until melted. Pack meat mixture into peppers. Place in oven-proof pan and top with buttered crumbs. Bake at 425° for 30 minutes or until bubbly.

Carolyn Adriaansen, Marion, NY

Slow Cooker Cabbage Rolls

1 large head cabbage
2 pounds ground beef
1 cup cooked rice
¼ teaspoon pepper
½ teaspoon salt
3 tablespoons brown sugar
½ teaspoon cinnamon
½ teaspoon nutmeg
1 (6-ounce) can tomato paste
1 (12-ounce) can tomato sauce
½ cup water

Place cabbage in boiling water for 5 minutes. Cut leaves off of core. (You may have to submerge the head again as needed to cook inner leaves). Combine everything except tomato paste, sauce, and water. Place 2–3 tablespoons meat mixture on a cabbage leaf and wrap like a burrito (fold ends in and roll). Combine tomato paste, tomato sauce, and water. Place cabbage rolls in layers into a slow cooker, pouring tomato mixture over each layer. Cook on LOW for 8 hours.

Linda Hess-Layne, Tulsa, OK

Forget-the-Meat Meatballs

4 tablespoons olive oil, divided
1 large eggplant, peeled and
  diced small
¼ cup water
1 tablespoon minced garlic
2 tablespoons dried parsley
2 tablespoons dried minced onion

2 teaspoons salt
1 teaspoon grated black pepper
¼ cup grated cheese
2 cups Italian-style bread crumbs
2 eggs, beaten
1 (16-ounce) can tomato sauce

Heat 2 tablespoons olive oil in a 12-inch sauté pan over medium heat. Add eggplant and sauté gently, about 5 minutes. Add water, minced garlic, parsley, minced onion, salt, and pepper, and simmer, stirring occasionally, until eggplant falls apart and reaches a purée texture, about 20 minutes.

Remove from heat and add additional seasoning as necessary. Transfer to bowl and let cool. Stir in grated cheese and bread crumbs. Add eggs. Add additional bread crumbs, if necessary, until mixture is firm enough to hold a ball shape. Mold by tablespoons into balls. Preheat oven to 375°.

Heat remaining 2 tablespoons oil in sauté pan. Lightly brown meatballs. Arrange in a shallow 14x16-inch baking dish. Bake 30 minutes. Cover with tomato sauce and bake an additional 15 minutes.

Linda Maslowski, Greenwood Lake, NE

Editor's Extra: I used a (26-ounce) jar of spaghetti sauce instead of tomato sauce. Yum! More saucy . . . good both ways.

Easy Cheesy Microwave Potatoes

1 stick butter or margarine,
   divided
3 or 4 large baking potatoes,
   peeled, thinly sliced

1 large onion, thinly sliced
9 slices American cheese (or
   cheese of choice)
Salt and pepper to taste

In a 2-quart glass casserole, melt 3 pats of butter. Layer potatoes, onion, and cheese. Salt and pepper each layer, if desired. Continue layering to top of casserole, ending with cheese. Pour remaining melted butter over all. Cover and cook in microwave on HIGH 20–25 minutes or until potatoes are tender and cheese is browned. Let stand 5 minutes before serving.

June Rees, Shickshinny, PA

Surprising Mashed Potatoes

This is a wonderful recipe that I made up because I love cauliflower, and it is a great way to get others (like my kids) to eat it!

2 heads cauliflower, cooked
1 cup instant mashed potato
   flakes
1 cup grated Cheddar cheese
Pepper to taste

1 clove garlic, minced
½ cup mayonnaise
Milk (as needed)
Crumbled cooked bacon

Drain cooked cauliflower. Mash cauliflower as you would potatoes. Add potato flakes, Cheddar cheese, pepper, minced garlic, and mayonnaise. Stir till cheese is melted and potato flakes are absorbed into cauliflower. Stir well until consistency of mashed potatoes is reached. Add warm milk, if needed, to obtain correct consistency. Stir bacon in, or put into serving dish and sprinkle with bacon on top.

Sarah Brackett, Manassas, VA

Editor's Extra: Good to fix ahead, then reheat in 350° oven about 15 minutes till heated throughout.

Spicy Hot Parsley Potato Pie

This is a spicy dish—equally as good hot or cold.

5–6 potatoes (large fist size),
  peeled and cubed
½–1 stick margarine
1 egg, beaten
¼ teaspoon hot pepper flakes,
  or to taste

½ cup grated cheese (pecorino,
  Asiago, or Parmesan)
Salt and pepper to taste
Milk as needed
½ cup finely chopped Italian
  leaf parsley

Boil, then drain potatoes, but not dry. Mash potatoes with margarine. Add beaten egg, hot pepper flakes, cheese, salt and pepper. (I add a triple dose of pepper.) Mix with milk until the consistency of thick mashed potatoes. Add parsley and mix well.

Spoon into 8- or 9-inch pie plate, which has been coated with margarine or butter. Looks better when baked if you leave many tiny peaks instead of smoothing the top. Bake in 350° oven for 45 minutes, or when "peaks" turn golden brown.

Lisa LaBrake, Lancaster, NY

Spicy Potato Slices

3 large gold potatoes, scrubbed
½ cup butter, melted
1 tablespoon Greek seasoning

2–3 tablespoons chipotle hot
  sauce

Preheat oven to 425°. Slice potatoes into ¼-inch disks. Spread slices in a single layer on baking sheet (you may need to use two). In a small bowl, combine remaining ingredients. Brush potato slices with sauce. Flip slices, then brush other side. Cook 25–30 minutes, turning once. Slices will be golden brown and slightly crispy around edges when done.

Sandra Kortjohn, Yelm, WA

Cinnamon Holiday Apples

1 (28-ounce) bag cinnamon bits
  or red hots
12 medium-firm apples, such as
  California Gala or Golden Rome

2 (8-ounce) packages cream
  cheese, softened
1½ cups chopped pecans
1½ teaspoons apple pie spice

Fill a large pot (large enough for 12 apples) about ¾ full of water. Add bag of cinnamon bits and stir on low heat until bits are melted. Peel and core apples and place in saucepan. Simmer, covered, on medium-low heat about one hour, basting tops of apples with liquid every few minutes. About halfway through cooking time, turn apples over and continue basting until apples turn a bright red color and are tender to the touch. (If apples are not deep enough in color to suit, add a few drops of red food coloring.) Remove apples to a paper towel-lined plate with a slotted spoon or tongs and refrigerate immediately.

While apples cool, mix cream cheese, pecans, and apple pie spice together in a small bowl. Stuff chilled apples with cream cheese mixture, slightly mounding the top. (I mold an elongated shape with my hands and stuff in hollowed-out part of apple, then mound extra on top.)

Betty Murray, Cape Girardeau, MO

Editor's Extra: Also good to cut apples in half and mound stuffing on top.

My friend, Betty Murray, used to make these apples every Christmas for family and neighborhood friends. She always placed them on a tray in the shape of a pyramid or Christmas tree, and decorated the rims of the plate with holly sprigs. That was her rule, and now it doesn't seem like Christmas without them served that way. Beautiful AND delicious!
—Melinda Burnham

Pineapple Cheese Casserole

2 (20-ounce) cans pineapple
  chunks, drained
1 cup sugar
5 tablespoons flour
1½ cups grated Cheddar cheese
1 stack butter-flavored crackers,
  crushed

¾–1 stick margarine, melted
⅓ cup chopped pecans
  (optional)
⅓ cup shredded coconut
  (optional)

Put drained pineapple in casserole dish. Mix sugar and flour, and sprinkle over pineapple. Add cheese and mix well. Mix together the crackers and margarine. Sprinkle over top of casserole. Sprinkle with pecans and coconut, if desired. Bake at 350° for 30 minutes.

Jean Born, Phoenix, AZ

Fruit Compote

Good served with any meat dish.

1 (20-ounce) can peach halves
1 (20-ounce) can pear halves
1 (20-ounce) can pineapple
  chunks
1 (20-ounce) can apricot halves
1 (20-ounce) can purple plums
1 (10-ounce) bottle maraschino
  cherries

1 dozen almond macaroons,
  or vanilla wafers, crushed
1 stick butter or margarine
¾ cup brown sugar
1 tablespoon cornstarch
½ cup sherry
Slivered almonds

Drain all fruits. Place crushed macaroons in bottom of large casserole dish. Add drained fruit. Melt butter or margarine; add brown sugar, cornstarch, and sherry. Pour over fruit and top with slivered almonds. Bake at 325° for 1½ hours.

Paula Fondren, Clinton, MS

Pasta, Rice, Etc.

Marco's Bella Tortellini

1 (2-pound) bag fresh tortellini
  (cheese filled)
1 (1.3-ounce) package dry
  Prima Rosa Sauce mix
3 large Italian sausages
  (precooked, cut into pieces)
10 marinated and jarred sun-
  dried tomatoes, slightly drained
  and sliced

1 (6-ounce) jar marinated
  artichokes, drained
½ teaspoon minced garlic
1 teaspoon parsley flakes
1 (8-ounce) package shredded
  mozzarella cheese

Bring water to a boil in 8-quart pot. Add tortellini. Cook for 7 minutes. While tortellini is cooking, make spaghetti sauce according to package directions in 1-quart saucepan. Let mixture simmer as directed.

In 10-inch saucepan, heat on low for 3 minutes the sausage, sun-dried tomatoes, artichokes, garlic, and parsley. Add drained tortellini and prepared spaghetti sauce to sausage mixture. Cover top with cheese. Place sauté pan in 350° oven for 3–4 minutes, or until cheese melts. Serves 4–6.

Note: You can use chicken breast filets in place of sausage, just cook cubed chicken in a dab of oil before adding to pot.

MarkCharles Misilli, QVC Guest, Philadelphia, PA

MarkCharles Misilli is very familiar to QVC viewers, demonstrating how a variety of popular gadgets work.

Crawfish Tortellini

2 (9-ounce) packages tortellini
   (cheese is good)
1 medium onion, finely chopped
2 cloves garlic, finely chopped
1 stick butter
1 pound crawfish tails (slightly
   rinsed)
$\frac{1}{2}$ cup Parmesan cheese
1 pint whipping cream
2 teaspoons cornstarch mixed in
   $\frac{1}{4}$ cup cold water
$\frac{1}{8}$ cup chopped fresh parsley
Salt and red pepper to taste
Parmesan for sprinkling

Prepare tortellini as directed and drain. Sauté onion and garlic in butter. Add crawfish and cook 5 minutes. Add Parmesan cheese, cream, cornstarch mixture, and parsley. Heat until cheese melts and sauce thickens. Fold tortellini into sauce. Season to taste with salt and red pepper. Pour all into casserole, and sprinkle with more Parmesan cheese. Bake at 375° till hot and bubbly, 20–30 minutes.

Note: May substitute chicken or shrimp for crawfish.

Shawn Alexander, Haughton, LA

Firehouse Spaghetti

1 pound hamburger meat
1 onion, chopped
1 (12-ounce) package spaghetti
   noodles
1 (10-ounce) can tomatoes with
   green chiles
1 ($10\frac{3}{4}$-ounce) can cream of
   mushroom soup
1 (5-ounce) jar processed cheese
   spread

Cook hamburger meat with onion until browned. Cook spaghetti according to package directions. Mix all ingredients together in a greased 9x13-inch baking dish, and cover with foil. Bake 30 minutes. Uncover and let stand 5 minutes.

Heather Massey, Odessa, TX

Editor's Extra: I used a roll of garlic cheese instead of the processed cheese spread—delicious!

Shrimp with Pasta, Peppers, and Pesto

2 tablespoons olive oil
4 garlic cloves, minced
1 medium yellow bell pepper, seeded and julienned
1 medium red bell pepper, seeded and julienned
1 medium orange bell pepper, seeded and julienned
1 cup sun-dried tomatoes, in olive oil and herbs, cut into small pieces

1 pound raw frozen shrimp, peeled and deveined
1 pound pasta (spaghetti or linguini)
½ cup pesto
Freshly grated Parmesan cheese

In a large skillet over medium-high heat, warm olive oil, then add garlic and sauté for 2 minutes. Add peppers and toss to coat; cook until tender. Add sun-dried tomatoes and shrimp. Cook until shrimp turn pink.

Meanwhile, cook pasta al dente, about 3 minutes in boiling water. Place pesto in microwave-safe bowl. Microwave on HIGH for 45 seconds. Drain pasta and place in a large bowl. Add shrimp mixture and pesto, tossing to coat. Serve immediately with Parmesan cheese.

Frank Negro, Gaithersburg, MD

Toss and Serve Onion Basil Pasta

¼ cup olive oil
2 tablespoons butter
3 medium onions, halved, then
    sliced thinly
½ pound spaghetti, broken
1 teaspoon minced garlic
¾ teaspoon dried basil

½ teaspoon black pepper
1 teaspoon beef bouillon
    granules
½ cup hot water
¾ cup Parmesan-Romano
    cheese (refrigerated, home-
    style kind is best)

Put oil and butter into skillet; add sliced onions, stir, and sauté till golden, about 5 minutes. Add garlic, basil, pepper, and beef bouillon dissolved in hot water; stir and cook about 10 minutes.

Meanwhile, boil pasta in salted water. Drain pasta and add to onions, then sprinkle with Parmesan. Toss and serve to 5 or 6 people. Offer more Parmesan at table.

Karen Tosten, Yorktown, VA

Easy, Cheesy White Lasagna

12 lasagna noodles
1 pound hot sausage
2 cups whipping cream
4 ounces shredded Parmesan
    cheese, divided

16 ounces ricotta cheese
8 ounces shredded Swiss cheese
8 ounces shredded mozzarella
    cheese
4 eggs

Cook lasagna noodles per package instructions. Drain and rinse with cold water for ease of handling. While noodles are cooking, brown sausage in skillet. Drain fat and add the whipping cream. Stir and set aside. Combine cheeses, reserving ¼ cup Parmesan for topping, and eggs, stirring by hand.

Place 4 noodles on bottom of a 9x13-inch baking dish, overlapping noodles. Spoon ½ of cheese mixture over noodles. Spoon ⅓ of sausage mixture over cheese. Repeat. For third layer, add remaining 4 noodles and top with remaining sausage mixture and additional Parmesan cheese. Bake uncovered in 350° oven for 30–45 minutes. Remove from oven and let sit for 5 minutes before serving. Serves 8.

Kristina Ash, Fort Wayne, IN

Lisa's Award-Winning Zesty Pasta Sauce

This recipe won second place at the 2003 Nevada State Fair.

3 cloves garlic, minced
1 small onion, finely chopped
$\frac{1}{2}$ pound mild Italian sausage
$\frac{1}{2}$ pound lean ground beef
1 (28-ounce) can crushed
  tomatoes
2 (6-ounce) cans tomato paste
1$\frac{1}{4}$ cups spicy tomato juice
$\frac{1}{2}$ cup Marsala wine

1 tablespoon granulated sugar
$\frac{1}{2}$ teaspoon salt
1 teaspoon oregano
1 teaspoon thyme
$\frac{1}{2}$ teaspoon crushed red pepper
$\frac{1}{4}$ cup grated Parmesan cheese
$\frac{1}{2}$ cup loosely packed, coarsely
  chopped fresh basil leaves
1 bay leaf

Sauté garlic, onion, Italian sausage, and ground beef in Dutch oven until well-browned, breaking up sausage and ground beef to desired size. Drain excess fat. Add all ingredients. Bring sauce to a boil, stirring well to mix ingredients. Reduce heat to a simmer, cover, and cook approximately 30 minutes. Remove bay leaf and serve over hot pasta. Sauce is just as good, if not better, refrigerated and served the next day. Makes 7 cups.

Lisa Strasser, Reno, NV

My interest in cooking began while helping my mom in the kitchen. I soon realized I had my grandmother's "baking thumb." My love for cooking and baking continued to grow while working in the food service industry. I still enjoy cooking and baking and appreciate the compliments even more. This recipe "evolved" nine times before I felt it was worthy for competition. My taste-testers were invaluable for this (now) award-winning recipe.
—Lisa Strasser

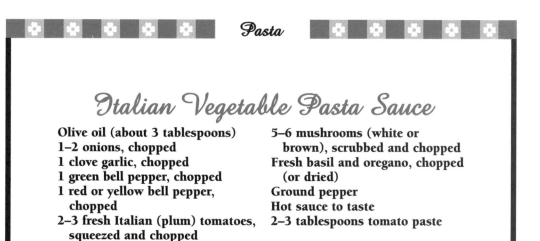

Italian Vegetable Pasta Sauce

Olive oil (about 3 tablespoons)
1–2 onions, chopped
1 clove garlic, chopped
1 green bell pepper, chopped
1 red or yellow bell pepper, chopped
2–3 fresh Italian (plum) tomatoes, squeezed and chopped
1–2 zucchini, scrubbed and chopped
5–6 mushrooms (white or brown), scrubbed and chopped
Fresh basil and oregano, chopped (or dried)
Ground pepper
Hot sauce to taste
2–3 tablespoons tomato paste

Heat olive oil in a saucepan. Add chopped onions and garlic and cook until somewhat limp; add chopped peppers, tomatoes, zucchini, and mushrooms. Sauté together over medium heat approximately 15–20 minutes. Add basil, pepper, hot sauce, and tomato paste. Cook another 5 minutes or so. Serve over pasta.

Linda Grassie, Silver Spring, MD

Sheila Simmons, Associate Publisher for Quail Ridge Press, and Stacy Parker, buyer for QVC, get down to business in one of the many conference rooms in the main hallway.

Spinach Noodle Casserole

½ pound fine egg noodles
2 (10-ounce) packages frozen
  spinach soufflé
1 cup cottage cheese
1 cup sour cream

1–1½ teaspoons garlic salt
1–1½ teaspoons onion powder
1 tablespoon Worcestershire
½ cup grated Parmesan cheese

Cook egg noodles according to package directions. Defrost spinach soufflé according to package directions. Mix together cottage cheese, sour cream, garlic salt, onion powder, Worcestershire, and Parmesan cheese. Add cooked, drained noodles and stir to coat.

Pour noodle mixture into greased 9x13-inch glass dish. Spread spinach soufflé over top of noodle mixture. Bake in preheated 350° oven 40 minutes. Cool slightly, then spoon out individual servings or cut into squares. This recipe may be prepared in advance and frozen.

Terri Warth, Sarasota, FL

Editor's Extra: A pound of ground beef, cooked, may be added to beef it up!

Spinach and Bacon Pizza

Pizza sauce or tomato sauce
1 (10- to 14-inch) prebaked
  pizza crust
Whole mozzarella, sliced
  (5–6 slices)

5 slices cooked bacon, crumbled
2–3 Roma tomatoes
10 leaves fresh spinach
Grated fresh Parmesan

Preheat oven according to the pizza crust packaging. Pour sauce on the crust. Top with sliced cheese, crumbled bacon, sliced tomatoes, and spinach. Sprinkle with Parmesan. Bake in preheated oven (usually 450°) until melted and bubbly.

Lori Evans, Riverview, FL

Editor's Extra: For crispy crust, place directly on oven rack.

No Bake Chicken, Bacon, Pineapple Pizza

½ cup (4 ounces) cream cheese, softened
¼ cup sour cream
¼ cup ranch salad dressing
1 (10- to 14-inch) prebaked pizza crust

½ cup real bacon bits
1 (10-ounce) can chicken breast, drained
1 (8-ounce) can pineapple tidbits, drained

In a bowl, combine cream cheese, sour cream, and ranch dressing. Mix well; spread over baked pizza crust. Top pizza with bacon bits, chicken, and pineapple tidbits. Cut into wedges and serve.

Denise Sickel, Clarksville, TN

Editor's Extra: We baked our packaged pizza crust at 375° till crusty (10–15 minutes). Also yummy with Mandarin oranges.

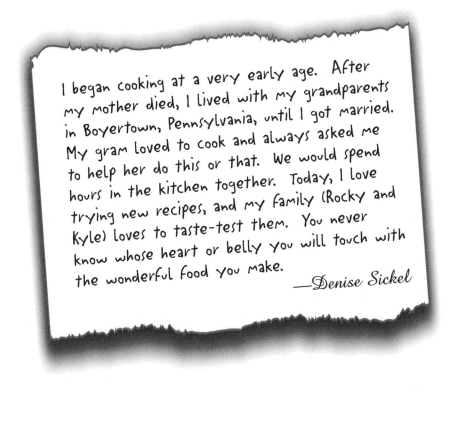

I began cooking at a very early age. After my mother died, I lived with my grandparents in Boyertown, Pennsylvania, until I got married. My gram loved to cook and always asked me to help her do this or that. We would spend hours in the kitchen together. Today, I love trying new recipes, and my family (Rocky and Kyle) loves to taste-test them. You never know whose heart or belly you will touch with the wonderful food you make.

—Denise Sickel

Smoked Sausage Roll-Ups

8 lasagna noodles
1 pound smoked sausage

1 (26-ounce) jar spaghetti sauce
Shredded mozzarella cheese

Cook lasagna noodles according to box directions; drain. Cut sausage into 8 sections, and cut down the middle without cutting all the way through. Add cheese to the middle of each piece of sausage. Hold sausage together and wrap lasagna noodle around it (use toothpicks if needed). Continue this with remaining sausage pieces. Place roll-ups in greased baking dish, and cover with spaghetti sauce. Bake at 350° for 20–25 minutes.

Note: We used smoked sausage with jalapeños—absolutely fabulous!

Lucinda Alexander, Hagerstown, IN

Sinfully Delicious Mac and Cheese

1 (1-pound) box elbow macaroni
1 (2-pound) box processed cheese
2 sticks butter, divided
1 (8-ounce) carton sour cream
1 (8-ounce) carton half-and-half
Ground pepper to taste

1 (8-ounce) package sharp yellow
  or white Cheddar cheese
  (or half of each)
1 (8-ounce) package shredded
  mozzarella
2½ cups plain bread crumbs

Cook macaroni until al dente; drain and put back in pot. Add cut-up pieces of cheese and 1 stick butter. Mix thoroughly until cheese and butter are melted. Add sour cream and half-and-half, and mix with ground pepper to taste. Put mixture into a buttered casserole dish and place in 300° oven for approximately 15 minutes. (If you are not putting casserole immediately into oven, then you might want to bake longer than 15 minutes so as to heat through).

Remove from oven and sprinkle over top the combination of shredded Cheddar and mozzarella cheeses. Put back in oven until cheese melts. In the meantime, melt remaining 1 stick butter; add bread crumbs and mix well. After cheese melts on top of casserole, remove from oven and put bread crumb mixture over top. Put under broiler just until it browns slightly.

Yvonne Cipollone, Wolcott, CT

Tonia's Louisiana Red Beans

They're better if you cook 'em the day before you want to serve 'em.

1 pound dried red beans
1 cup chopped onion
1 cup chopped celery
½ cup chopped bell pepper
¼ cup diced garlic
2 cups chopped green onions,
   divided
2 cups diced smoked ham

½ cup rendered bacon fat
1 pound andouille sausage or
   quality smoked sausage
1–2 quarts chicken broth
½ cup chopped parsley
Salt, pepper, and hot sauce to
   taste

Cover beans with water and soak overnight in refrigerator. Next afternoon, get a really cold beer or glass of wine. In large saucepot, sauté onion, celery, bell pepper, garlic, 1 cup green onions, and smoked ham in rendered bacon fat. Add sliced sausage and drained beans. Cook 2 or 3 minutes. Add enough broth to cover beans by approximately 2 inches. Bring to a rolling boil and cook for 30 minutes, stirring occasionally to avoid scorching.

Get second beer or wine. Reduce heat to a simmer and cook approximately one hour or until beans are tender. Stir occasionally.

Add chopped parsley and remaining cup of green onions. Season to taste. Mash some of the beans on the side of the pot . . . well . . . because it's just what you do.

Call some friends and family over and tell them to bring their own "take home" containers just in case. Serve over steamy rice. Enjoy!

Tonia Thibodeaux, Madison, MS

Leaving my home in Brusly, Louisiana, wasn't easy; neither is cooking for one . . . so what better way to make everyone happy? I cooked and my new co-workers ate. So did other stray folks from the building. These Red Beans were only the beginning of many lunches to come!

—Tonia Thibodeaux

Bringing-Up-Three-Boys Spanish Rice

1 pound lean ground meat
  (sirloin is best)
1 small onion, chopped
1 small bell pepper, chopped
1 clove garlic, minced (optional)
1¼ cups uncooked rice
  (not instant)

1 (16-ounce) can stewed
  tomatoes (regular or Spanish
  style)
1 (8-ounce) can tomato sauce
Salt and pepper to taste

In a skillet, brown beef, then add onion and bell pepper (you can use frozen, already chopped version, but fresh is better) and garlic, if desired. Cook until slightly done; add rice and continue cooking on medium heat for about 2 minutes. Add stewed tomatoes and tomato sauce. Refill each of the cans with water and add to mixture along with salt and pepper (Cajun seasoning adds zip, or a little red pepper). When it comes to a boil, cover and simmer on low heat until liquid is absorbed and rice is done, about 30 minutes. Time for supper!

Pat Abernathy, Biloxi, MS

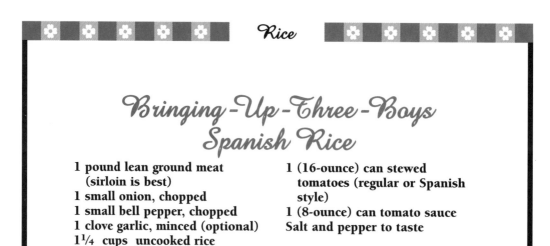

While the boys were growing up, I made this recipe often, and the whole family loved it. It's my version of Spanish rice . . . a quick and easy main dish casserole. When my daughter came along years later, she loved it, too. It's still a family favorite.

—Pat Abernathy

Can't-Be-Beat Broccoli Rice Casserole

1 small onion, chopped
1/2 cup chopped celery
1 (10-ounce) box frozen
  chopped broccoli, thawed
1 tablespoon butter
1 (8-ounce) jar processed cheese
  spread
1 (10³/₄-ounce) can condensed
  cream of mushroom soup
1 (5-ounce) can evaporated milk
3 cups cooked rice

In a large skillet over medium heat, sauté onion, celery, and broccoli in butter for 3–5 minutes. Stir in cheese, soup, and milk until smooth. Place rice in a greased 8-inch-square baking dish. Pour cheese mixture over top—do not stir. Bake uncovered at 325° for 25–30 minutes, or until hot and bubbly.

Debbie Crocetto, Sanatoga, PA

Cheesy Beefy Rice Bake

1 pound ground beef
1 cup rice, uncooked
2 tablespoons butter
3 cups water
1 cup shredded carrots
2 teaspoons instant beef
  bouillon granules
1 teaspoon dried parsley flakes
1/2 teaspoon minced dried onion
1/2 teaspoon salt
1/2 teaspoon dried basil
1/2 cup shredded cheese

Brown ground beef, drain, and set aside. Blend uncooked rice, butter, water, carrots, bouillon, parsley flakes, minced onion, salt, and dried basil in saucepan. Bring to a boil, then reduce heat, cover, and simmer 5 minutes. Add ground beef; mix. Pour into greased casserole dish. Cover and bake at 375° for 45 minutes, stirring twice. Sprinkle with cheese; bake 5 minutes more, uncovered.

Barbara Ann Mason, Underhill, VT

Pantry Jambalaya

1 pound smoked sausage, cut
  in ½-inch slices
1 (12-ounce) package frozen
  seasoning blend (onions, celery,
  and bell pepper)
1 pound shrimp, peeled
1 (6-ounce) box long grain and
  wild rice
1 (6-ounce) box chicken-flavored
  rice (or plain)
1 chicken, boiled and diced
  (reserve broth)

1 (10-ounce) can diced tomatoes
  and green chiles
1 (10¾-ounce) can cream of
  onion soup
1 (10¾-ounce) can cream of
  chicken soup
¼ teaspoon hot sauce, or
  ½ teaspoon crushed red
  pepper (optional)

Sauté sausage; remove from pan. In pan drippings, sauté seasoning blend and shrimp. In saucepan, cook both rices per directions on box, using chicken broth as part of the liquid. Mix all ingredients together and bake at 350° for one hour. For a spicier taste, add hot sauce or red pepper.

Margret Montgomery, West Monroe, LA

Editor's Extra: To make this even easier, use already cooked chicken chunks and a can of chicken broth. Easy and good!

Poultry

Crunchy Fried Chicken

Oil (enough to fill deep fryer)
2 pounds chicken, cut up
40 saltine crackers
1 cup flour
2 tablespoons seasoned salt

2 teaspoons pepper
$\frac{1}{2}$ cup milk
2 eggs
2 tablespoons paprika
1 teaspoon salt

Put oil in deep fryer heated to 325°. Rinse chicken with cold water, pat dry, and set aside. Get a bag that you can seal. Crush crackers into crumbs in bag. Add flour, seasoned salt, and pepper, and shake until well blended. Whisk together milk, eggs, paprika, and salt. Dip chicken pieces into egg mixture. Then place chicken pieces one at a time in plastic bag and shake up until well coated. Deep-fry chicken 10–15 minutes, until golden brown.

Suzanne Holovka, Staten Island, NY

Crunchy Baked Chicken

$\frac{1}{2}$ cup yellow cornmeal
$\frac{1}{2}$ cup flour
$1\frac{1}{2}$ teaspoons salt
$1\frac{1}{2}$ teaspoons chili powder
$\frac{1}{2}$ teaspoon dried oregano

$\frac{1}{4}$ teaspoon pepper
1 (3- to $3\frac{1}{2}$-pound) fryer, cut up
$\frac{1}{2}$ cup milk
$\frac{1}{3}$ cup butter or margarine, melted

Combine cornmeal, flour, salt, chili powder, oregano, and pepper. Dip chicken pieces in milk, then roll in cornmeal mixture. Place in greased 9x13-inch baking pan. Drizzle with melted butter. Bake uncovered at 375° for 50–55 minutes. Yields 4–6 servings.

Marlene Svasek, Columbus, NE

Onion Ring Parmesan Chicken

2½–3 pounds chicken breasts
1 large egg
1 tablespoon milk
1 (3.5-ounce) can French fried
  onion rings, crushed
½ cup grated Parmesan cheese
¼ cup fine dry bread crumbs
1 teaspoon paprika
½ teaspoon salt
Dash pepper
¼ cup margarine, melted

Rinse chicken and pat dry. Beat together egg and milk; set aside. In separate bowl, combine onions, cheese, bread crumbs, and spices. Dip chicken in egg mixture, then coat with crumb mixture. Place in 9x13-inch greased baking dish. Pour melted margarine over chicken. Bake at 350° for 55–60 minutes. (Pictured on cover.)

Jean Born, Phoenix, AZ

Creamy Jalapeño Chicken

1 tablespoon butter
1 green pepper, chopped
1 clove garlic, chopped
1 jalapeño pepper (more or less),
  chopped
4 boneless, skinless chicken
  breasts, cubed
1 (15-ounce) can tomato sauce
Salt and pepper to taste
1 (8-ounce) package cream
  cheese
2 cups cooked rice

Preheat oven to 350°. In a large saucepan, heat butter. Sauté green pepper, garlic, and jalapeño pepper. Add chicken and sauté until chicken is no longer pink. Add tomato sauce, salt and pepper. Simmer for 5 minutes.

Cut cream cheese in cubes. Put in bottom of a casserole dish sprayed with cooking spray. Pour chicken mixture on top of cream cheese. Bake covered for 25 minutes. Stir mixture and bake covered for 10 minutes more. Serve over rice.

Penny Kratochwil, Stratford, CT

Pink Flamingo Chicken

4 boneless skinless chicken
  breasts
Seasoned flour
Oil for frying

1 (8-ounce) carton sour cream
1 (16-ounce) jar salsa (mild
  or hot)
Rice or pasta

Dredge chicken breasts in flour, and fry in oil until slightly browned on each side; drain. Mix sour cream and salsa together and pour over chicken. Simmer with lid on for 20 minutes; serve over rice or pasta. Good with tossed green salad and bread.

Colleen Batty, Buellton, CA

Chicken Enchilada Casserole

6–7 boneless skinless chicken
  breast halves
1/3 stick butter
1 medium onion, chopped
1 (10¾-ounce) can condensed
  cream of chicken soup
1 (10¾-ounce) can condensed
  cream of mushroom soup

1 (8-ounce) can diced green
  chiles
10 corn tortillas, torn into
  2-inch sizes
¾ pound grated Cheddar
  cheese, divided

After boiling chicken breasts, reserve 2 cups broth. Melt butter in Dutch oven. Add chopped onion and sauté. Add condensed soups and about 2 cups reserved chicken broth. Then add torn chicken breast meat and diced green chiles. Heat through.

Line bottom of greased 9x13-inch pan with torn tortillas. Layer half of chicken mixture over tortilla shells. Then layer half of grated cheese over chicken. Repeat with tortilla pieces, chicken mixture, and cheese. Refrigerate till ready to serve. When ready to serve, heat through in 350° oven until cheese melts, 20–30 minutes.

Annette Brumbaugh, Pueblo, CO

Sweet and Sassy Salsa Chicken

4 frozen skinless chicken breasts
2 cups salsa
¼ cup packed light brown sugar

2 tablespoons Worcestershire
4 cups cooked white rice

Cook frozen chicken breasts, uncovered, in greased casserole dish at 350° for one hour; remove grease/juice. Mix salsa, brown sugar, and Worcestershire together in a bowl. Add salsa mixture to chicken and bake an additional ½ hour, uncovered. Serve with rice. Place chicken and salsa sauce on rice. Enjoy!

Chris Snyder, Jefferson Hills, PA

Southwest Chicken Bundles

2 whole boneless, skinless
chicken breasts
1 or 2 cans jalapeño peppers
1 (4-ounce) block Monterey
Jack cheese

1 envelope dry taco seasoning
1 (16-ounce) jar salsa of choice
4 ounces shredded Monterey
Jack cheese

Wash and dry chicken breasts. Separate into 4 pieces. Pound each piece until flat, being careful not to tear meat. Place a jalapeño pepper on underside of each pounded chicken piece. Put a 1-ounce chunk of cheese at narrow end of chicken piece. Roll into "bundle," tucking sides in as you roll. Roll each bundle in dried taco seasoning. Place in casserole dish sprayed with oil. Pour salsa over chicken bundles. Bake uncovered in 350° oven 50–60 minutes, sprinkling shredded cheese over bundles during last 5 minutes of baking time. Serve with white rice and a mixed green salad. Serves 4.

Kathleen Swaffield, Essexville, MI

Texas Heaven

Make these ahead of time and refrigerate, then bake when guests arrive. Enjoy your share of Texas Heaven!

2 boneless, skinless chicken breasts
6 fresh jalapeños

12 slices raw bacon
¹/₂ cup teriyaki sauce

Slice each breast lengthwise 3 times, then once across to make 6 pieces for each breast. Slice each stemmed jalapeño in half lengthwise and pull out seeds. Lay one piece bacon on flat surface. Put one slice chicken and one half jalapeño at one end of bacon strip and roll up. Secure with toothpicks. Brush each piece with teriyaki sauce.

Place Texas Heaven on foiled-lined cookie sheet and bake at 400° for 25 minutes, or grill outside on a pit over open flame until bacon is crisp.

Susan Carter, Corpus Christi, TX

Editor's Extra: Great to serve as appetizers, too. Cut into smaller pieces (after baking) with more toothpicks to feed more guests. Offer a small bowl of teriyaki sauce for extra dipping. Superb!

You're not seeing double—Chris Moretzsohn and Paula Bower are twins. Both are in the culinary business; Chris is a pastry chef, and Paula is QVC's Culinary Manager. These experienced chefs are often directly responsible for bringing good-looking food to the QVC audience.

Chicken with Dried Cherry Sauce

MARINADE:

1 cup olive oil
½ cup dry white wine
1 tablespoon minced fresh garlic

2 teaspoons minced fresh
rosemary
2 teaspoons minced fresh thyme

Combine Marinade ingredients in large bowl with cover.

4 boneless skinless chicken
breast halves
1 teaspoon salt

1 teaspoon freshly ground
black pepper
1 tablespoon olive oil

Marinate chicken in refrigerator, covered, 4–6 hours, or overnight.

Remove chicken from Marinade. Pat chicken dry and season with salt and pepper. Heat olive oil in a large skillet over moderately high heat until hot but not smoking, then sauté chicken until golden brown, about 3 minutes on each side. Transfer chicken to a plate and keep warm.

DRIED CHERRY SAUCE:

1 tablespoon olive oil
¼ cup chopped shallots
¾ cup chopped shiitake
mushrooms
5 cups rich brown chicken stock
1 teaspoon grated orange zest

1½ cups hearty red wine
½ cup dried cherries
½ cup fresh orange juice
2 teaspoons chopped fresh thyme
⅓ cup port wine, or to taste
Salt and pepper to taste

In same skillet, add 1 tablespoon olive oil. Sauté shallots and shiitake mushrooms in oil until very lightly browned. Add stock, zest, and wine, and reduce by half. Add half the cherries, orange juice, thyme, and port, and reduce to a light sauce consistency.

Strain, and add remaining cherries. Correct seasoning with salt and pepper. Spoon over chicken and serve.

Paula Bower, QVC Culinary Manager, Downingtown, PA

Italian Stuffed Chicken Over Spinach

4 (4-ounce) skinless, boneless
   chicken breasts, halved
1 (4-ounce) package feta cheese
1 (8-ounce) carton ricotta cheese
1/2 cup plus 2 tablespoons
   chopped basil, divided
1/2 cup chopped Roma tomatoes
1/4 cup minced seeded jalapeño

Dash of oregano
3/4 teaspoon black pepper,
   divided
1 cup tomato sauce
Salt and pepper to taste
4 cups torn baby spinach
3 tablespoons balsamic vinegar
3 teaspoons olive oil

Place each chicken breast half between 2 sheets of heavy-duty plastic wrap; flatten to 1/4-inch thickness, using a meat mallet or rolling pin. Combine feta cheese, ricotta cheese, 2 tablespoons chopped basil, chopped tomatoes, minced jalapeño, oregano, and 1/4 teaspoon pepper. Spoon generous portion of this mixture onto each piece of chicken; fold chicken in half. Top with any leftover cheese mixture and tomato sauce. Salt and pepper as desired. Place folded breast halves in a baking dish coated with cooking spray. Bake, uncovered, at 350° for 35 minutes or until chicken is done.

Combine spinach and remaining 1/2 cup chopped basil in a bowl; drizzle with vinegar and oil. Sprinkle remaining 1/2 teaspoon pepper over salad; toss well. Serve chicken over spinach.

Stephen Collins, Baltimore, MD

Not Just for Company Chicken

4 boneless, skinless chicken
  breasts
1 cup seasoned bread crumbs
1/2 pound mushrooms, sliced
  thin
3 tablespoons butter

1/4 cup whipping cream
1/2 cup dry sherry
4 thin slices Italian ham
  (prosciutto)
4 slices Swiss cheese

Coat chicken with bread crumbs. Arrange in a single layer in casserole dish. Bake at 400° for 20–30 minutes, till just done.

    Sauté mushrooms in butter until tender (about 2 minutes). Stir in cream and sherry; heat, then pour over chicken. Top chicken with a piece of ham, then a slice of cheese. Bake 5 minutes longer or until cheese just begins to melt. Serves 4.

Merritta Dane, Naples, FL

Lemon Chicken

4–6 boneless, skinless chicken
  breasts
Salt and pepper to taste
1 tablespoon olive oil

1 (14.5-ounce) can chicken broth
1/3 cup lemon juice
1/3 cup white Worcestershire
1 large can French fried onions

Season chicken breasts with salt and pepper. Brown in olive oil; set aside. In same pan, add chicken broth, lemon juice, and Worcestershire. Add chicken back to pan. Top with onions. Cover and simmer until chicken is done, about 45 minutes. The onions should soften and thicken the broth. Creates a "smothered" effect over chicken. Serve over rice or pasta.

Note: Pork or veal cutlets are also good this way.

Melinda Burnham, Brandon, MS

Mike's Fabulous Chicken

4 boneless, skinless chicken breasts
Greek seasoning (which incidently would taste good on a stick)

4 ounces feta cheese, plain or flavored
3 ounces ham, prosciutto, or pepperoni, chopped

Preheat oven to 400°. Put each breast between 2 pieces of plastic wrap and pound out to about ¼ inch. Season each side with Greek seasoning. In a small bowl, blend feta cheese and ham with a fork. Spoon about 3 tablespoons onto each breast; roll and secure with toothpicks. Put in glass baking dish, seam-side-down. Bake for 25–30 minutes. After placing on serving dish, pour pan drippings on top of chicken.

James Lamb, Jackson, MS

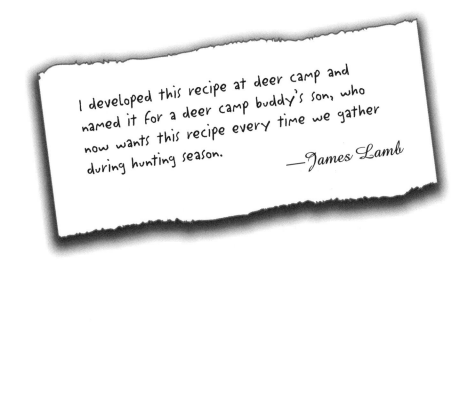

I developed this recipe at deer camp and named it for a deer camp buddy's son, who now wants this recipe every time we gather during hunting season.

—James Lamb

Aloha Hawaiian Chicken

1 pound skinless, boneless
  chicken breasts
2 tablespoons canola oil
½ cup orange juice
½ cup mayonnaise-style salad
  dressing
2 tablespoons brown sugar

1 medium green pepper, diced
1 cup raw minute rice
1 (11-ounce) can Mandarin
  oranges, drained
1 (8-ounce) can pineapple tidbits,
  drained

Cube chicken breasts; heat in oil till cooked; drain. Combine orange juice, salad dressing, and brown sugar; mix well. Reduce heat to medium and add to cooked chicken. Add green pepper and minute rice. Bring to a boil. Remove from heat and add Mandarin oranges and pineapple tidbits. Let stand 5 minutes. Serves 4.

Belinda Logan, Fremont, OH

Sweet & Sour Chicken

4 boneless chicken breasts
Garlic powder, salt and pepper
  to taste

2 eggs, beaten
¼ cup cornstarch

Cut chicken into bite-size pieces. Sprinkle with garlic powder, salt and pepper. Place in refrigerator for 1 hour or longer. Coat pieces with egg, then cornstarch. Deep-fry quickly until lightly browned. Preheat oven to 350°. Drain chicken and line single layer in greased shallow pan.

SAUCE:
1 cup sugar
¼ cup water
1 tablespoon soy sauce
½ cup vinegar

4 tablespoons catsup
1 teaspoon MSG (optional)
Dash salt

Heat all ingredients until smooth, making sure not to boil. Spoon half of mixture over chicken. Bake 10 minutes. Turn and add remaining Sauce. Bake an additional 10 minutes. Serve while hot.

Rhonda Glass, Lubbock, TX

Deep-Fried Coconut Chicken

1 pound boneless, skinless chicken breasts

MARINADE:

¼ cup soy sauce	2 teaspoons grated ginger root
¼ cup dry sherry	¼ teaspoon curry powder
3 tablespoons fresh lime juice	

Cut chicken into 1-inch squares. In 9-inch-square baking dish, combine Marinade ingredients. Add chicken and toss to coat. Cover and chill at least 1 hour, turning occasionally.

BATTER:

½ cup all-purpose flour	⅛ teaspoon salt
2 tablespoons cornstarch	1 egg, lightly beaten
½ teaspoon baking powder	½ cup cold water

Combine flour, cornstarch, baking powder, and salt. In small bowl, combine egg and water. Stir into dry ingredients until smooth; let stand 15 minutes.

SAUCE:

⅔ cup apricot preserves	2 tablespoons dry sherry
1 tablespoon plus 1 teaspoon soy sauce	¼ teaspoon curry powder
	¼ teaspoon grated ginger root

In 1-quart saucepan, combine apricot preserves, soy sauce, sherry, curry powder, and ginger root. Cook over medium heat, stirring constantly, until heated through. Cover and keep warm over low heat, stirring occasionally. Yields about 1 cup.

Oil for frying	**3 cups flaked or shredded coconut**

Fill a deep fryer or 3-quart saucepan with oil to come 2½ inches up sides. Heat oil to about 335°. Meanwhile, drain Marinade from chicken; discard. Dip chicken first into Batter to coat well. Roll in coconut. Fry ¼ of the chicken pieces at a time, about 1½–2 minutes or until golden and cooked through. Drain chicken on paper towels. Serve immediately with Sauce.

Linda Seaman, Grand Junction, MI

Quick Fix Chics

6–8 skinless, boneless chicken
  breasts
1 (8-ounce) bottle Italian
  dressing

1 package dry onion soup mix
1 (4-ounce) can mushrooms,
  drained

Place chicken in 8- to 10-inch greased pan. Combine soup mix, dressing, and mushrooms. Pour over chicken. Bake covered for 1–1½ hours at 325°.

Lottie Taylor, Canton, MS

Chickensicles

This easy recipe is wonderful for snacks, appetizers, or as a picnic entrée.

Boneless, skinless chicken
  breasts
Garlic salt and lemon pepper
Flour

Olive oil
Soy sauce
Bacon fat or oil

Pound breasts lightly between sheets of wax paper so they are of even thickness (about ¼ inch thick). Slice vertically in 1-inch-wide strips. Thread strips on skewers and roll in seasoned flour. Marinate chicken in equal parts olive oil and soy sauce for an hour.

Place oil in large skillet and heat to a medium-high temperature. Place "chickensicles" in hot oil and cook, turning with tongs, until browned on outside and tender inside. Drain on paper towels. Serve with favorite dipping sauce. These are also good chilled, and make an easy carry-along for a hike or picnic.

Kay Plowman, Rapid City, SD

TLC–Tender Lovin' Chicken

This chicken is so incredible and oh! so tender. Enjoy!

1–1½ pounds frozen chicken tenders
1 stick (½ cup) butter

1¼ cups 100% grated Parmesan cheese (dry style)

Preheat oven to 350°. Melt butter in skillet. Pour Parmesan cheese onto a dinner plate. Roll each frozen chicken tender in butter, then in Parmesan cheese, patting cheese so it sticks. Place chicken onto a baking sheet; do not overlap. Pour any remaining butter around (not on) cheesy chicken tenders. Pat on any remaining Parmesan cheese. Bake 30–35 minutes until golden brown.

Shelley Joy Menzel, Suisun, CA

Cha-Cha Chicken in a Biscuit

1½ pounds boneless, skinless chicken breasts
1 (3-ounce) package cream cheese, softened
1 (5½-ounce) jar garlic and herb (spreadable) cheese

½ cup Parmesan cheese
About 2 tablespoons milk
3 (8-count) cans crescent rolls
⅛ stick margarine, melted
Italian bread crumbs

Boil or sauté chicken. Allow to cool slightly. Cut chicken into small pieces. In a medium bowl, mix cream cheese, soft garlic and herb cheese, and Parmesan cheese until creamy. You may need to add milk to achieve the desired consistency. Stir chicken into cheesy mixture.

Unroll crescent rolls and pinch perforations together. Cut rolls into 8 equal squares (using a ruler is not necessary). Divide chicken mixture evenly among the centers of each square. Pull the 4 corners of the rolls up and pinch together. Then pinch the sides together. Place on ungreased cookie sheet, pinched-side-down. Brush with melted butter and sprinkle with bread crumbs. Bake until golden brown following directions on crescent roll can.

Terri Warth, Sarasota, FL

The Bestest Chicken and Dumplings

This is sooo good—and easy, too.

**4–5 large chicken breasts, or
  10–15 chicken tenders**
**1 (10¾-ounce) can cream of
  chicken soup**

Salt and pepper to taste

Place thawed chicken in crockpot. Add cream of chicken soup, salt and pepper. Add just enough water to cover chicken. Stir. Cover and cook on LOW 8–9 hours. When done (it will pull apart easily), remove bones and cut up chicken; return to crockpot.

Note: If you use boneless chicken, simply cut up the chicken inside the crockpot, saving you a step.

DUMPLINGS:
2 (10½-ounce) cans chicken broth   **Salt and pepper to taste**
1 (12- to 16-ounce) can biscuits

Pour chicken broth into a large saucepan; bring to a boil. Cut each biscuit into 4 pieces, then drop into boiling broth. Cut temperature down to medium heat, so it doesn't boil over. Continue to stir. Add some salt and pepper. When Dumplings are tender and sauce is creamy (about 15 minutes), pour into crockpot with cut-up chicken. Stir. Cover for just a minute.

Donna Hutcherson, Danville, VA

Editor's Extra: Though you can use any kind of biscuits, I like to use the butter-flavored variety, cut into 8 pieces. You'll make this again and again.

Quick and Easy Chicken Pot Pie

2 (9-inch) deep-dish pie crusts
2 cups cooked, finely chopped
  chicken
1 (15-ounce) can mixed
  vegetables, undrained

1 (10¾-ounce) can cream
  of potato soup
½ cup chicken broth
½ teaspoon poultry seasoning
2 (9-inch) regular pie crusts

Preheat oven to 350°. With a fork, poke a few holes in deep-dish pie crusts and bake just until starting to brown, about 10 minutes. Mix remaining ingredients, except 2 remaining pie crusts. Pour half of mixture in each browned crust. Cover with regular pie crusts and crimp edges. Cut a few slits in top of crust, brush lightly with milk, and bake at 350° about 30 minutes, till brown. Cool a few minutes and serve.

Note: Can freeze filling till ready to use. Also very good served over toast or biscuits.

Connie McGhee, Bowling Green, KY

To get the perfect lighting for laser shots of products, draped chambers are sometimes used to diffuse the lighting.

Poppy Seed Chicken Casserole

1 (10¾-ounce) can cream of
    chicken soup
1 (8-ounce) carton sour cream
2 cups diced, cooked chicken

1 stick butter
1 sleeve round crackers
Poppy seeds

Mix soup and sour cream together in 8x8-inch baking dish. Add cooked chicken and fold into mixture. Melt butter in microwave. Crumble crackers into melted butter. Sprinkle butter/cracker topping over chicken mixture. Sprinkle poppy seeds over top. Bake at 350° for 30–40 minutes.

Amy Miller, Birmingham, AL

Southern Chicken Casserole

1 cup chopped celery
½ cup chopped onion
½ cup water
2 cups cut-up chicken breasts,
    uncooked
1 cup instant rice

1 cup water chestnuts, drained
    and coarsley chopped
½ cup slivered almonds
½ cup mayonnaise
1 (10¾-ounce) can cream of
    chicken soup

Cook celery and onion in water until fork-tender. Add remaining ingredients, and mix well. Place in a greased 2½-quart casserole dish.

TOPPING:
1 cup cornflake crumbs
½ cup margarine, melted

¼ cup chopped almonds

Mix cornflake crumbs, margarine, and almonds until crumbly. Place on top of chicken mixture and bake at 350° for 50–60 minutes.

Judy Pieczonka, Seminole, FL

Ta-Dah! Chicken Tetrazzini

2 tablespoons minced onion
1 tablespoon butter
1 (10¾-ounce) can cream of
  mushroom soup
½ (10¾-ounce) cream of
  chicken soup
½ (15-ounce) can condensed
  chicken broth

2 teaspoons curry powder
Dash white pepper to taste
2 cups cooked broad noodles
2 cups cubed cooked chicken
½ cup shredded sharp Cheddar
  cheese
2 tablespoons chopped parsley

Sauté onion in butter until golden. Add soups, chicken broth, curry powder, and white pepper. Cook over low heat, stirring constantly until well blended. Arrange layers of noodles, chicken, and soup mixture in a greased baking dish, ending with a layer of noodles. Cover; bake in preheated 350° oven for 30 minutes. Uncover; sprinkle cheese over top. Bake 10 minutes longer or until cheese is melted and golden. Garnish with parsley. Serve at once.

Margaret Plitt, Hanover, PA

Editor's Extra: For added flavor, before boiling chicken, sprinkle with poultry seasoning or celery salt, and boil noodles in broth. You can also use this broth in place of canned.

Spicy Chicken Casserole

2 (7-ounce) cans chunk-style
  chicken
1 (16-ounce) can chili without
  beans
1 (15-ounce) can diced tomatoes
1 (10¾-ounce) can cream of
  celery soup
1 (10¾-ounce) can cream of
  chicken soup
1½ cups salsa
1 (10-count) package corn
  tortillas, cut into eighths
1 (8-ounce) package shredded
  Cheddar cheese
1 cup crunched taco chips for
  topping (optional)

Mix all ingredients into a 4-quart bowl, except tortillas, cheese and
chips. Spray a 9x13-inch casserole dish with nonstick spray. Make
2 layers of tortillas, chicken mixture, and cheese; repeat and end
with cheese. Top with crunched chips, if desired. Bake at 375° for
45 minutes.

Note: Use mild, medium, or hot salsa for spicy, spicier, or wake-up-your
taste buds spiciest casserole.

Carolyn Etzler, Thurmont, MD

Mo Turkey

*Makes its own gravy. The flavor of the seasoned turkey and onion cook into the
potatoes to make a delicious meal.*

1 (3-pound) frozen boneless
  turkey breast roast, with
  gravy packet, thawed
Creole seasoning to taste
1 large onion, coarsely chopped
1 small package steak-cut fries

Rub turkey all over with gravy packet (do not add water) and
Creole seasoning. Make a boat with heavy-duty aluminum foil.
Place turkey, onion, and 'taters in boat, then cover completely with
foil. Cook on infrared burner on grill (or in your oven) at 375° for
2 hours, rotating ½ turn every ½ hour or so (or until roast reaches 170° on meat thermometer).

Trey Moseley, Braxton, MS

Spicy Maple Chicken Wings

5 pounds chicken wings	4 tablespoons minced garlic
2–4 cups maple syrup	2 tablespoons garlic powder
⅔ cup teriyaki sauce	2 tablespoons onion powder
1 cup soy sauce	4 tablespoons red pepper flakes

Preheat oven to 350°. Cut off chicken wing tips and snip the skin between the joints. Place in a large bowl. Add maple syrup, teriyaki sauce, soy sauce, garlic, garlic powder, onion powder, and red pepper flakes; toss to coat. Place on a disposable baking pan, reserving half of liquid. Place pan on baking sheet and bake approximately one hour, tossing every 15–20 minutes. (The liquid will gradually evaporate the longer you cook it.)

After one hour, increase temperature to 425°. Turn wings to coat evenly and cook an additional 45 minutes. You may need to add more of the liquid at this point. Keep a close eye on the wings during the last 45 minutes, as they have a tendency to burn easily.

John Lichtenberg, Biddeford, ME

Tango Tangy Chicken Wings

3–5 pounds frozen chicken wings

Preheat oven to 400°. Place frozen chicken wings in baking dish.

MARINADE MIXTURE:

2 cups soy sauce	2 cups brown sugar
2 tablespoons dry mustard	Crushed garlic for a little kick
(may substitute regular mustard)	(optional)

Pour Marinade Mixture over chicken. It may seem like there is not enough marinade, but as the wings cook, they sink into the marinade. Bake about 2 hours, being sure to turn wings every so often. If you want a darker, crispier wing, cook at 425° for the last 30 minutes. Enjoy.

Connie Stuhr, Weston, FL

Seafood

"Carbsidered" Crab-Stuffed Portobellos

4–6 portobello mushrooms
2 tablespoons olive oil, divided
1 medium onion, chopped
1 medium red bell pepper, chopped
1 stalk celery, chopped
Butter or light margarine for toast

2 slices whole-wheat bread, toasted
$\frac{1}{2}$–1 cup chicken broth
1 pound lump crabmeat
1 tablespoon seafood seasoning
1 teaspoon Worcestershire
Salt and pepper to taste

Lightly brush mushrooms with olive oil and place on a baking sheet. Heat in oven at 400° for 15 minutes. Meanwhile, in a sauté pan, heat remaining olive oil. Add onion, pepper, and celery, and sauté until soft, not brown. Butter toast and slice into 4 pieces; turn and slice 4 ways again until cubed. Add to pan and stir. Begin adding chicken broth a little at a time, until bread absorbs it and mixture is moist. Add crabmeat and mix lightly just until combined. Add seasoning, Worcestershire, and salt and pepper to taste. Remove pan from heat. Mixture should be "rustic" and chunky. With an ice cream scoop, stuff a heaping scoop into each mushroom. Enjoy.

Note: If you like, you may sprinkle Parmesan cheese (or any cheese you like) on top and broil for a few minutes.

Faith-Anne Wagner, Toms River, NJ

Editor's Extra: We usually think of stuffed mushrooms as appetizers, but this can be an elegant main dish with a green vegetable, salad, and crusty bread.

Baked Seafood Au Gratin

1 onion, chopped
1 green bell pepper, chopped
1 cup butter, divided
1 cup all-purpose flour, divided
1 pound fresh crabmeat
4 cups water
1 pound fresh shrimp, peeled and deveined
1/2 pound small scallops
1/2 pound flounder fillets
3 cups milk
1 cup shredded sharp Cheddar cheese
1 tablespoon distilled white vinegar
1 teaspoon Worcestershire
1/2 teaspoon salt
1 pinch ground black pepper
1 dash hot pepper sauce
1/2 cup grated Parmesan cheese

In a heavy skillet, sauté onion and pepper in 1/2 cup butter. Cook until tender. Mix in 1/2 cup flour, and cook over medium heat for 10 minutes, stirring frequently. Stir in crabmeat, remove from heat, and set aside.

In a large Dutch oven, bring water to a boil. Add shrimp, scallops, and flounder; simmer for 3 minutes. Drain, reserving 1 cup liquid, and set seafood aside. In a heavy saucepan, melt remaining 1/2 cup butter over low heat. Stir in remaining 1/2 cup flour. Cook and stir constantly for 1 minute. Gradually add milk plus 1 cup reserved cooking liquid. Raise heat to medium; cook, stirring constantly, until mixture is thickened and bubbly. Mix in shredded Cheddar cheese, vinegar, Worcestershire, salt, pepper, and hot sauce. Stir in cooked seafood.

Preheat oven to 350°. Lightly grease a 9x13-inch baking dish. Press crabmeat mixture into bottom of prepared pan. Spoon seafood mixture over crabmeat crust, and sprinkle with Parmesan cheese. Bake for 30 minutes, or until lightly browned.

Katy B. Minchew, Waycross, GA

This was my mom's favorite seafood recipe, and is mine, too. I have had guests, who, when invited to dinner, specifically requested this to be served.
—Katy B. Minchew

Cheesy Seafood Enchiladas

1 onion, chopped
2 tablespoons butter
1 pound fresh crabmeat
$\frac{1}{2}$ pound shrimp, peeled,
  deveined, cooked, and chopped
4 cups shredded colby Jack or
  Monterey Jack cheese, divided
10 (10-inch) flour tortillas

$1\frac{3}{4}$ cups half-and-half
1 cup sour cream
$\frac{1}{2}$ cup butter or margarine,
  melted
1 tablespoon chopped parsley
$1\frac{1}{2}$ teaspoons garlic salt
1 bunch green onions, chopped

Sauté onion in butter. In a bowl, combine onion with crabmeat, shrimp, and 2 cups cheese. Divide mixture evenly among each tortilla. Roll tortillas enchilada style, and place in a 9x13-inch casserole dish. Over medium heat, combine half-and half, sour cream, and butter. When thoroughly combined and heated through, pour mixture over enchiladas. Sprinkle with remaining cheese, parsley, and garlic salt. Bake covered at 350° for 30–35 minutes, then uncover and bake 10–15 minutes longer. Sprinkle with green onions, and serve immediately.

Larry Lollar, Pinson, AL

There's a lot of scampering going on to prepare each new set during road shows like here in Islamorada, Florida. Everybody has to function as a family to make it all come together . . . and it always does.

Garden by the Sea

1 pound shrimp
1 packet (mesh) seafood
    seasoning
1½ pounds claw crabmeat
½ stick butter
½ onion, diced
1 tablespoon chopped garlic
1 (26-ounce) can and
    1 (10¾-ounce) can cream
    of mushroom soup

2 (8-ounce) blocks sharp
    Cheddar cheese, divided
2 cans whole or French-style
    green beans
Salt and pepper to taste
1 cup slivered almonds
1 tablespoon paprika

Boil shrimp, with shells on, with the mesh seafood seasoning pouch for 5 minutes. Take off heat and let sit for about an hour (put a few ice cubes in pot to cool it down and prevent shrimp from becoming overcooked). Clean shells from crabmeat. Put both of these aside. Melt butter in a heavy skillet. Add onion and garlic and sauté until clear. Put aside.

In a large saucepan, empty cans of soup. Cut one block of sharp Cheddar cheese into ½-inch chunks and add to soup. Cook over medium heat until creamy and all cheese is melted. At this time, add onion and garlic mixture and mix well. Now add shrimp and crab mixture, and mix well; add green beans, season, and mix well. Take off heat, add slivered almonds, and pour into a slightly greased casserole dish. Top with the other block of cheese that has been finely grated. Sprinkle with paprika. Bake at 350° for 20–30 minutes until bubbly.

Hayden Markowitz, Saint Simons Island, GA

Easy, Peas-y Oriental Shrimp

This recipe is super quick and superbly delicious. The magical combination of snow peas and shrimp in this delicious sauce will have you making this recipe over and over again.

1¹⁄₂ cups water	Salt and pepper to taste
2 chicken bouillon cubes	2¹⁄₂ tablespoons cornstarch
2 pounds medium shrimp, peeled and deveined	2¹⁄₂ tablespoons cold water
¹⁄₄ cup chopped green onions	1 tomato, chopped
2 tablespoons soy sauce	1 cup snow peas

Add bouillon cubes to boiling water, allowing bouillon cubes to dissolve over medium-high heat. Stir in the shrimp, green onions, soy sauce, salt and pepper. Cook 3–5 minutes, just until shrimp curl and turn pink. Stir cornstarch into cold water, then add to shrimp mixture (this will thicken the sauce). Add chopped tomatoes and snow peas, and allow to heat through. Serve hot over pasta or rice. Serves 4–6.

Scott Anderton, Collierville, TN

Simple Shrimp Scampi Parmigiana

Great served by itself, or with fettuccine and a green salad.

¹⁄₂ cup butter (not margarine)	1¹⁄₂ cups shredded (not grated) Parmesan cheese
2 tablespoons minced garlic	
1 pound (15-count) raw shrimp, peeled	

Melt butter over low heat in a 10-inch skillet, then add garlic. Add shrimp to butter and cook over low heat until shrimp are pink, turning once. Smother shrimp with Parmesan cheese, then turn off heat, cover, and let Parmesan melt.

Kitty Harris, Cascade, MT

Succulent Shrimp Creole

This recipe is absolutely fabulous!

1 cup chopped onion
3 garlic cloves, minced
½ cup chopped celery
½ cup chopped bell pepper
⅓ cup butter
½ cup vegetable oil
½ cup flour
1 bay leaf
1½ tablespoons lemon juice
½ (6-ounce) can tomato paste

1 (10-ounce) can diced tomatoes
  with green chiles
1½ teaspoons Worcestershire
2 pounds shrimp, peeled,
  deveined
Salt and pepper to taste
½ teaspoon chili powder, or
  to taste
Hot sauce to taste

Sauté onion, garlic, celery, and bell pepper in butter until onion is translucent. In a heavy skillet, make a roux from oil and flour. Cook over medium heat until golden brown. Stir in sautéed vegetables, bay leaf, lemon juice, tomato paste, tomatoes, Worcestershire, and shrimp. Add water just to cover mixture. Cook over medium heat until shrimp are pink and tender; stirring occasionally. Adjust seasoning to your liking with salt, pepper, chili powder, and hot sauce.

Carroll Dawkins, Wichita, KS

Being from South Louisiana, I am often asked to explain the difference between Creole and Cajun cooking. I think of Cajun food as South Louisiana one-pot dishes, and Creole as more aristocratic New Orleans-style prepared dishes. Cajun food may not be as pretty as fancy Creole recipes, but Cajuns think a big pot of dark, murky gumbo is beautiful. One day I asked a Cajun the difference and he said, "How should I know? Just eat it—it's all good!" And I agree.
—Gwen

Buffalo Shrimp

This is the BEST . . . you can adjust the intensity of the buffalo sauce to your liking. We like it HOT!

BUFFALO SAUCE:
4 cloves garlic, minced
2½ tablespoons butter
6 ounces hot pepper sauce
(or to taste)

1 teaspoon ground cayenne
   pepper (or to taste)

In a mixing bowl, whisk together garlic, butter, hot sauce, and cayenne pepper; set aside.

2 cups all-purpose flour
2 tablespoons Creole-style
   seasoning
1 tablespoon garlic powder
1 tablespoon ground cayenne
   pepper

1 teaspoon onion powder
1 teaspoon freshly ground black
   pepper
1 pound large shrimp, peeled and
   deveined with tails attached
4 cups oil for frying

In a large re-sealable plastic bag, combine flour, Creole-style seasoning, garlic powder, ground cayenne pepper, onion powder, and ground black pepper. Seal the bag and shake a few times to combine ingredients well.

Rinse shrimp under cold water and place in plastic bag with flour mixture. Seal the bag and shake to coat all shrimp well with flour mixture. Place coated shrimp on a cookie sheet and in refrigerator 15–20 minutes. Save remaining flour mixture in the bag.

In a pot, heat oil to 375°. Remove shrimp from refrigerator and shake a second time in flour mixture. Fry shrimp in hot oil until pink, about 2–3 minutes. Immediately coat with Buffalo Sauce.

Janet Roetzel, Lakeland, FL

Crispy Coconut Shrimp

¾ cup self-rising flour, divided
½ teaspoon paprika
¼ teaspoon salt
¼ teaspoon red pepper
1 (12-ounce) can beer
2 pounds large shrimp
1 (16-ounce) bag flaked coconut

Combine ½ cup flour, paprika, salt, and red pepper in medium bowl. Gradually add beer, stirring constantly until well combined. Place remaining ¼ cup flour in separate bowl. Then, place coconut in another bowl. Dredge shrimp first in flour, then in beer batter, allowing excess to drain. Finally, roll in coconut.

Heat oil to 375°, and fry shrimp in hot oil until golden brown on both sides. Drain, and serve warm with your favorite dipping sauce. Enjoy!

Clarence Ray, DeRidder, LA

Chilled Grilled Shrimp

1½ pounds large shrimp
1 cup Italian salad dressing, divided
½ cup olive oil, divided
2 tablespoons balsamic vinegar
2 garlic cloves, chopped
1 small red onion, chopped
1 red bell pepper, sliced
1 green bell pepper, sliced

Peel and devein shrimp, leaving the tails on. Marinate in ½ cup salad dressing and ¼ cup olive oil for at least 2 hours (overnight is best).

Grill shrimp 2–3 minutes on each side or until shrimp are just pink. Cool in refrigerator. Combine remaining ingredients in large re-sealable bag. Add shrimp, and chill for at least 2 hours. When shrimp are sufficiently chilled, pour contents of bag onto a serving plate and serve immediately.

Sheila Tylus, Danvers, MA

Honey Shrimp Kabobs

1½–2 pounds large shrimp,
  peeled, deveined
1½ tablespoons dry white wine
2½ tablespoons Italian dressing
⅓ cup Worcestershire, divided

½ teaspoon garlic powder
¼ teaspoon salt
¼ teaspoon freshly ground
  black pepper

Marinate shrimp in a covered container in refrigerator for 1–2 hours in a combination of wine, Italian dressing, Worcestershire, garlic salt, salt, and pepper, tossing to coat well.

HONEY SAUCE:
¼ cup margarine or butter,
  melted

¼ cup honey
2 tablespoons Worcestershire

Combine margarine or butter, honey, and Worcestershire; set aside.

Onions
Peppers

Mushrooms

Cut vegetables into bite-size portions. Soak wooden skewers in water for 1 hour. Place shrimp, onions, peppers, and mushrooms onto bamboo skewers, alternating as such, until the skewer is full. Baste each kabob with Honey Sauce. On a hot grill, cook each kabob 2–3 minutes per side, basting as desired, until shrimp are done (curled and pink); do not overcook. Serves 4–6.

Note: For those who don't like their vegetables crunchy, you may wish to sauté them as desired before placing onto skewers.

Sherry Girard, Navarre, FL

Tangy Shrimp & Scallops

½ cup butter, softened
7 tablespoons lemon juice
5 tablespoons Worcestershire
1–2 teaspoons garlic powder

1 teaspoon paprika
28 large shrimp (about 1½
   pounds peeled and deveined)
28 sea scallops (about ½ pound)

Combine butter, lemon juice, Worcestershire, and spices. Microwave until butter is melted. Set aside ⅓ cup for basting. Add shrimp and scallops and let marinate for 1 hour in refrigerator.

Drain and discard marinade. Alternately thread shrimp and scallops on skewers. Grill, uncovered, over medium-hot heat for 6 minutes. Brush with remaining marinade. Grill an additional 8–10 minutes.

Victoria Stohr, Branchville, NJ

Quick and Easy Scallops

3 green onions, chopped, tops
   included
8 ounces baby portobello
   mushrooms, sliced
3 slices bacon, chopped
4 tablespoons butter

Salt and pepper to taste
1 pound sea scallops
Red pepper flakes to taste
Angel hair pasta
1 tablespoon olive oil
3 tablespoons Parmesan cheese

Sauté green onions, mushrooms, and bacon in butter until tender. Salt and pepper each scallop, then add to pan. Cook 1–2 minutes, then turn, making sure scallop is slightly brown. Cook 2–3 minutes longer, or until scallops are cooked through. Add red pepper flakes and let simmer 1 minute. Serve over angel hair pasta. Drizzle with olive oil and a sprinkle of Parmesan cheese.

Kelly Williams, Hickman, TN

Seafood Crèpe Filling

This is the BEST crèpe filling!

1 pound scallops
1 pound sliced mushrooms
5 tablespoons butter, divided
2 tablespoons fresh lemon juice
1 cup dry white wine
¼ teaspoon thyme leaves
1 bay leaf

½ teaspoon salt
Dash of pepper
3 tablespoons flour
1 cup light cream
Prepared crèpes
¼ cup Parmesan cheese

Thaw scallops, if frozen. Cut large ones in quarters. Sauté mushrooms in 2 tablespoons butter till golden. Stir in lemon juice and set aside.

In saucepan, combine wine, thyme, bay leaf, salt, pepper, and scallops. Bring to a boil, lower heat, and simmer 10 minutes. Drain and reserve 1 cup of the broth. Make a cream sauce with remaining 3 tablespoons butter, flour, reserved scallop broth, and cream. Cook until smooth and thickened; do not boil. Add scallops and mushrooms to sauce. Spoon into prepared crèpes and sprinkle with cheese. Bake in 400° oven till golden, about 10 minutes. Serves 6.

Julie Hamric, Mount Airy, MD

Editor's Extra: Crèpes are not that hard to make, but they can be bought at the supermarket in a package of ten. Not easy to find—I recently saw them in the produce department near the strawberries—do ask your grocer for them. They are nice to have on hand for a quick meal or fruit dessert.

Seafood Newburg

Wonderful for a party dish.

1 stick butter or margarine
1 (8-ounce) package cream
  cheese
1 (10¾-ounce) can Cheddar
  cheese soup
White wine (splash to taste)

Garlic powder to taste
Paprika (1–2 teaspoons for color)
2 tablespoons chopped fresh
  parsley or dried parsley
Shellfish or white fish without
  bones

Melt butter or margarine in saucepan. Add cream cheese into butter and stir until smooth and well blended. Add Cheddar cheese soup. Whisk mixture until well blended. Add white wine, garlic powder, paprika, and parsley. Cook fish; add to butter-cheese mixture. Stir until all ingredients are blended well. Heat until fish is hot (do not overcook). Serve over pasta, rice, toast points, puff pastry shells, or by itself.

Karen Delduce, Latham, NY

Creamy Pesto-Topped Fish

¼ cup pesto sauce
1 (3-ounce) package cream
  cheese, softened
1 tablespoon lemon juice

6 firm, white-fleshed fish fillets
¼ cup grated Parmesan cheese
¼ cup bread crumbs

Preheat oven to 400°. Butter a 9x13-inch baking pan. Sprinkle fish pieces with lemon juice and place in pan. Combine pesto sauce and cream cheese thoroughly and spread evenly on top of fish pieces. Combine bread crumbs and Parmesan cheese and sprinkle over pesto. Bake 10 minutes or until fish flakes easily with a fork.

Sue Soteriou, Berrien Springs, MI

Crispy Fried Catfish

No cornmeal? No problem! Instant potatoes are all you need to fry up some perfectly seasoned catfish. Make some hushpuppies and cole slaw and serve this with a pitcher of sweet iced tea . . . talk about perfect!

2 cups instant potato flakes	2 teaspoons cayenne pepper,
1 cup all-purpose flour	or to taste
1 tablespoon garlic powder	½ teaspoon Greek seasoning
1 tablespoon seasoning salt	½ teaspoon paprika
1 tablespoon ground black	4 (6-ounce) catfish fillets
pepper	2 cups butter-flavored shortening

Combine instant potato flakes with flour and seasonings. Rinse fish in cold water. Heat shortening to 350°. Coat fish in potato flake mixture. Fry in hot oil 4–5 minutes, turning to brown both sides evenly. Fish is done when it flakes easily with a fork. Drain on paper towels, and serve piping hot!

Amanda Mize, St. Joseph, LA

Cajun Catfish with Sauce

You'll never purchase tartar sauce again . . . this is the best!

TARTAR SAUCE:

1 cup mayonnaise	2 teaspoons hot sauce, or to taste
½ cup sweet pickle relish	2 teaspoons Cajun seasoning
1 tablespoon horseradish sauce	

Mix well and chill until ready to serve with catfish.

1 large egg	½ cup cornmeal (white or
2 tablespoons hot sauce	yellow)
1¼ pounds catfish fillets, cut	Salt to taste
diagonally in ½-inch strips	1 teaspoon Cajun seasoning
½ cup flour	2 quarts vegetable oil

Mix egg and hot sauce in bowl. Add catfish strips and let sit 10–30 minutes. Stir together flour, cornmeal, salt, and Cajun seasoning. Dredge catfish in mixture. Deep-fry in oil at 350°. Serves 4.

Joel Timmons, Piedmont, SC

First Choice Grilled Salmon

MARINADE:
¹/₃ cup soy sauce ¹/₃ cup bourbon
¹/₃ cup vegetable oil

Mix ingredients well.

4 salmon steaks **¹/₂ teaspoon garlic salt**
¹/₂ teaspoon salt

Sprinkle salmon with salt and garlic salt. Place in heavy self-sealing plastic storage bag; add Marinade. Marinate in refrigerator for 30 minutes, turning after 15 minutes to coat both sides.

Prepare grill. When coals are white, place salmon on grill, 5–6 inches above coals. Grill for 7–8 minutes. Turn over and grill for an additional 7–8 minutes. Baste with Marinade while salmon cooks. Fish will flake when done. Do not overcook. Serves 4.

Linda Seaman, Grand Junction, MI

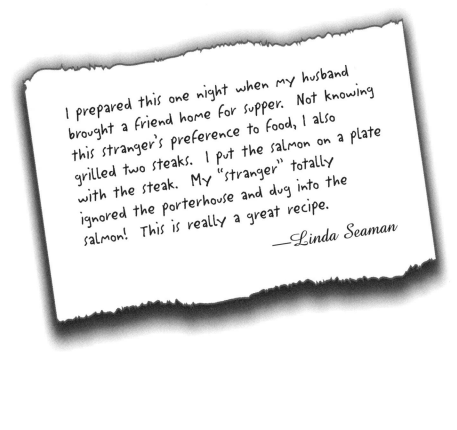

I prepared this one night when my husband brought a friend home for supper. Not knowing this stranger's preference to food, I also grilled two steaks. I put the salmon on a plate with the steak. My "stranger" totally ignored the porterhouse and dug into the salmon! This is really a great recipe.

—Linda Seaman

Salmon Florentine

4 (1½-pound) salmon fillets
1 (10-ounce) package frozen
  spinach, thawed and moisture
  squeezed out
1 egg, beaten
1 (8-ounce) container soft-style
  cream cheese with chives
  and onion

¼ cup grated Parmesan cheese
¾ cup herb stuffing cubes
2 tablespoons milk
2 tablespoons dry white wine
¼ teaspoon finely chopped
  garlic

Rinse fish and pat dry. Place in shallow baking dish. Drain spinach. Combine egg, ½ the cream cheese, and Parmesan. Stir in drained spinach and stuffing cubes. Spoon ¼ over each fillet. Bake at 350° for 20–25 minutes.

Combine remaining cream cheese, milk, wine, and garlic in saucepan over medium-low heat, cooking until smooth and creamy. Serve over fillets. Makes 4 servings.

Jane Stroschin, Fremont, MI

My husband makes this for me. It is one of my favorite dishes.

—Jane Stroschin

Broiled Salmon with Shrimp Curry Sauce

This is delicious!

1 (1-pound) salmon fillet, cut in
  4 pieces
¼ cup olive oil

3 teaspoons soy sauce
4 teaspoons lime juice

Place salmon pieces in flat dish with meaty side up. Combine olive oil, soy sauce, and lime juice in small bowl. Mix thoroughly. Drizzle mixture over salmon pieces. Allow to marinate in refrigerator for at least 3 hours; overnight is better.

Preheat oven broiler. Place marinated salmon in greased baking dish and place in broiler. Cook for about 5–7 minutes and remove from broiler; turn salmon over on other side. Cook another 5–7 minutes or until fish is cooked. Serve with Shrimp Curry Sauce. Serves 3–4.

SHRIMP CURRY SAUCE:

2 tablespoons extra virgin
  olive oil
2 cloves garlic, minced
2 medium onions, diced
2 tablespoons curry powder
3 cups chicken stock
2 bay leaves
3 tablespoons tomato paste,
  mixed with ¾ cup water

½ cup lite coconut milk
1 tablespoon lime juice
½ teaspoon honey
½ teaspoon diced hot pepper
¼ teaspoon freshly grated ginger
6 ounces shrimp, cleaned,
  deveined, and diced
Salt to taste

Heat olive oil in large skillet on low heat. Stir in garlic and onions. Sauté 5–7 minutes or until garlic starts to change color; do not burn. Stir frequently. Stir in curry; add chicken stock, bay leaves, tomato paste mixture, and coconut milk. Bring to a boil on medium-high heat. Then reduce heat to medium and simmer, covered, about 45 minutes or until mixture thickens. Stir frequently.

Stir in lime juice, honey, hot pepper, ginger, and shrimp. Add salt to taste. Simmer another 3–5 minutes. Remove sauce from heat. Serve with broiled salmon or any other fish, meat, or poultry, or over rice. Yields 3 cups.

Sara Friday, Hollywood, FL

Bonnie's Tasty Salmon Patties

1 (14- to 15-ounce) can salmon,
   drained, deboned, and skinned
1 cup plain bread crumbs
½ small onion, finely chopped
1 egg
¼ cup milk
1 tablespoon dried parsley flakes
1 teaspoon lemon juice

Dash of pepper
¼ teaspoon celery seed
¼ teaspoon dry mustard
¼ teaspoon dill weed
1 hard-cooked egg, finely
   chopped
Butter as needed for sautéing

Combine all ingredients except butter, and form into patties. Sauté in butter until browned on both sides. Serve with sauce.

DILLY HORSERADISH SAUCE:
⅓ cup mayonnaise
⅓ cup sour cream
½ small onion, finely chopped
1 teaspoon dried parsley

½ teaspoon dill weed
1 teaspoon horseradish
½ teaspoon lemon juice
½–1 teaspoon sugar

Combine sauce ingredients; serve with salmon patties.

Bonnie M. Davis, Easton, PA

Halibut Enchiladas

1 pound halibut
½ cup mayonnaise
½ cup sour cream
1 (7-ounce) can chopped green
  chiles
¼ cup chopped onion

1 (16-ounce) can green or red
  enchilada sauce, divided
1 cup shredded cheese, divided
1 package (10-inch) flour
  tortillas

Bake fish at 350° for about 20–25 minutes. When cool, flake with fork. In a bowl, mix mayonnaise, sour cream, green chiles, onion, ½ cup cheese, and flaked halibut. Grease a 9x13-inch pan, and pour ½ the enchilada sauce on the bottom. Spoon a row of mayonnaise mixture down center of tortilla, then roll up and place in greased pan. Pour remaining enchilada sauce over tortillas, and bake at 350° for 30–35 minutes. During last 5 minutes, sprinkle with remaining cheese. Serve with a spoonful of sour cream on top.

Jeanie Steinman, Newton, MA

Editor's Extra: If you can't find halibut, orange roughy is a good substitute.

Baked Halibut Olé

¼ cup butter, melted
1½–2 pounds halibut fillets
Lemon pepper to taste
Garlic salt to taste

1 cup salsa
¾ cup mayonnaise
¾ cup sour cream
1 tablespoon olive oil

Pour melted butter in a casserole dish, then add fillets. Season fillets with lemon pepper and garlic salt. Combine salsa, mayonnaise, sour cream, and olive oil, and spoon over fillets. Bake in a preheated 350° oven 25–30 minutes, or until fish flakes easily with a fork.

Note: If you like it even spicier, add red pepper flakes to taste.

Lisa Flynt, Jackson, MS

Fancy Stuffed Sole

Delicious!

4 (8-ounce) sole fillets
Salt and pepper to taste
16 fresh spinach leaves
1 clove garlic, minced
8 ounces feta cheese
1 tomato, sliced

Rinse sole fillets, and pat dry. Season with salt and pepper. Rinse fresh spinach leaves and lay on fillets (4 leaves per fillet). Add minced garlic clove to feta cheese. Spread equal amounts onto fillets. Place sliced tomatoes on top. Fold fillets in half and secure with a toothpick. Cook at 350° for 20 minutes.

Cynthia Palmer-Poirier, Holland, MA

Tasty Tilapia Medley

1 large zucchini squash
1 large yellow squash
16 ounces crimini mushrooms
2 serrano chiles
4–6 green onion
1 nectarine
2 tablespoons butter
$1/4$ cup extra virgin olive oil
8 tilapia fish fillets
Kosher salt and freshly cracked
    black pepper to taste

Thinly slice squash, mushrooms, serrano chiles, and green onions; set aside. Slice nectarine into $1/2$-inch chunks, and set aside. In a large skillet, add butter and olive oil. Heat till melted. Add tilapia fillets to pan. Fry 2 minutes, then turn over. Top with vegetables and nectarine, then season to taste with the salt and pepper. Cover and let cook 6–10 minutes, till squash is tender. Remove from heat and serve.

Tina McKinney, Seaside, OR

Editor's Extra: I used drained Mandarin oranges instead of a nectarine—yummy!

Meats

Stove Top Hawaiian Ribs

1 cup packed brown sugar
1/2 cup vinegar
1 cup soy sauce
8 cloves garlic, chopped
6 stalks green onions, chopped

1 (20-ounce) can crushed
 pineapple
3 slabs pork ribs, sliced into
 individual ribs

Combine brown sugar, vinegar, soy sauce, garlic, green onions, and pineapple. Place ribs in Dutch oven or large covered skillet. Pour mixture onto ribs; bring to a boil. Turn heat down, cover, and simmer for 1 hour and 15 minutes.

Joni Sliwoski, Honolulu, HI

Sweet-Sour Spare Ribs

This dish is easy to make, and one that my whole family asks for often. Using a pressure cooker shortens the cook time to under one hour, including the browning. Deeeeelicious!

3 pounds country-style pork ribs
1 tablespoon olive oil
1 clove garlic, minced
1/4 teaspoon ginger
1 teaspoon salt

1/4 teaspoon pepper
1 1/2 tablespoons sugar
3/4 cup vinegar
2 tablespoons soy sauce

In a pressure cooker, brown ribs in oil on all sides. Combine garlic, ginger, salt, pepper, sugar, vinegar, and soy sauce, and pour over ribs. Follow pressure cooker directions to seal the lid. Set pressure on HIGH and cook 45 minutes. Release pressure and remove lid. Cook on MEDIUM heat another 10 minutes or until liquid thickens. Serve over rice or noodles.

Note: You can make it on top of the stove in a heavy saucepan, or in an electric frying pan, but it takes 2–3 hours to slowly simmer so that the meat is tender.

Arlene Juratovac, Mayfield Heights, OH

Scrumptious Country-Style Ribs

This is a wonderful change from standard barbecued ribs.

3 pounds country-style spareribs
1½ cups ketchup

1 cup brown sugar
2½ cups cola beverage

Put ribs in roasting pan. Mix remaining ingredients in bowl and pour over ribs. Cover and bake in 350° oven about 3 hours.

Natalie Leon Golankiewicz, Pittsburgh, PA

Mom's Favorite Barbecued Spareribs

2 medium onions, sliced
2 teaspoons salt
¼ teaspoon pepper
½ teaspoon cayenne pepper
1 teaspoon chili powder

¾ cup ketchup
¾ cup water
2 teaspoons Worcestershire
3–4 pounds country-style
  Western spareribs

Mix all ingredients except ribs in roaster. Add ribs and turn to coat with sauce. Cover and bake at 350° for 1½–2 hours, basting with sauce as it cooks. This sauce is spicy and gets thick as it bakes.

Chris Sikorski, Granger, IN

This is one of my mom's favorite recipes that I found written in her own handwriting. I remember her preparing these for us when I was growing up.

—Chris Sikorski

Root Beer Ribs

4–6 pounds pork ribs, cut into
  individual riblets
1 teaspoon garlic salt
1 teaspoon chili powder
2 teaspoons Cajun seasoning

1 teaspoon red pepper
1 teaspoon black pepper
2 tablespoons Worcestershire
2 tablespoons hot sauce
2 tablespoons cooking oil

RIB SAUCE:
2 tablespoons Worcestershire
2 tablespoons hot sauce
1 (12-ounce) can root beer

1 cup ketchup
1½ teaspoons prepared mustard
1 cup brown sugar

Rub ribs with the seasonings and sauces. Heat oil in a Dutch oven and brown ribs on all sides, then drain off excess oil. While ribs are browning, mix Rib Sauce ingredients together in a large bowl. Pour over browned ribs. Bring mixture to a boil, then lower heat and cover. Simmer on low heat, stirring occasionally until ribs are tender (about 1½ hours). Serves 4–6.

Pamela East, Hackberry, LA

Beer-Basted Babyback Ribs

6 cups beer
2½ cups packed brown sugar
1½ cups apple cider vinegar
1½ tablespoons chili powder
1½ tablespoons ground cumin
1 tablespoon dry mustard

2 teaspoons salt
2 teaspoons dried crushed red
  pepper flakes
2 bay leaves
8 pounds baby back ribs, cut
  into 4-rib sections

Bring all but ribs to a boil in very large pot or roasting pan on stove top. Reduce heat. Simmer one minute to blend flavors. Add ribs to liquid. Cover pot and simmer until ribs are tender, turning frequently, about 25 minutes. Transfer ribs to baking dish. Pour half the liquid over the ribs. Cover and roast in 300° oven 4–5 hours. Serve remaining sauce with ribs.

Karen Saracusa, North Canton, OH

One-Pot Pork Chop Dinner

What a wonderful blend of flavor in a one-pot meal!

4 tablespoons oil	1 green pepper, sliced
Flour to coat chops	1 onion, chopped
4 thick pork chops	Salt and pepper to taste
1 cup rice (uncooked)	2½ cups water

Heat oil and fry floured pork chops in frying pan. Take chops out of pan and drain excess oil. Place chops back in pan and put in rice, green pepper, onion, salt, pepper, and water. Turn heat to low, cover, and cook 30 minutes, or till rice is done. Serves 4.

Nona McLean, Mitchellville, MD

Mimi's Pork Chops

Before my mom passed away in 2002 from breast cancer, it was important to her that I continue the tradition of her recipes to be passed down to her children and grandchildren. I am happy to share this recipe with others.

6 pork chops	1 cup vegetable juice
1 egg, beaten	1 cup ketchup
1½ cups bread crumbs	2 teaspoons sugar
½ cup butter	1–2 teaspoons salt
1 cup water	1–2 teaspoons pepper

Bread pork chops by coating in beaten egg and shaking in bread crumbs. Brown in butter. Move to a baking dish. Mix water, vegetable juice, ketchup, and seasonings to taste. Pour mixture over pork chops and bake at 350° for one hour. If thickening is needed, add cornstarch mixed with water to gravy and bring to a boil to thicken. Ready to serve.

Linda Downs-Ash, Medford, NJ

Sweet-n-Sour Pork Chops

1 (6-ounce) can tomato sauce
1 tablespoon Worcestershire
½ cup barbecue sauce (your
    choice)
¼ cup packed brown sugar
1 (8-ounce) can mushrooms,
    drained

1 small onion, diced
3 cloves garlic, minced
¼ teaspoon pepper
12–14 trimmed loin pork chops

Mix all ingredients, except chops, together to make a sauce. Pour over pork chops. Layer chops alternately with sauce in a crockpot. Cook 8 hours on LOW.

Sharon Brenneman, Lima, OH

Tex-Mex Chops

4 (¾-inch) boneless pork chops
1 teaspoon vegetable oil
1 cup salsa, chunky style

1 (4-ounce) can diced green
    chiles, undrained

In large skillet over medium-high heat, brown chops in oil on one side about 2 minutes; turn chops. Add salsa and chiles to skillet; lower heat, cover, and simmer gently for 20 minutes or until desired doneness is achieved. Serves 4.

Ruthann Dulovich, Monongahela, PA

Stir-Fry Pork with Peanut Sauce

This recipe has never let me down! It's always a hit with family and friends.

3 tablespoons peanut oil
1 pound boneless pork, cut
   into strips
1 onion, chopped
1 red bell pepper, cored, seeded,
   and sliced
1 clove garlic, minced
1½ teaspoons ground ginger
2–3 teaspoons ground coriander
1 teaspoon ground cumin

2 tablespoons soft dark brown
   sugar
Grated zest and juice of 1 lemon
4–5 tablespoons crunchy
   peanut butter
3 tablespoons dark soy sauce
1 tablespoon Worcestershire
Salt and pepper to taste
⅓ cup chopped cocktail peanuts
   (optional, for extra crunch)

Heat oil in large skillet or sauté pan. Add pork and stir-fry 1–2 minutes to seal. Add onion, red pepper, garlic, ginger, and other spices, and cook 3 minutes longer, stirring constantly. Add remaining ingredients to pan, and stir well to mix; lower heat. Cover and simmer about 20 minutes, until pork is tender. Serve over white rice and garnish with fresh parsley. Doubles easily.

Nicole Watkins, Alpharetta, GA

The studio garage provides the ideal setting for a tailgating party to help demonstrate the first QVC cookbook.

Honey-Bourbon Pork Tenderloins

2–3 pork tenderloins
3–4 green onions, chopped
1 clove garlic, minced
³⁄₈ cup honey

¹⁄₄ cup bourbon
¹⁄₂ cup vegetable or olive oil
¹⁄₂ teaspoon freshly ground
    black pepper

Combine all ingredients, except pork, in a small saucepan. Simmer for 10–15 minutes. Place tenderloins in a shallow dish and pour marinade over; cover. Marinate for about one hour. Grill over indirect heat until done. Makes 4–6 servings.

Val Early, Birmingham, AL

Moe's Pork and Pineapple Stir-Fry

1 pound pork tenderloin,
  sliced thin
1 tablespoon oil
1 cup thinly sliced onion
2 medium zucchini, sliced
1 stalk celery, sliced diagonally
1 carrot, sliced diagonally
1 crown broccoli florets,
  broken up

¹⁄₂ cup orange juice
3 tablespoons soy sauce
Salt and pepper to taste
Pepper to taste
1 tablespoon cornstarch
2 tablespoons water
2 cups pineapple chunks
Cooked rice

Fry pork in hot oil in wok 3–5 minutes. Remove pork. To oil in wok, add vegetables and cook for 2 minutes. Add pork back to wok along with orange juice, soy sauce, salt and pepper. Reduce heat, cover, and simmer 2 minutes. Add cornstarch dissolved in water. Stir-fry till thick and clear. Add pineapple chunks. Serve hot over cooked rice. Serves 4–6.

Jane F. Clapp, Berwick, ME

Honey Pork Oriental

2 pounds pork shoulder steak
   or pork tenderloin
2 tablespoons vegetable oil
1 envelope brown gravy mix
3/4 cup water
1/4 cup honey
3 tablespoons soy sauce
3 tablespoons red wine vinegar

1 teaspoon ginger
1/2 teaspoon garlic salt
4 small carrots, thinly sliced
1 medium onion, cut in wedges
1 green pepper, cut in thin strips
1 cup rice (or more), or 1 small
   can Chinese noodles (optional)

Cut pork into 1-inch squares, discarding fat and bones. Brown pork in oiled skillet, stirring frequently for about 15 minutes, then drain. Combine brown gravy mix, water, honey, soy sauce, red wine vinegar, ginger, and garlic salt. Pour over chops, cover, and cook 10 minutes. Add carrots; cook 10 minutes. Add onion and green peppers; cook 5–15 minutes. If you want your veggies softer, add 1/4 cup (or less) water and cook an additional 10 minutes. Serve over cooked rice or Chinese noodles. Enjoy!

Wendy Beaney, Mosheim, TN

Glazed Corned Beef

1 (4- to 5-pound) first-cut
  (thin-cut) corned beef
$2/3$ cup mustard

1 (11-ounce) can Mandarin
  oranges, with $1/4$ cup juice
1 cup brown sugar

Boil corned beef until tender, 2–2½ hours. Cool meat, then slice. Combine remaining ingredients for glaze; pour over sliced meat. Cover and bake at 350° for 35 minutes. Can be made a day or two ahead.

Barbara Thomas, Levittown, PA

Perfect-Every-Time Prime Rib

1 (3-rib) roast
Flour

Salt and pepper

Preheat oven to 500°. Immediately after removing roast from refrigerator, coat lightly with flour and rub it into the meat. Season generously with salt and pepper. Place roast in roasting pan and place a tent of heavy-duty foil loosely over top. Roast for precisely 8 minutes per pound for rare, 9 minutes per pound for medium. For larger roast, cook 9 minutes per pound for rare and 10 minutes per pound for medium. When roasting time is up, turn oven off—do not open the door. Let roast stay in the oven for at least 1 hour or more. It will cook perfectly every time.

Judith Laino, Old Tappan, NJ

Creole Garlic Prime Rib

This recipe is a very simple and delicious beef recipe that has won us many awards through the years.

**1 (6- to 8-pound) rib roast, with
or without the bone**
**1 (16-ounce) jar Cajun Injector
Creole Garlic Marinade**

**1 (8-ounce) can Cajun Shake
Creole Seasoning**

Inject 2 ounces of marinade per pound evenly throughout roast. Rub outside of roast generously with Cajun Shake Creole Seasoning. Cook covered in 350° oven for 2 hours, then uncover and cook another 30 minutes for browning.

Chef Reece Williams, QVC Guest, Clinton, LA

Chef Reece Williams and Gwen McKee are Cajun buddies from Louisiana. He knows how to inject flavor into most anything to make it taste great! Talk about good!

Mmmmm Good Baked Brisket

When I serve this, it disappears—you just can't stop till it's gone!

1 (5-pound) brisket	**Salt and pepper to taste**
Garlic salt to taste	**4–5 beef bouillon cubes**
Garlic powder to taste	

Place brisket in a roasting pan, fatty side up. Season to taste. Cover meat almost to top of brisket with water; cover and bake at 425° for 1 hour. Lower oven to 350°; turn meat over, adding more water, if needed, to keep half covered. Add bouillon cubes. Continue to turn meat over every hour to keep it moist, and bake approximately 4 hours more. Test for tenderness. When nice and tender, remove meat from liquid to platter and cool. Cover and refrigerate overnight or till cold. Refrigerate liquid in original pan.

When cold, spoon fat off top of liquid and discard. Slice brisket, then put back into pan, spooning juice over meat slices. Cover and heat and hold in 350° oven 30–60 minutes till warm and you're ready to serve. Serve with mashed potatoes and salad. You can use the juice as is to spoon over potatoes, or thicken with flour to make gravy. This freezes nicely. Mmmmm good!

Paula Schmidt, Fort Wayne, IN

Spoon Bread Beef Stroganoff

STROGANOFF:

½ cup flour
Salt and pepper to taste
2 pounds cubed beef steaks,
  cut in serving-size portions
3 tablespoons vegetable oil
1 large sweet onion, chopped

1 (10¾-ounce) can cream of
  mushroom soup
1 (8-ounce) carton sour cream
1 cup half-and-half
¼ cup ketchup

Flour, salt and pepper cubed steaks and brown in oil on both sides. Add onion and sauté till soft. Mix together soup, sour cream, half-and-half, and ketchup. Pour over steaks. Cover and simmer until steaks are tender, 1–2 hours.

SPOON BREAD:

1½ cups grits
6 cups water
Salt and pepper to taste

5 eggs, separated
½ cup butter

Prepare grits according to directions on box. Salt and pepper to taste. Whisk in egg yolks and butter, until well mixed. Beat egg whites until close to stiff and fold into grits. Bake in greased soufflé dish at 350° until brown and raised, 20–25 minutes.

Spoon hot Spoon Bread onto plate and add Stroganoff over top. Add a dollop of sour cream and chives, if desired.

Linda Bell, Greenwood, IN

Wok-a-Meal

1½ pounds sirloin steak tips,
  cut to bite-size
2 or 3 cloves garlic, minced
1 tablespoon olive oil
1 pound button mushrooms,
  sliced
1 red bell pepper, large dice
1 green bell pepper, large dice
1–2 cups celery, sliced thin on
  diagonal
1 cup carrots, sliced thin on
  diagonal
2 bunches green onions, sliced
  2 inches long, most of tops
  remaining
Baby corn, if you like
¾–1 cup lite soy sauce
3–4 tablespoons orange
  marmalade to taste
Cooked rice or noodles

Sauté beef and garlic in olive oil until beef is cooked through.
Remove from pan. In the same pan, sauté vegetables until al dente
(still firm). When vegetables are done, add beef and garlic mixture; stir. Add soy sauce and orange marmalade, and stir until
sauce is heated. Serve over egg noodles or rice.

Eileen Thompson, Rumford, RI

Slow Cooked Beef Tips

Throw-in-the-pot easy—please-the-whole-family good!

2 pounds beef tips
1 envelope onion soup mix
1 (10¾-ounce) can cream of
  mushroom soup or golden
  mushroom soup

Cooked rice or noodles

Spray the inside of a 4- to 5-quart crockpot with cooking spray.
Place beef tips inside. Add onion soup mix and stir to coat. Add
soup and stir to coat. Do not add water. Cook on LOW about 8
hours. Serve over cooked rice or noodles. Serves 4–6.

Note: Can substitute 2 pounds beef stew cut into smaller sections. Can
double the dry onion soup mix and cream of mushroom soup, if more
gravy is desired.

Mika Williams, Salisbury, NC

Steak Tips Linguini

1½ pounds tender steak tips
3 ounces burgundy wine
½ (15-ounce) can chicken broth
½ (10¾-ounce) can tomato
  soup
1 package onion soup mix
½ teaspoon black pepper

4 ounces water
1 tablespoon browning sauce
1 (10¾-ounce) can cream of
  mushroom soup
1 (6-ounce) can mushroom
  stems and pieces, drained
1 pound linguini, cooked

Combine steak tips, wine, chicken broth, tomato soup, onion soup mix, pepper, water, and gravy in large saucepan. Simmer for one hour. Add mushroom soup and mushrooms at end of cooking time. Serve hot over cooked linguini.

Denise Xanthakis, North Smithfield, RI

The-Simpler-the-Better Pepper Steak

1–2 pounds lean round or sirloin
  steak, about ½ inch thick
Black pepper to taste
1 medium onion, cut up

1 green or red bell pepper, cut
  into bite-size pieces
1 (24-ounce) bottle ketchup

Remove all visible fat from meat and cut into serving sizes. Arrange in casserole or baking pan and sprinkle with black pepper. Top with onion and bell pepper. Pour entire bottle of ketchup on top. Place lid on dish or cover tightly with foil. Bake at 350° approximately 1½ hours or until meat is fork-tender and ketchup has thickened. No salt is needed since ketchup has plenty in it. Serve with mashed potatoes or rice and a vegetable. No one would ever guess that the sauce is plain ketchup. If you want more sauce, use more ketchup.

Kay Reynolds, Red Oak, TX

Tender Oven-Baked Pepper Steak

2 medium onions, sliced into
  chunk pieces
1 green bell pepper, sliced into
  chunk pieces
2 red bell peppers, sliced into
  chunk pieces
2 tablespoons olive oil

Garlic powder to taste
Red pepper flakes to taste
1 (1- to 2-pound) London broil
1 (28-ounce) can crushed
  tomatoes
Soy sauce
White or brown rice

Sauté onions and peppers in olive oil until tender; drain and set aside. Slice London broil (better if slightly frozen); put in same pan you cooked onions and peppers. Sprinkle lots of garlic powder on slices of steak, add crushed red pepper flakes for taste (to your liking), then brown. Drain juices from meat after it is cooked. Place steak, peppers, and onions in roaster pan. Pour in crushed tomatoes and pour enough soy sauce so the color turns a reddish brown. Mix all together, cover, and cook in preheated 350° oven 50 minutes or until meat is tender. Uncover and cook another 10 minutes. Serve over brown or white rice.

Nan Angerman, Suffern, NY

Chuck Steak Pizziola

2–3 boneless chuck steaks, cut
  in serving pieces
Salt and pepper to taste
3 tablespoons oil, or more
1 onion, cut in half, then sliced
1 (4-ounce) can sliced
  mushrooms, drained

4 garlic cloves, minced
1 (16-ounce or 28-ounce) can
  Italian stewed tomatoes,
  to taste
2 teaspoons Italian seasoning
1/4 cup red wine (optional)

Season steak pieces with salt and pepper and brown on both sides in oil. Remove to a well-greased baking dish. To same skillet, add a little more oil if needed, then onion, mushrooms, and garlic. Sauté a couple of minutes, then add stewed tomatoes with juice, Italian seasoning, and wine, if desired. Cook a few more minutes. Pour over the steaks in baking dish, then cover. Bake at 350° for 1 hour and 30 minutes until tender. Serve sauce over mashed potatoes, rice, or pasta.

Mary Pin, Covington, WA

Quick & Easy Shepherd's Pie

Everyone will think you've been cooking all day!

1 (19-ounce) can beef stew
1 cup potato flakes

1 cup shredded Cheddar cheese

Preheat oven to 350°. Pour beef stew into casserole dish. Prepare potato flakes in mixing bowl according to directions on package. Whip with a spoon or mixer until smooth and spreadable. Spread mashed potato mix evenly over beef stew. Sprinkle with cheese. Bake uncovered in oven 20–30 minutes, or until cheese is completely melted and stew is bubbling on sides of casserole dish. Let cool 10 minutes and dig in! Great served with rolls and a salad.

Leslie Barnette, Allen Park, MI

South of the Border Meat Loaf

1½ pounds ground beef
1 (8-ounce) can Mexicorn, drained, or 1 cup regular corn mixed with ¼ cup chopped green pepper
¼ cup chopped onion
¼ cup cornmeal
½ teaspoon chili powder
1 (8-ounce) can tomato sauce
½ teaspoon oregano
1 teaspoon salt, or more to taste
⅛ teaspoon pepper

Mix ingredients for meat loaf and press into a large round pie pan or square baking dish. Bake at 425° for 25–30 minutes.

TOPPING:
1 egg
¼ cup milk
½ teaspoon dried mustard
½ teaspoon Worcestershire
1–1½ cups shredded Cheddar cheese
½ teaspoon chopped chile pepper (optional)

Combine Topping ingredients and spread on top of cooked meat loaf. Return to oven for 5 minutes or until cheese melts. Let stand 10 minutes before serving.

Bev Moe, Gwinn, MI

Easy Cheesy Meatloaf Ole!

1 pound ground chuck or ground turkey
1 extra large egg
½ cup oatmeal
½ package taco seasoning
2 cups salsa
1 cup grated sharp Cheddar cheese

Preheat oven to 350°. Mix meat, egg, oatmeal, and taco seasoning. Add salsa and mix well. Shape into loaf and place in loaf pan. Bake for 45 minutes. Remove from oven and top with cheese. Let sit 10 minutes on cooling rack before serving. Serve with salad and bread for a great simple meal.

Glenda Wood, Lillington, NC

Mexican Lasagna

1 pound ground beef
1 package taco seasoning mix
1 (16-ounce) jar salsa
1 (16-ounce) can refried beans
1 (10-count) package corn
  tortillas, cut in fourths

1 (16-ounce) container sour
  cream
1 (2-cup) package shredded
  sharp Cheddar cheese

Brown ground beef and drain. Add taco seasoning mix, but do not add water. In a 9x13-inch pan, layer half of each: ground beef mixture, salsa, refried beans, tortillas, sour cream, and cheese; repeat, ending with sour cream and topping with cheese. Bake at 350° for 30 minutes. Let sit 5 minutes before serving.

Cynthia Jones, Belpre, OH

Messy Burritos

1½ cups sour cream
1 (10¾-ounce) can cream of
  mushroom soup
1 cup salsa
1 pound ground beef
1 medium onion, chopped

1 (1¼-ounce) package taco
  seasoning mix
1 (16-ounce) can refried beans
10 soft flour tortillas
4 cups shredded Cheddar cheese

Mix together sour cream, soup, and salsa. Put ½ mixture in bottom of 9x13-inch baking pan. Fry ground beef and onion. Add taco seasoning mix and refried beans. Divide mixture onto tortillas. Roll up tortillas and place on top of sour cream mixture in pan. Spread remaining sour cream mixture on top. Sprinkle with cheese. Bake at 350° for 30–35 minutes.

Sandra Mirando, Depew, NY

Enchilada Casserole

2½ pounds ground beef
3 tablespoons chili powder
2 (16-ounce) jars salsa
½ stick butter or margarine
18–24 corn tortillas
1 (4-ounce) can sliced olives

1 (16-ounce) can whole-kernel
  corn, drained, or 1¼ cups
  frozen corn
4 cups shredded Cheddar cheese
1 cup water

In large skillet, brown ground beef, then drain. Cover all meat with a layer of chili powder, then pour salsa over meat. Mix well and set aside. In a 9x13-inch glass or aluminum pan, spread a thin layer of meat mixture on bottom. Butter one side of corn tortillas, and place over meat mixture with butter side up. Add more meat mixture on top of tortillas, then continue layering in the following order 3 times: olives, corn, tortillas, meat, cheese, etc. There should be 6 buttered tortillas on each layer. Pour 1 cup water around sides of casserole, then cover with foil. Bake at 350° for 30 minutes. Remove foil and continue baking for 15 minutes more, until cheese is bubbly.

Robyn Minnetti, Stockton, CA

Corn Bread Skillet Casserole

1 pound ground beef
l cup cornmeal
1 (15-ounce) can cream-style
  corn
½ cup vegetable oil

1 cup milk
½ teaspoon salt, or to taste
1 large onion, chopped
1 (16-ounce) bag shredded
  Cheddar cheese

Brown ground beef; drain. Mix cornmeal, corn, vegetable oil, milk, and salt in bowl. Pour ½ of mixture into greased, hot iron skillet, then top with ground beef, onion, and cheese. Pour remaining mixture over top. Bake at 350° approximately 1 hour or until done.

Judi Swilling, New Tazewell, TN

Cliff's Jazzy Casserole

1 large onion, chopped
1 large bell pepper, chopped
3 (or more) jalapeño peppers,
  finely chopped
1 tablespoon olive oil
2 pounds ground chuck
1 (8-ounce) can water chestnuts,
  drained
1 teaspoon salt
1 teaspoon freshly ground pepper
1 (1-pound) loaf processed
  cheese
1 (10¾-ounce) can cream of
  mushroom soup
1 (4-ounce) can mushroom
  stems and pieces, drained
1½ cups water
1 large package wide egg noodles
6 slices processed cheese

In large nonstick pot, sauté onion and peppers in olive oil until semi-firm. Add ground chuck, and brown. Drain grease, then add remaining ingredients, except water, noodles, and cheese slices. Stir until cheese melts, then add water. Let cook on low for 30 minutes, stirring every 10 minutes.

While this is simmering, cook egg noodles according to package directions, but only cook for ¾ of the specified time. Drain noodles and pour into greased casserole dish. Add mixture to noodles and combine. Place cheese singles on top and bake for 30 minutes at 350°. Best served with garlic bread.

Note: You can substitute ham for the beef, but leave out the salt.

James Lamb, Jackson, MS

My father Cliff was a great cook, and this was his crowning achievement. My friends still beg me to cook this all the time.

—James Lamb

Glorious Mess

3 onions, chopped
1 stalk celery, chopped
4 pounds hamburger
½–1 teaspoon each: oregano,
   marjoram, and thyme
1 bay leaf
2 (15-ounce) cans tomatoes
1 (16-ounce) can Mexican-style
   beans

1 (10¾-ounce) can cream of
   mushroom soup
1 (16-ounce) bag corn chips
Chopped tomatoes, shredded
   lettuce, shredded cheese, and
   chopped green onions

Sauté onions and celery with hamburger meat. Cook until meat is browned. Add oregano, marjoram, thyme, bay leaf, and tomatoes. Cook over medium-low heat one hour. Add beans and cream of mushroom soup. Heat through. In a baking dish, layer corn chips and beef mixture. Top with tomatoes, lettuce, cheese, and green onions.

Dorothy Bock, Conyers, GA

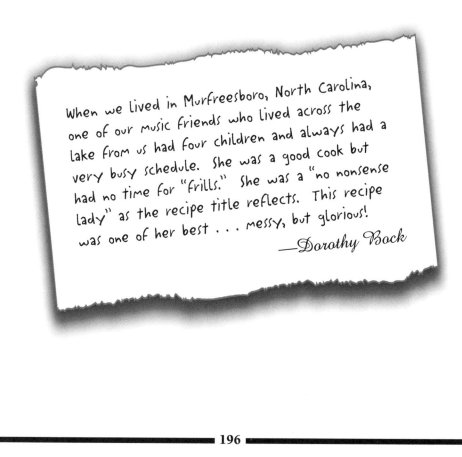

When we lived in Murfreesboro, North Carolina, one of our music friends who lived across the lake from us had four children and always had a very busy schedule. She was a good cook but had no time for "frills." She was a "no nonsense lady" as the recipe title reflects. This recipe was one of her best . . . messy, but glorious!

—Dorothy Bock

Dinner In a Dish

1 pound ground chuck or hamburger
1 cup chopped or sliced green pepper
1 medium onion, chopped
1½ teaspoons salt (optional)
¼ teaspoon pepper (optional)
2 eggs, beaten

2 cups whole-kernel corn, drained, divided
4 medium tomatoes, or 2 cups canned tomatoes, drained, divided
2 tablespoons margarine
½ cup dry bread crumbs, plain or seasoned

Lightly brown meat. Drain fat. Add green pepper, onion, and seasonings, if desired. Remove from heat and add beaten eggs. Put 1 cup corn in baking dish, ½ of meat mixture, and ½ of tomatoes. Repeat with remaining corn, meat mixture, and tomatoes. Melt margarine in same skillet and add bread crumbs. Spread buttered crumbs over casserole. Bake at 375° for 45 minutes. Serves 6.

Jan Siefert, Kankakee, IL

All Together Slow-Pot Dinner

1 pound ground beef
¾ pound bacon, cut into small pieces
1 cup chopped onion
1 (31-ounce) can pork and beans
1 (16-ounce) can kidney beans, drained
1 (16-ounce) can lima beans, drained

1 (16-ounce) can butter beans, drained
1 cup ketchup
¾ cup brown sugar
1 tablespoon liquid smoke
3 tablespoons vinegar
½ teaspoon salt
Dash of pepper

Brown ground beef in skillet; drain fat. Place in a slow cooker. Fry bacon and onion together; drain fat. Add to ground beef mixture. Add remaining ingredients to slow cooker; stir well. Cover and cook 8–10 hours on LOW.

Glenda Juris, Belvidere, IL

Favorite Family Casserole

1 pound lean ground beef
2 cups cooked noodles (any kind)
1 (16-ounce) can white corn, drained
1 (8-ounce) can tomatoes, drained
1 (4-ounce) can mushrooms, drained
1 (8-ounce) can tomato sauce
Salt and pepper to taste
1 cup grated Cheddar cheese

Preheat oven to 350°. Brown ground beef; drain, if necessary. Combine with remaining ingredients, adding cheese last. Bake in greased casserole dish for 45 minutes.

Leigh Ann McRoy, Alton, IL

Burgers Divan

3 slices bacon
1 teaspoon Worcestershire
3/4 teaspoon salt
1/4 teaspoon dried crushed oregano
1/2 teaspoon dry mustard
1 pound hamburger meat
1/4 cup mayonnaise
2 teaspoons milk

Cook bacon until crisp, then drain; reserve drippings in pan. In a bowl, combine crumbled bacon with Worcestershire, salt, oregano, dry mustard, and hamburger meat. Make into 4 patties and fry in reserved bacon drippings. Mix mayonnaise and milk. Top burgers with mixture. Serve with buns and trimmings as desired.

Barbara Ann Mason, Underhill, VT

Juicy Burgers

These are the best!

1 pound hamburger meat
1 (3.5-ounce) can French fried
   onions, crushed
1 tablespoon Worcestershire

1 (4-ounce) can chopped
   mushroom pieces, drained
$\frac{1}{4}$ teaspoon salt

Mix all ingredients well. Shape into 4 patties. Grill to desired doneness. Serve on toasted buns.

Janet Parslow, Pleasant Valley, NY

A-Step-Above Burgers

1 pound ground chuck
$\frac{1}{4}$ cup seasoned bread crumbs
1 package dry onion soup mix
2 eggs

1 teaspoon Worcestershire
$\frac{1}{4}$ teaspoon garlic salt
1 ($10\frac{3}{4}$-ounce) can golden
   mushroom soup

Combine first 6 ingredients; mix well. Shape into 4 patties. Place in an ungreased baking dish. Spoon soup on top. Bake at 350° for about 40 minutes. Serve open-face on toasted buns or French bread. Omit the bread for low-carb diets.

Betty Lou Wright, Goodlettsville, TN

Best Ever Quick Sloppy Joes

This recipe is very simple and totally delicious.

1 medium onion
1 bell pepper
1 rib celery
$1\frac{1}{2}$ pounds ground beef
2–4 tablespoons brown sugar

1 tablespoon Worcestershire
1 (12-ounce) bottle prepared
   chili sauce
2 tablespoons cider vinegar

Chop onion, bell pepper, and celery into medium dice. Cook with meat until slightly browned. Drain, then add all remaining ingredients and simmer gently for 15 minutes. Serve on buns.

Norma Wright, Albuquerque, NM

Sweet & Tangy Chili BBQ

2 pounds ground sirloin
⅓ cup diced onion
1 tablespoon black pepper
1 (20-ounce) bottle ketchup

½ cup yellow mustard
1 cup brown sugar (not packed)
3 tablespoons chili powder

Brown meat with onion and black pepper; drain, breaking into fine pieces. In crockpot, mix meat mixture with enough ketchup to coat the hamburger well. Mix in remaining ingredients and simmer on LOW heat for at least 1½ hours. Serve on hamburger or hoagie buns.

Carrie Korthals, Sun Prairie, WI

Sausage and Cabbage La Rue

I always brought this to church gatherings, and everybody loved it. It's a winner!

2 pounds Polish sausage, cut in
  chunks
1 medium bell pepper, cut in
  strips
1 medium onion, quartered
3 baking potatoes, peeled, cubed

3 medium carrots, sliced
1 small cabbage, cored and
  quartered
1 cup water
Salt and pepper to taste

Fry sausage and drain. In large Dutch oven or electric skillet, layer vegetables and sausage. Salt and pepper between layers. Add water, and bring to a quick boil. Lower heat, and simmer, covered, for 45 minutes, till cabbage is cooked. Check the water during cooking; add more, if necessary. Serves 6–8.

La Rue Dunagin, Austin, TX

Beer-Braised Italian Sausages

3 tablespoons olive oil
3 pounds Italian sausage links, skinned
3 red bell peppers, sliced
2 green bell peppers, sliced
2 large red onions, sliced
3 cloves garlic, chopped
2 (12-ounce) bottles beer
1 (6-ounce) can tomato paste
3 tablespoons chopped fresh basil
2 tablespoons hot sauce
Salt and pepper to taste

Heat olive oil in a large heavy skillet over medium-high heat. Sauté sausage until browned on all sides. Remove sausage from pan, and set aside. Place red peppers, green peppers, onions, and garlic in pan and cook 3 minutes. Stir in beer and tomato paste. Season with basil, hot sauce, salt and pepper. Cover, and simmer until onions and peppers are tender. Slice sausage into bite-size pieces, and add to peppers. Cover; simmer until sausage is cooked through. Makes 6 servings.

Jill Gioia, New Milford, NJ

Editor's Extra: Good served over pasta or on hoagie buns.

Fabulous Dinner in a Biscuit

1 (10- to 12-count) can refrigerator biscuits
1 pound bulk sausage
1 (4-ounce) can sliced black olives, drained
1 cup ranch dressing
1/2 green bell pepper, chopped
1/2 red bell pepper, chopped
Shredded Cheddar cheese

Flatten each biscuit and fit in a muffin tin. Fry sausage until done; crumble. Mix in remaining ingredients except cheese. Fill each "muffin" with sausage mixture; top with cheese. Bake at 350° for 10–15 minutes or until muffins are golden brown.

Darlene Powell, South Cle Elum, WA

Cheesy Ham and Asparagus Casserole

This is wonderful!

5 tablespoons butter, divided
1½ tablespoons flour
Salt and pepper to taste
1 cup milk
1½ cups grated Cheddar cheese

1 (15-ounce) can asparagus, drained
½ pound boiled ham, diced
2 tablespoons minced onion
20 saltine crackers

In a saucepan, melt 2 tablespoons butter; whisk in flour, salt and pepper. When bubbly, slowly add milk, constantly stirring with a whisk. With spoon, stir in grated cheese till melted.

In a greased 8x8-inch glass or ceramic baking pan, layer asparagus, diced ham, onions, and sauce. Crush crackers in blender or food processor; melt and add remaining 3 tablespoons butter. Spread this on top of casserole and bake at 350° for 30 minutes or until hot and bubbly. Serves 4.

Note: This recipe doubles easily; use an 11x15-inch baking dish instead. You may also substitute fresh or frozen broccoli for the asparagus.

Carol Seay, Boiling Springs, SC

Good Old Ham and Broccoli Bake

1 (8-ounce) jar processed cheese spread
2 (10¾-ounce) cans cream of chicken soup
½ cup milk
½ cup chopped onion

4 tablespoons margarine
2 (10-ounce) packages frozen chopped broccoli
4 cups diced cooked ham
2 cups minute rice
½ teaspoon Worcestershire

In a large bowl, blend cheese spread, soup, and milk. Sauté onion in margarine until tender. Cook broccoli as directed on box until almost tender; drain. Add onion, broccoli, ham, uncooked rice, and Worcestershire to soup and cheese mixture. Blend. Bake in greased 9x13-inch pan at 350° for 35–40 minutes.

Linda Lehman, Belvidere, IL

Cakes

Lemon Pie Sheet Cake

1 (18¼-ounce) package lemon
  cake mix
4 eggs
1 (21-ounce) can lemon pie filling
1 (3-ounce) package cream
  cheese, softened

½ cup butter or margarine,
  softened
2 cups confectioners' sugar
1½ teaspoons vanilla extract

In large mixing bowl, beat cake mix and eggs until well blended;
fold in pie filling. Spread into a greased 10x15-inch baking pan.
Bake in preheated 350° oven for 18–20 minutes or until a toothpick inserted comes out clean. Cool on wire rack. In a small mixing bowl, beat cream cheese, butter, and confectioners' sugar until
smooth. Stir in vanilla. Spread over cake. Store in refrigerator.
Yields 30–35 servings.

Jody Strecker, Falls City, NE

Polish Apple Cookie Sheet Cake

3 cups flour
1 cup sugar
½ teaspoon salt
1 cup butter, softened
2 egg yolks, beaten

3 tablespoons sour cream
½ teaspoon vanilla
5 large apples
1 cup sugar mixed with 1½
  teaspoons cinnamon

Mix flour, sugar, salt, and butter. In a cup, lightly blend in egg
yolks, sour cream, and vanilla. Add to dry ingredients and make a
crumb mixture. Pat onto greased cookie sheet. Pare and slice
apples. Toss apples in sugar-cinnamon mixture, then place in rows
on crumb mixture. Bake at 350° for 25–35 minutes. Cut into
squares, and serve plain or with vanilla ice cream; sprinkle with
cinnamon.

Carol Birtic, Wadsworth, OH

Butterscotch Apple Cake

1 cup oil
2 eggs
2 cups sugar
2½ cups flour
1 teaspoon baking soda

1 teaspoon salt
1 teaspoon cinnamon
1 cup broken pecans (optional)
3 cups chopped apples
1 cup butterscotch chips

Mix oil, eggs, and sugar in large bowl. Sift dry ingredients and add to oil mixture. Stir in apples and nuts and mix well. Batter will be stiff. (You may add a few drops of water if needed.) Spread in greased 9x13-inch pan. Sprinkle butterscotch chips on top of cake. Bake at 350° for 55–60 minutes.

Cheryl Sowards, Germantown, OH

Holiday Cake

Unbelievably good!

1 (20-ounce) can crushed
  pineapple
1 (18¼-ounce) white cake mix
1 (8-ounce) package cream
  cheese, softened
1 (5-ounce) package vanilla
  instant pudding

1–2 tablespoons milk
1 (12- to 16-ounce) container
  whipped topping (regular or
  strawberry)
Shredded coconut
Chopped nuts

Drain crushed pineapple and save juice to make the liquid portion for cake mix. Follow cake mix instructions and spread batter onto greased cookie sheet or jellyroll pan; bake until golden brown (about 20 minutes).

Combine cream cheese and dry instant pudding with a little milk. Add drained pineapple. Mix until creamy. Spread mixture onto cooled cake. Spread whipped topping over top of cream cheese layer. Finally, sprinkle coconut and chopped nuts over whipped topping.

Jean Ives, Fort Edward, NY

Heavenly Caramel Carrot Cake

1 (17-ounce) box cinnamon swirl
  cake mix (or coffee cake mix)
1 cup water
$\frac{1}{3}$ cup butter, melted
3 eggs
1 cup grated carrots
1 cup chopped walnuts

$\frac{1}{2}$ (16-ounce) jar caramel ice
  cream topping
$\frac{1}{2}$ (16-ounce) tub caramel
  frosting
1 (8- to 12-ounce) tub whipped
  topping, thawed

In a large bowl, mix cake mix and cinnamon package with water, butter, and eggs until blended, about 2 minutes. Fold in carrots and nuts. Pour into a greased 9x13-inch pan. Bake at 350° for 35–45 minutes or until toothpick comes out clean. Cool 15 minutes.

Poke holes in top of cake. Warm ice cream topping and drizzle over top of cake. Let cake sit 10 minutes to absorb topping. Mix $\frac{1}{2}$ can of caramel frosting with whipped topping. Spread on top of completely cooled cake and refrigerate until serving.

Brenda Pittman, Richmond, KY

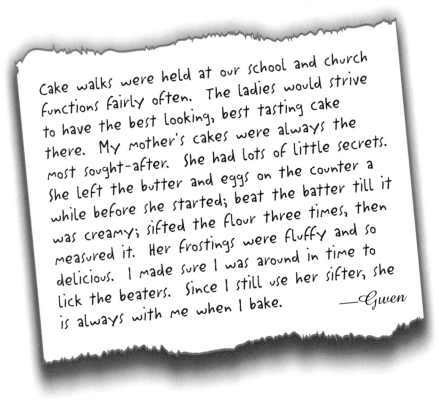

Cake walks were held at our school and church functions fairly often. The ladies would strive to have the best looking, best tasting cake there. My mother's cakes were always the most sought-after. She had lots of little secrets. She left the butter and eggs on the counter a while before she started; beat the batter till it was creamy; sifted the flour three times, then measured it. Her frostings were fluffy and so delicious. I made sure I was around in time to lick the beaters. Since I still use her sifter, she is always with me when I bake.

—Gwen

Cool Tropical Cake

Delicious! Melts in your mouth. The longer it sits, the better it tastes.

1 (18¼-ounce) yellow cake mix
1 (16-ounce) can crushed
  pineapple, drained
1 (8-ounce) can piña colada mix
1 (14-ounce) can sweetened
  condensed milk
1 (16-ounce) carton whipped
  topping
8 ounces shredded coconut

Mix cake mix as directed, but add pineapple. Bake in 9x13-inch cake pan as directed. While cake is hot, punch holes in top using a straw or fork. Mix piña colada mix with condensed milk; pour over cake and let mixture sink into holes. Cool completely. Cover with whipped topping and coconut. Refrigerate overnight.

Barbara Jefferson, Talbott, TN

Frosted Pumpkin Delight

1 (30-ounce) can pumpkin pie
  mix (not canned pumpkin)
3 eggs
1 cup sugar
½ teaspoon salt
½ teaspoon pumpkin pie spice
2 cups dry yellow cake mix
1 stick margarine, melted
1 (16-ounce) container whipped
  topping
¾ cup chopped pecans

Preheat oven to 350°. Thoroughly mix first 5 ingredients. Pour into a greased 9x13-inch pan. Sprinkle dry cake mix on top. Drizzle melted margarine over top. Bake for 45 minutes. Let cool. Frost with the whipped topping. Sprinkle with chopped pecans. Keep refrigerated.

Donna Howell, Supply, NC

Pineapple Angel Food Cake

No fat, low sugar, high taste.

1 (20-ounce) can crushed
   pineapple, in its own juice
1 (16-ounce) box angel food
   cake mix

1 carton low-fat (or no fat)
   whipped topping (optional)

Mix crushed pineapple (with juice) and cake mix. Bake according to directions on cake box. When cool, top with whipped topping.

Mable Fuselier, Eunice, LA

Banana-Sour Cream Crunch Cake

¹/₂ cup butter
1 cup sugar
2 eggs
1 cup mashed bananas (2–3
   very ripe bananas)
1 teaspoon vanilla
¹/₂ cup sour cream

2 cups flour
1 teaspoon baking powder
1 teaspoon baking soda
¹/₄ teaspoon salt
1 (10-ounce) bag cinnamon
   chips*

In a bowl, cream butter with sugar. Beat in eggs. Add bananas, vanilla, and sour cream. In a separate bowl, sift together flour, baking powder, baking soda, and salt. Fold dry ingredients into banana mixture; stir to blend.

Preheat oven to 350°. Grease and lightly flour Bundt or tube cake pan. Sprinkle half of chips in pan. Add cake batter and sprinkle remaining chips on top. Bake for 45 minutes or until toothpick inserted comes out clean. Cool in pan for 10 minutes.

Note: If cinnamon chips can not be found, use 1 teaspoon cinnamon with praline or butterscotch chips. May be dusted with confectioners' sugar or simple vanilla glaze, if desired, but I like it just plain!

JoAnn Peek, Brigantine, NJ

Nanny's Banana Cake

GLAZE:

1 tablespoon or so milk

1 cup confectioners' sugar

Gradually add milk to confectioners' sugar. Set aside.

2 cups sifted cake flour, or 2
   cups less 4 tablespoons
   regular flour
2 teaspoons baking powder
1/4 teaspoon salt
1/4 cup shortening

1 cup white sugar
1 egg, unbeaten
3/4 cup milk
1 teaspoon vanilla
2–3 large very ripe bananas,
   divided

Sift flour, baking powder, and salt. Cream shortening thoroughly in large bowl. Add white sugar gradually and cream well. Add egg and beat thoroughly. Add flour mixture alternately with milk, beating after each addition, till smooth. Stir in vanilla; blend.

Bake in 2 (8-inch-round) greased and floured cake pans at 375° for 25–30 minutes. Cool 10 minutes, then carefully place one cake layer on a serving plate; cover top with banana slices. Glaze first layer before topping with second cake layer. After second layer is placed on top, slice another banana for top and sides. Glaze entire cake. The Glaze will set or harden. Enjoy!

Sharon A. Younkins, Boonsboro, MD

My great grandmother started cooking for her family and company before she was a teen. She was a born cook who measured by handfuls, and never cooked on anything but a wood stove. She lived to be ninety-six years old and was loved by everyone for miles around.

—Sharon A. Younkins

Sticky Toffee Date Cake

2 cups pitted and chopped dates
1¼ cups water
1 teaspoon baking soda
1 cup all-purpose flour
1½ teaspoons baking powder
1 teaspoon salt

6 tablespoons (¾ stick) butter, softened
¾ cup sugar
2 large eggs
1 teaspoon pure vanilla extract

Stir together dates and water in a medium saucepan; bring to a boil. If dates don't dissolve completely, use an immersion blender to smooth mixture. Remove from heat, stir in baking soda (it will bubble), and let stand until cooled and softened to a lukewarm slurry, about 20 minutes.

Preheat oven to 350°. Spray 8-inch square baking pan with non-stick spray. In a small bowl, whisk together flour, baking powder, and salt. With an electric mixer on medium speed, cream butter with sugar until fluffy. Add eggs, one at a time, then vanilla, beating well. Stir in cooled date slurry, then fold in flour mixture a little at a time until just combined. Pour into prepared pan, and bake on center oven rack until a toothpick inserted into center comes out clean, with a few fudgy crumbs, 35–40 minutes. Cool slightly on a rack. While cake cools, prepare sauce.

CARAMEL SAUCE:

¾ cup packed brown sugar
½ cup heavy cream

4 tablespoons (½ stick) butter
1 teaspoon pure vanilla extract

Combine brown sugar, cream, butter, and vanilla in a small, heavy saucepan. Bring to just below boiling, reduce heat, and simmer gently, stirring 1 minute. Remove from heat and let stand a few minutes to thicken slightly.

Prick warm cake all over, plunging all the way through to bottom (you are making little channels for sauce to penetrate cake—leave no spot unpricked). Spread warm sauce over warm cake, letting it sink in at least 10 minutes. Serve warm and gooey, or let cool to room temperature and freeze, covered with foil. To thaw, let stand at room temperature about 2 hours or until soft; or warm it, with foil on, in a 250° oven until heated through, about 30 minutes.

Alice Kasman Fixx, New York, NY
and Joyce Hendley, Minneapolis, MN

Mango Upside-Down Cake

1 ripe mango, peeled, thinly
   sliced
2 tablespoons fresh lemon juice
2 tablespoons butter
¼ cup brown sugar, firmly
   packed
1¼ cups all-purpose flour
¾ cup sugar
⅓ cup unsweetened cocoa
   powder

1 teaspoon baking soda
¼ teaspoon salt
½ cup buttermilk
¼ cup vegetable oil
1 large egg
½ teaspoon vanilla extract
¼ cup apricot preserves

Preheat oven to 350°. In a bowl, combine mangoes and lemon juice; set aside. In a saucepan over medium heat, combine butter and sugar, stirring until bubbling. Pour mixture into bottom of an 8-inch baking pan; arrange mangoes decoratively in pan.

Onto wax paper, combine flour, sugar, cocoa powder, baking soda, and salt. In a mixing bowl, combine buttermilk, oil, egg, and vanilla. Stir into dry ingredients. Pour over mangoes; bake 35–40 minutes. Invert onto serving platter. In a saucepan over medium heat, warm preserves. Brush over top of cake. Allow to sit 10 minutes. Serves 8.

Deirdre Todd, Honolulu, HI

Perky Poppy Seed Cake

1 (18¼-ounce) yellow cake mix
1 (3-ounce) package French
   vanilla instant pudding
4 eggs
½ cup oil

½ cup water
1 cup sour cream
1 teaspoon rum flavoring
2–4 tablespoons poppy seeds

Put cake mix in bowl; add remaining ingredients except poppy seeds. Mix well. Stir in seeds by hand. Pour into greased and floured Bundt pan. Bake at 350° for 50 minutes. Remove from oven; let stand 10–15 minutes. Place on plate.

TOPPING:

2 tablespoons orange juice
              1 cup powdered sugar

Poke holes in cake. Mix orange juice with powdered sugar and pour over cake.

Debbie Dean, Cross Lanes, WV

Lemon Ginger Ale Cake

1 (18¼-ounce) box white cake
   mix
1 (3-ounce) box lemon instant
   pudding mix

1 cup oil
3 eggs, beaten
1 cup ginger ale
1 teaspoon lemon zest

In a mixing bowl, combine cake mix, pudding mix, oil, eggs, ginger ale, and lemon zest. Pour into a greased angel food or Bundt cake pan. Bake at 350° for 50–60 minutes. Cool in pan for 10 minutes; turn out on wire rack for additional cooling.

LEMON CREAM CHEESE GLAZE:

1½ cups powdered sugar
1 teaspoon vanilla
1 tablespoon butter, softened
4 ounces cream cheese

1 teaspoon lemon zest
3 tablespoons lemon juice
   (juice of 1 lemon)

Mix all ingredients. Pour on cooled cake.

Terri Hammond, Monroe, OH

Delicious Butter Rum Cake

2 sticks (1 cup) margarine
2½ cups sugar
6 eggs, separated
3 cups flour
¼ teaspoon baking soda

8 ounces sour cream
1 tablespoon rum
1 teaspoon vanilla
½ cup sugar

Cream margarine and sugar; add egg yolks one at a time. Add flour and soda alternately with sour cream, beginning and ending with flour. Stir in rum and vanilla. Beat egg whites with sugar till stiff, then stir into batter. Pour into a greased and floured tube pan, and bake 1½ hours at 325°. When cake is cool, remove to a plate. Poke holes in top of cake, and pour Butter Rum Glaze over.

BUTTER RUM GLAZE:
¼ cup plus 2 teaspoons
   margarine

6 tablespoons rum
¾ cup sugar

Cook over low heat till sugar dissolves. Pour over top of cake.

Kathie Landrum, Louisville, KY

QVC's Studio Park is big! Besides the "family rooms"—kitchen, sunroom, garage, bedroom, bathroom, living room—where appropriate products are demonstrated, there are several annexes like this one, where big products have room to stretch out.

Family Classic Fudge Delight

2 cups sugar
2 cups self-rising flour
1 stick margarine
½ cup oil
1 cup water
4 tablespoons cocoa

½ cup buttermilk
2 eggs, slightly beaten
1 teaspoon baking soda
1 teaspoon vanilla
1½ teaspoons cinnamon

Mix sugar and flour in mixing bowl; set aside. Melt margarine, oil, water, and cocoa in boiler. Pour mixture over sugar and flour mixture, stirring well. Add buttermilk, eggs, baking soda, vanilla, and cinnamon; mix well. Bake in 15x11-inch sheet pan that has been greased and floured. Bake 20 minutes at 400º.

ICING:

1 stick margarine
4 tablespoons cocoa
6 tablespoons milk
1 teaspoon vanilla

1 (1-pound) box confectioners' sugar
1 cup chopped pecans

Five minutes before cake is done, melt margarine, cocoa, milk, and vanilla; bring just to boil. Take off heat and add sugar and pecans. Spread on cake while hot.

Kay Williams, Clinton, MS

Comin' Home Chocolate Frosting

1 stick margarine, divided
2 cups sugar
5 tablespoons cocoa

¼ teaspoon salt
½ cup milk
1 teaspoon vanilla

Spread a small amount of margarine around inside of saucepan. Combine sugar, cocoa, salt, milk, and remaining margarine in saucepan. Cook over medium heat, stirring occasionally, for 10 minutes or until a firm ball forms in cold water. Let cool 5–10 minutes, then add vanilla. Spread over prepared cake.

Note: If you overcook the frosting, don't worry; just add a tablespoon or so of white corn syrup.

Katie Sue Meredith, Brantley, AL

My Granny Meredith always makes her famous chocolate cake whenever one of her grandchildren comes home for a visit. When I was old enough to understand (and ask), she apologetically explained that the cake itself is a mix, and proudly proclaimed that it is her frosting that makes it so good. A trip home wouldn't be the same without her comforting chocolate cake there to welcome me.

—*Granddaughter, Keena*

Chocolate Cream Puff Cake

DOUGH:

1 cup water
½ cup margarine

1 cup flour
4 eggs

Heat water and margarine to a boil. Stir in flour over heat until a ball forms. Remove from heat and add eggs one at a time. Beat until creamy smooth. Spread in lightly greased cookie sheet with sides. Bake at 400° for 30 minutes, or until browned; cool completely.

FILLING:

1 (8-ounce) package cream
  cheese, softened
1 (5-ounce) box vanilla instant
  pudding

1 cup heavy cream, whipped, or
  2–2½ cups whipped topping
Chocolate syrup

Cream the cream cheese; prepare pudding as directed and mix with cream cheese. Spread over Dough. Top with whipped cream, then drizzle chocolate syrup on top. Refrigerate. Cut into squares. Enjoy!

Jean Ives, Fort Edward, NY

If you were a guest selling a product in the annex, where visitors are sometimes invited to sit in the audience, you would have this view of the monitors.

Chocolate Kahlúa Cake

1 (18¼-ounce) package super
  moist German chocolate
  cake mix
1 (3.4-ounce) package chocolate
  instant pudding
1 (16-ounce) container sour cream

4 eggs
¾ cup vegetable oil
⅓ cup plus 2 tablespoons
  Kahlúa, divided
1 teaspoon vanilla
1 cup mini-chocolate chips

Preheat oven to 350°. Grease Bundt pan by spraying it with non-stick spray. Pour contents of German chocolate cake mix and chocolate pudding together into mixer. Mix for a minute to get lumps out. Now add sour cream and mix another minute. Turn off machine. Add eggs one at a time, beating after each. Scrape down sides of bowl. Turn mixer on low and slowly pour in oil, ⅓ cup Kahlúa, and vanilla. Mix well. Scrape down sides of bowl one more time. Add mini-chocolate chips. Mix about 1 minute. Pour into prepared Bundt pan and bake 55–65 minutes. Do not over-cook. When cake is done, let it cool on counter for about 10 minutes. Remove from pan. Drizzle remaining 2 tablespoons Kahlúa over warm cake.

GLAZE:
1⅓ cups semisweet chocolate
  chips

½ cup heavy whipping cream
1 teaspoon vanilla

In a small saucepan, combine chocolate chips, heavy whipping cream, and vanilla. Cook over low heat until melted. Spoon over cooled cake.

Mckall Cuffel, Rancho Palos Verdes, CA

Toffee Kahlúa Cake

1 cup butter, softened
2 cups sugar
5 large eggs, separated
2 cups all-purpose flour
1 teaspoon baking soda

¼ teaspoon salt
1 cup buttermilk
1 teaspoon vanilla extract
1 tablespoon Kahlúa

Beat butter at medium speed until creamy; gradually add sugar, beating well. Add egg yolks, one at a time. Combine flour, soda, and salt, and add to butter mixture alternately with buttermilk, beginning and ending with flour mixture. Mix at low speed until all blended. Stir in vanilla and Kahlúa. Beat egg whites at high speed until stiff peaks form. Gently fold into batter. Pour into 2 greased and floured 9-inch cake pans. Bake at 350° for 30–35 minutes or until a wooden pick inserted in center comes out clean. Cool in pans on wire racks 5 minutes; remove from pans and cool completely on wire racks.

TOFFEE KAHLÚA FROSTING:

1 (8-ounce) package cream
  cheese, softened
1 stick butter, softened
1 (2-pound) bag confectioners'
  sugar, sifted

Whole milk, as needed
1½ tablespoons Kahlúa
1 cup crushed toffee bits

Mix cream cheese and butter until well blended. Add confectioners' sugar, a little at a time. If mixture is too stiff, add a little whole milk. Add Kahlúa and toffee bits, mixing well.

Ruth Wetmore, Madison, FL

Coffee & Cream Praline Cake

This cake is so rich and good, everybody who tries it thinks it must be difficult to make, but it is really so simple!

1 (18¼-ounce) box white
  cake mix
3 eggs
1 cup coffee liqueur
¼ cup oil
1 cup butter
1 cup packed brown sugar
1¼ cups chopped pecans

1 (3-ounce) package vanilla
  instant pudding
1 (8-ounce) package cream
  cheese, softened
1¼ cups milk
1 (12-ounce) carton whipped
  topping, or 1 pint whipped
  cream

Grease and flour a 9x13-inch pan. Combine cake mix, eggs, liqueur, and oil in large bowl. Mix on medium speed for 2–3 minutes. Pour into greased pan. Bake at 350° for 25 minutes or until done.

When cake is almost done, start making praline topping by combining butter and brown sugar in a saucepan. Boil for 2 minutes, stirring constantly. Pour in pecans; remove from heat and stir well. Pour over baked cake and spread evenly. Cool cake in the refrigerator.

To make frosting, combine pudding and softened cream cheese, then mix with milk until smooth; fold in whipped topping or whipped cream. Spread frosting on cake. Keep in the refrigerator.

Brenda Harrison, Chattanooga, TN

Cream Top Black Bottom Cupcakes

CREAM CHEESE FILLING:

1 (8-ounce) package cream
   cheese, softened

¹⁄₃ cup sugar
¹⁄₈ teaspoon salt

Beat together cream cheese, sugar, and salt until creamy. Set aside.

BATTER:

1¹⁄₂ cups unsifted flour
1 cup sugar
¹⁄₄ cup cocoa
1 teaspoon baking soda
1 cup water

¹⁄₃ cup vegetable oil
1 teaspoon vanilla
1 (6-ounce) bag semisweet
   chocolate chips

Mix together dry ingredients. Add water, oil, and vanilla; mix until smooth. Stir in chocolate chips. Insert paper muffin cups into muffin pans, and fill each ¹⁄₃ full with Batter. Top each with a heaping teaspoon of Cream Cheese Filling. Bake at 350° for 30 minutes. Makes 24.

Tammy Maldonado, Millbrae, CA

Red Velvet Bon Bons

This gem is admittedly a bit of work, but so outstanding in taste and presentation that you will get compliments galore. Imagine being able to eat candy-coated cake and icing in a neat pop-in-your-mouth bon bon! Outstanding!

1 (18¹⁄₄-ounce) box red velvet
   cake mix, prepared as directed
1 (16-ounce) container cream
   cheese icing

1 pound almond bark (white or
   chocolate)

Bake cake per package directions in a greased 9x13-inch pan. When cool, crumble into a big bowl and mix in icing (may do better with fingers). Form into ping-pong-size balls and place on cookie sheet. Refrigerate till firm.

Melt almond bark over hot water and stir till smooth. Dip firm balls in melted bark and place on wax paper to dry.

Note: This also works with other cake mixes, but so pretty and tasty with red velvet.

Kristin Spencer, Baton Rouge, LA

Family Secret Pound Cake

CAKE:

1 cup butter, softened
½ cup shortening
2½ cups sugar
5 eggs, well beaten
3 cups flour
½ teaspoon baking powder

1 cup milk
1 teaspoon coconut flavoring
1 teaspoon rum flavoring
1 teaspoon butter flavoring
1 teaspoon lemon flavoring
1 teaspoon vanilla extract

Cream together butter, shortening, and sugar. Add eggs and mix well. Combine flour and baking powder in a separate bowl. Alternately add flour mixture and milk to creamed mixture. Add all flavorings. Pour into a well-greased and floured tube pan and bake for 1½ hours at 325°. When cake is done, pour Glaze over top. Let sit until cool. Invert cooled cake onto cake plate.

GLAZE:

1 cup sugar
½ cup water
1 teaspoon coconut flavoring
1 teaspoon rum flavoring

1 teaspoon butter flavoring
1 teaspoon lemon flavoring
1 teaspoon vanilla extract
1 teaspoon almond flavoring

While cake is baking, mix Glaze ingredients together in saucepan over medium flame until sugar is dissolved and it starts to bubble. Remove from stove and set aside.

Sarah Wimer, Leesburg, VA

Family Heirloom Sour Cream Pound Cake

2 sticks margarine, softened	1 cup sour cream
3 cups sugar	6 eggs, divided
¼ teaspoon baking soda	3 cups flour, sifted, divided
1½ teaspoons vanilla	Powdered sugar
½ teaspoon lemon juice	

Cream margarine; add sugar, and beat. Add baking soda, vanilla, lemon juice, and sour cream, and beat until completely smooth. Add 2 eggs, then beat; add 1 cup flour, then beat; add 2 more eggs, then beat; add 1 more cup flour, then beat; add remaining 2 eggs, and beat; finally add remaining 1 cup flour, and beat. (Important to follow the above steps by combining the eggs and flour as noted—consistency of batter is better.)

Bake in greased tube pan at 325° for 1 hour and 15 minutes. Let cake cool in pan. When cake is cooled, sprinkle powered sugar all over and enjoy!

Jackie Courtney, Bridgeport, PA

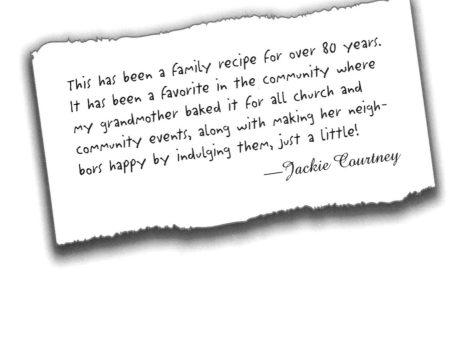

This has been a family recipe for over 80 years. It has been a favorite in the community where my grandmother baked it for all church and community events, along with making her neighbors happy by indulging them, just a little!

—Jackie Courtney

Sunshine Lemon Glaze Pound Cake

3 cups all-purpose flour	3 cups sugar
1 teaspoon baking powder	6 eggs, room temperature
1/4 teaspoon salt	1 teaspoon lemon extract
3 sticks butter, softened	1 cup buttermilk

Preheat oven to 325°. Grease and flour a standard tube pan. Sift flour, baking powder, and salt; set aside. In a large bowl, using an electric mixer, cream butter until smooth. Add sugar in several additions, beating until mixture is light and fluffy. Add eggs, one at a time. Scrape down sides of the bowl. Add lemon extract, and combine well.

At low speed, alternately stir in dry ingredients and buttermilk. Begin and end with dry ingredients. Increase speed to medium and beat until consistency is like creamy butter. Pour batter into prepared pan. Bake 1 hour and 15 minutes. Cool 25 minutes, then remove from pan. Glaze cake while warm.

SUNSHINE LEMONADE GLAZE:

3 lemons	3 cups sugar
1 stick butter	1 tablespoon vanilla extract

Using a vegetable peeler, remove the zest from lemons, being careful not to remove white part of lemon, only yellow part. Place lemon zest in a food processor and process until very finely chopped. Squeeze juice from lemons into small bowl. In medium-size saucepan on low heat, combine butter, sugar, lemon juice, and lemon zest. Stirring continuously, cook until glaze has a thick consistency and sugar has dissolved completely. Remove pan from heat, add vanilla extract, and stir well to combine. Pour glaze through a strainer to remove any butter solids. Spoon glaze over entire cake, repeating again with remaining glaze.

LaVern Ward, West Bloomfield, MI

Heavenly Hint of Lemon Cheesecake

CRUST:

1½ cups graham cracker crumbs
   or ginger snap crumbs
¼–½ cup confectioners' sugar

6 tablespoons butter, melted
Cinnamon or nutmeg to taste
   (optional)

Mix Crust ingredients together and pat into bottom and up sides of a 12-inch springform pan or 9x13-inch pan (if using smaller pan, halve topping). Preheat oven to 350°. Put a small pan of boiling water in the oven on another shelf (keeps cake from cracking).

FILLING:

5 (8-ounce) packages cream
   cheese, softened
½ tablespoon vanilla extract
   (not imitation)
2 tablespoons grated lemon peel
1½ cups granulated sugar

3 tablespoons all-purpose flour
¼ teaspoon salt
4 or 5 eggs (to equal 1 cup)
2 egg yolks
¼ cup heavy cream

Very important to have all ingredients at room temperature. Beat cream cheese until creamy. Add vanilla and lemon peel. Mix sugar, flour, and salt gradually into cream cheese mixture. Add eggs and egg yolks one at a time, beating in after each. Gently stir in heavy cream. Pour into Crust and bake at 350° for one hour; cake will be jiggly but not runny. Remove from oven for 15 minutes.

TOPPING:

1 quart sour cream
1 tablespoon vanilla extract
8 tablespoons granulated sugar

1 tablespoon grated lemon peel
Dash of ground cinnamon
   (optional)

Mix while cake is baking. Pour on top of cake after being out of oven for 15 minutes. Return to oven for 10–15 minutes. Cool on rack for 15 minutes. Loosen around edges with a thin knife. Chill for 4 hours. Use whatever fruit topping you like, but it is awesome just by itself. Keeps well in refrigerator.

Variation: In a small saucepan, heat 1 (20-ounce) can crushed pineapple on low until it simmers. Add a little granulated sugar, a few drops of yellow food coloring (optional), and cornstarch to reach a spreadable consistency. Cover and cool mixture overnight. Spread onto Cheesecake the following morning.

Alberta Lee Kaiser, New Port Richey, FL

Peaches 'n Cream Cheesecake

BOTTOM:
¾ cup flour
1 teaspoon baking powder
½ teaspoon salt
1 (3.5-ounce) package dry vanilla
  pudding (not instant)

3 tablespoons butter or
  margarine, softened
1 egg
½ cup milk

Grease bottom and sides of 9-inch pie pan. Preheat oven to 350°. Combine ingredients in large mixing bowl; beat 2 minutes at medium speed. Pour into prepared pan.

FILLING:
1 (15- to 20-ounce) can sliced
  peaches or pineapple chunks,
  well drained (reserve juice)
1 (8-ounce) package cream
  cheese, softened

3 tablespoons reserved juice
½ cup sugar
1 tablespoon sugar
½ teaspoon cinnamon

In mixing bowl, combine peaches or pineapple chunks, cream cheese, reserved juice, and ½ cup sugar. Beat 2 minutes at medium speed. Spoon to within 1 inch of edge of batter. Combine sugar and cinnamon; sprinkle over fruit mixture. Bake at 350° for 30–35 minutes, until Bottom is golden brown (Filling will appear soft). Store in refrigerator.

Linda Seaman, Grand Junction, MI

The Best Strawberry Cheesecake

FILLING:

3 (8-ounce) packages cream
  cheese, room temperature
1–1½ cups sugar
1 cup heavy cream, room
  temperature
4 eggs, room temperature

1 (16-ounce) carton sour cream,
  room temperature
3 tablespoons flour
2 teaspoons vanilla
½ teaspoon almond extract

Mix cream cheese; gradually add sugar until fluffy. Add eggs one at a time, beating well after each addition. Add remaining ingredients and mix well.

CRUST:

2 cups crushed pecan cookies
2 tablespoons melted butter

2 tablespoons sugar

Combine ingredients and press into an 8- or 9-inch springform pan. Wrap pan in a collar of aluminum foil. Pour Filling over Crust. Bake at 350° for 1 hour, then leave cake in oven 1 hour after turning oven off. Do not open oven door at all during this time! Cool and Glaze.

GLAZE:

1 (20-ounce) package frozen
  strawberries, thawed completely
2 tablespoons sugar

1 tablespoon cornstarch
1 tablespoon water

Combine strawberries and sugar, and bring to a boil. Mix cornstarch and water; add to strawberries mixture. Cook until clear. Allow to cool. Spread over top of cooled cheesecake. Refrigerate overnight.

Margaret McGovern, Worcester, MA

White Chocolate Key Lime Mousse Cake

The combination of sweet white chocolate and tangy lime is heavenly. Simple, yet sophisticated, this is the dessert I prepare when I want to pull out all the stops!

CRUST:

1½ cups vanilla wafer or chocolate wafer crumbs

6 tablespoons butter, melted

Preheat oven to 325°. Butter a 9-inch springform pan. Mix crumbs and butter; press evenly onto bottom and part way up sides of pan. Bake 6 minutes. Cool.

FILLING:

8 ounces chopped white chocolate or white chocolate chips
½ cup heavy whipping cream
2 (8-ounce) containers mascarpone cheese, or
2 (8-ounce) packages cream cheese, softened
⅓ cup Key lime (or regular lime) juice

2 teaspoons grated lime zest
2 teaspoons vanilla
⅓ cup powdered sugar
1 (8-ounce) container frozen nondairy whipped topping, thawed

Place white chocolate in small bowl. Heat cream in microwave until hot, not boiling. Pour over white chocolate; whisk until smooth. Cool. In mixing bowl, beat mascarpone (or cream cheese), lime juice, lime zest, and vanilla until smooth. Beat in sugar until blended. Gradually beat in cooled white chocolate. Fold in whipped topping. Pour into Crust. Cover and chill until firm, 2 hours or overnight.

GARNISH:

White chocolate curls

Fresh berries

To serve, carefully remove sides of pan. Garnish with white chocolate curls and fresh berries. Makes 12 servings.

Edwina Gadsby, Great Falls, MT

Cheesecake on a Stick

1 frozen cheesecake, thawed
8 craft sticks
1 cup semisweet chocolate chips
1 cup butterscotch chips

2–3 tablespoons shortening
½ cup chopped pecans
  (optional)

Cut thawed cheesecake into 8 pieces. Insert craft stick into wide end of each piece. Cover a cookie sheet with wax paper, then place each piece on it. Freeze overnight.

Melt chocolate and butterscotch chips along with shortening in a small saucepan over very low heat, stirring often. Hold each piece of cheesecake over the saucepan and spoon coating over cheesecake, covering completely. Sprinkle with chopped pecans, if desired. Repeat until all cheesecakes are covered. Return to freezer until firm. Thaw slightly before serving. Makes 8 servings.

Kathy Missel, Streator, IL

Double Chocolate Peanut Butter Cheesecake

CRUST:

1 cup chocolate wafer cookie crumbs or chocolate graham cracker crumbs

3 tablespoons sugar
3 tablespoons butter, melted

Preheat oven to 300°. Mix crumbs, sugar, and butter, and press onto the bottom of a 9-inch dark nonstick springform pan. Bake for 10 minutes. Remove and set aside. Raise oven temperature to 325°.

FILLING:

4 (8-ounce) packages cream cheese, softened
1 cup sugar
1 teaspoon vanilla extract
4 eggs
4 squares semisweet baking chocolate, melted and slightly cooled

$\frac{1}{3}$ cup creamy peanut butter
$\frac{3}{4}$ cup mini-chocolate chips, tossed with 1 teaspoon flour

Mix cream cheese, sugar, and vanilla with electric mixer on medium speed until creamy and well blended. Add eggs, one at a time, on low speed just until blended. Pour $\frac{1}{2}$ of Filling into another bowl.

To one bowl of Filling, add melted chocolate and stir until blended. To other bowl of Filling, add peanut butter and mini-chocolate chips; stir until blended. Pour peanut butter Filling over Crust and smooth with spatula. Carefully pour chocolate Filling on top of peanut butter Filling and smooth with spatula. Bake at 325° for one hour or until center is almost set. Remove from oven and run knife around rim of pan to loosen cake.

TOPPING:

1½ cups semisweet chocolate chips
¼ cup milk

1 teaspoon vanilla extract
1 bag mini-peanut butter cups, chopped

Melt chocolate chips, either in double-boiler or in a glass bowl in microwave. Add milk and vanilla. Smooth over cake. Decorate with chopped mini-peanut butter cups.

Sarah LaFon, Franklin, TN

Peanut Butter Mousse Brownie Cheesecake Torte

1 (19.5-ounce) box brownie mix
2 (8-ounce) packages cream
 cheese, softened
1 cup sugar
1 (12-ounce) package peanut
 butter chips (set aside ¼ cup
 chips, and melt remaining
 chips)

1 cup creamy peanut butter
½ teaspoon vanilla
1 (12-ounce) container frozen
 whipped topping, thawed
1 cup hot fudge ice cream
 topping, divided
¼ cup chocolate chips

Mix brownies according to box directions and bake in a greased 9-inch springform pan at 350° for 35–40 minutes. Cool completely.

In a large mixing bowl, cream together cream cheese and sugar on high speed with electric mixer until mixture is light and creamy. Add melted peanut butter chips and peanut butter; mix well. Add vanilla and whipped topping, and beat on high speed only until mixture is light and fluffy.

Spread ½ cup hot fudge on top of brownies, then spread mousse on top of hot fudge. Heat remaining ½ cup hot fudge in microwave 20–30 seconds, then drizzle over mousse. Sprinkle with chocolate chips and remaining ¼ cup peanut butter chips. Refrigerate 2–3 hours before serving. Makes 10–12 servings.

Hilda Shepherd, Fort Wayne, IN

Cookies
and Candies

Cranberry Snowball Cookies

A tangy surprise on the inside makes these sweet confections extra special. Yum!

1 cup butter, softened	1¾ cups sifted flour
1 cup confectioners' sugar, divided	½ cup finely chopped dried cranberries
½ teaspoon vanilla	

Preheat oven to 350°. In a bowl, cream butter; gradually add ½ cup confectioners' sugar. Beat until light and fluffy. Blend in vanilla, and gradually add flour and finely chopped dried cranberries. Roll into 1-inch balls and place on nonstick baking sheet. Bake 20 minutes. While they are warm, put a few at a time into remaining ½ cup confectioners' sugar in a brown paper lunch bag, and shake gently to coat. Cool on a rack.

Carol Olson, Madison, WI

Nana's Glazed Sugar Cookies

1 stick butter, softened	1 egg
¾ cup sugar	1 tablespoon milk
2 teaspoons vanilla	2 cups self-rising flour

Cream butter and sugar together. Add vanilla, egg, and milk. Blend until smooth. Add flour and blend. Chill in fridge for one hour. Roll out dough onto floured surface to ¼-inch thickness. Cut out in desired shapes and place on greased pan. Bake 5–6 minutes (or until edges start to brown slightly) at 425°. Remove and cool.

GLAZE:

1 cup sifted powdered sugar	½ teaspoon vanilla
2 tablespoons water	Food coloring as desired

Mix all ingredients until smooth. Add water as needed. Invert cooled cookies and dip into bowl of Glaze until coated. Wipe off excess Glaze. Place on brown or parchment paper to harden.

Pat Abernathy, Biloxi, MS

Snowflake Cookies

These are so simple and so good!

2 egg whites	1 cup chocolate chips
¾ cup granulated sugar	1 cup chopped nuts

Beat egg whites until foamy; add sugar and beat until stiff. Fold in chocolate chips and chopped nuts. Drop by teaspoon onto lightly greased baking sheet. Preheat oven to 350°. Place cookies in oven and immediately turn oven off. Leave in oven overnight or at least 3–4 hours. Do not open oven door until time is up.

Vivian Ferguson, Gaston, NC

Sugar Cookies for Granddad

1 cup butter or margarine, softened	½ teaspoon salt
1 cup shortening	4 cups flour
2 eggs	1 teaspoon baking soda
1 cup sugar	1 teaspoon cream of tartar
1 cup powdered sugar	1 teaspoon vanilla
	1 teaspoon cinnamon

Combine butter, shortening, eggs, and sugars until creamy. Add dry ingredients. Use a spoon or an ice cream scooper to drop onto cookie sheet. Bake at 375° for 10 minutes. Serve with lots of kisses.

Jen Edwards, West Point, NY

My mom used to make these for her dad, and she would try to hide them in the freezer from my brother and me. We found out that they were quite good frozen.

—Jen Edwards

Mother's English Diamond Cookies

My mother's English shortbread cookies never fail to bring a flood of emotions. Transporting me to my very earliest memories, the heavenly aroma as they bake is, to me, the quintessential fragrance of Christmas. For pretty cookies, score the pan lengthwise at 1½-inch intervals. Next, make diagonal crosswise cuts to form diamonds. The cookies are light, crisp, and lovely. They freeze well, too, so I can bake them before the season gets too hectic.

1 cup (2 sticks) unsalted butter, softened
1 cup granulated sugar
1 large egg yolk

1 teaspoon vanilla extract
2 cups all-purpose flour
1 cup finely chopped pecans

Using paddle attachment of electric mixer, cream butter and sugar on medium speed until light and fluffy, about 5 minutes. Scrape bowl several times during mixing. Add egg yolk and vanilla, and beat until mixture is well blended and light in color. On low speed, gradually beat in flour. The dough will come together into a ball on the paddle. At this point, the dough can be wrapped tightly in plastic and frozen for up to one month; defrost before shaping.

Preheat oven to 350°. With your fingertips, spread dough in a thin layer about ¼ inch thick on unbuttered jellyroll pan. Do not push dough onto sides. Sprinkle dough with chopped pecans and very lightly press in. Bake 20–25 minutes, until sides are golden brown. Let cookies cool on baking sheet on a rack 5–10 minutes. Using a sharp knife, cut cookies into diamonds. Yields about 3 dozen 2-inch cookies.

Variation: For other seasons in the year, a delightful twist is to place crushed milk chocolate bars on top of cookies when they first come out of the oven. The warmth of the cookies melts the chocolate; then you can smooth it evenly over the entire top, sprinkle with pecans, and cut into diamond shapes. Enjoy!

Valerie Parr Hill, QVC Guest, Mountain Lakes, NJ

Valerie Parr Hill is quite familiar to the QVC audience. Her charming demeanor and lovely choices of home decor always brighten up the set.

Everything Oatmeal Cookies

2 cups all-purpose flour
1 teaspoon baking soda
1 teaspoon baking powder
1 teaspoon salt
$\frac{1}{2}$ teaspoon cinnamon
2 sticks butter (not margarine)
$\frac{3}{4}$ cup white sugar

$\frac{3}{4}$ cup brown sugar
2 eggs
1 teaspoon vanilla
2 cups rolled oats
1 cup raisins
1 cup chopped pecans
1 cup white chocolate chips

Mix together flour, baking soda, baking powder, salt, and cinnamon. Cream butter and sugars in a separate mixing bowl. Beat in eggs and vanilla. Gradually add flour mixture. Fold in oats, raisins, pecans, and chips. Shape into 1- to $1\frac{1}{2}$-inch balls, and bake at 325° for 10–12 minutes. Cookies should look a little underdone when they come out of the oven. Let cool on cookie sheet for just a few minutes, then transfer to wax paper or a cooling rack.

Kimberly Cornelison, Baton Rouge, LA

Blue Devil Wrestler Oatmeal Cookies

¾ cup oil
1 cup firmly packed brown sugar
2 eggs
1 teaspoon vanilla extract
1½ cups unsifted, unbleached
   all-purpose flour

1 cup oatmeal
1½ teaspoons baking powder
½ teaspoon cinnamon
½ cup wheat germ

In a large bowl, with mixer at medium speed, beat oil, sugar, eggs, and vanilla until thick. Add flour, oats, baking powder, and cinnamon. Beat at low speed until blended. Stir in wheat germ. Drop by tablespoonfuls onto ungreased cookie sheet (or parchment paper-covered sheet). Bake at 350° about 12 minutes or until light brown. Makes about 3½ dozen cookies.

Note: These cookies are low in fat, high in fiber, and may be made cholesterol free by using 3 egg whites instead of 2 whole eggs. The addition of wheat germ instead of nuts makes them lower in fat and higher in fiber. Any type oatmeal is okay, but old-fashioned rolled oats add a nice texture.

Gretchen Duynslager, St. Clair, MI

As the Family and Consumer Sciences teacher and team nutrition consultant, I developed this recipe especially for the Richmond High School Wrestling team (State Champs!). It is the result of much trial and sometimes rather delicious error.

—Gretchen Duynslager

Chocolate Macaroon Cookies

6 ounces semisweet chocolate,
  broken into pieces for melting
2 egg whites
1/3 cup sugar (or less)

1 pinch salt
1 teaspoon vanilla
6–7 ounces shredded sweetened
  coconut

Preheat oven to 375°. Melt chocolate in the top of a double boiler (or in microwave oven for 2 minutes on HIGH). Watch closely. Stir and set aside to cool.

    Beat egg whites to a stiff consistency, not peaks. Fold in sugar, salt, and vanilla. Fold in melted chocolate and shredded coconut. Drop small spoonfuls onto parchment-lined cookie sheets. Bake 10 minutes. Cookies will be soft in the center. Cool on wire racks. Makes around 32 cookies.

Variation: Add 2 tablespoons of strong, espresso coffee to enhance the chocolate flavor.

Allicin Rauzin, Palo Alto, CA

Lemon Cookie Dimes

1 lemon, seeded, cut into pieces
1 cup butter
2 cups white sugar
3 eggs
1 (1-ounce) bottle pure lemon
  extract

4 cups all-purpose flour
1 teaspoon baking soda
1 teaspoon cream of tartar
1/4 teaspoon salt
Powdered sugar

Preheat oven to 325°. In a food processor, grind lemon pieces (including the rind) into mush. Melt butter in a large bowl; add sugar, eggs, lemon extract, and lemon mush. Mix well. Sift together all dry ingredients, except powdered sugar. Add slowly to the wet mix to obtain a consistency appropriate for a cookie press. Press onto an ungreased cookie sheet in dime-size shapes. (A baby spoon can be used to drop small amounts on a cookie sheet, if you don't have a cookie press.) Bake approximately 12 minutes or until they start to turn brown. Coat with powdered sugar.

Debbie Wedgeworth, Pass Christian, MS

Pecan Cream Cheese Cookies

1 (3-ounce) package cream
   cheese, softened
1/3 cup soft butter
1 egg yolk
1 teaspoon vanilla

1 (18¼-ounce) box yellow
   cake mix
½ cup butterscotch toffee bits
1 cup chopped pecans

Cream together cream cheese, butter, egg yolk, and vanilla until well blended. Gradually add dry cake mix. Stir in toffee bits and pecans. Chill one hour.

Preheat oven to 350°. Shape into balls. Place on ungreased cookie sheet. Bake 12–15 minutes. Makes 24–30 balls.

Donna Howell, Supply, NC

Chocolate Mint Candy Cookies

¾ cup butter or margarine
1½ cups firmly packed brown
   sugar
2 tablespoons water
2 cups semisweet chocolate
   pieces

2 eggs
2½ cups all-purpose flour
1¼ teaspoons baking soda
½ teaspoon salt
Approximately 1 pound chocolate
   mint wafers

In a large saucepan over low heat, cook butter or margarine, sugar, and water until butter is melted. Add chocolate pieces and stir until partially melted; remove from heat, stir until melted, and pour into large mixing bowl. Let stand 10 minutes to cool slightly. With mixer at high speed, beat in eggs one at a time. Reduce speed to low and add combined dry ingredients, beating just until blended. Chill dough at least 1 hour for easier handling (very important).

Preheat oven to 350°. Line 2 cookie sheets with foil. Roll teaspoonfuls of dough into balls; place on cookie sheets with foil, about 2 inches apart. Bake at 350° for 12–13 minutes, no longer, as cookies crisp as they cool. After removing from oven, immediately place ½ mint on top of cookie and let sit a minute to melt, then spread like frosting with tip of a spoon. Let cool.

Jill Churchill, Crawfordsville, IN

Triple Chocolate Cookies

½ cup margarine
1 cup semisweet chocolate chips,
 divided
¾ cup sugar
¾ cup packed brown sugar
2 eggs
2 tablespoons strong coffee

2 teaspoons vanilla
2 cups flour
½ teaspoon baking powder
⅓ cup unsweetened cocoa
 powder
½ cup milk chocolate chips

Melt margarine and ½ cup semisweet chips together and cool. In mixer, mix sugars, eggs, cooled coffee, and vanilla. Stir in flour, baking powder, and cocoa powder. Stir in chocolate mixture. Stir in remaining ½ cup semisweet chips and milk chocolate chips. Drop by a teaspoon onto greased cookie sheet. Bake at 350° for 10 minutes or until tops look dry. Cool for 1 minute on sheet. Remove to wire rack. Yields 30.

Susan L. Anderson, Fort Madison, IA

Great Big Chocolate Chip Cookies

½ cup butter
½ cup shortening
1 cup brown sugar
½ cup granulated sugar
2 eggs
2 teaspoons good quality vanilla

1¼ cups all-purpose flour
1 cup bread flour
1 teaspoon baking soda
1 teaspoon salt
2 cups semisweet chocolate chips
1 cup chopped pecans (optional)

Mix butter, shortening, and sugars together until creamy. Add eggs one at a time, mixing well to incorporate. Mix in vanilla. Add dry ingredients slowly to combine, then mix at medium speed just until thoroughly mixed. Fold in chocolate chips and nuts by hand.

 Line a cookie sheet with aluminum foil. Using a 2-ounce ice cream scoop or tablespoon, place dough on cookie sheet, spacing well. Bake at 375° for 13–15 minutes, or until lightly browned on edges but still soft in the middle. Let cool 1–2 minutes on cookie sheet before removing to rack to completely cool. Makes 3–4 dozen, depending on size.

Robin Stevens, Marietta, GA

Mighty Peanut Butter Chip Cookies

These are GOOD!

2½ cups flour
½ cup ground oatmeal
1 cup chopped nuts
1 (12-ounce) package peanut
  butter chips
1 teaspoon salt
1 teaspoon cream of tartar
1 teaspoon baking soda

2 teaspoons cinnamon
1 cup unsalted butter, softened
1½ cups creamy peanut butter
1 cup light brown sugar
1 cup white sugar
2 jumbo eggs
1 tablespoon crème de cocoa
1 teaspoon pure vanilla

Preheat oven to 375°. In a bowl, mix flour, oatmeal, nuts, peanut butter chips, salt, cream of tartar, soda, and cinnamon; set aside.

With your electric mixer on slow speed, cream butter, peanut butter, and sugars until well blended. Mix together eggs, crème de cacao, and vanilla, then add to butter mixture; beat until very fluffy. Mix in dry ingredients one cup at a time, until thoroughly blended.

Line cookie sheets with parchment paper. Measure a good ⅓ cup of cookie mixture, form into balls, and place on cookie sheets 2 inches apart; flatten to a 3-inch circle with a fork that has been dipped in flour to keep from sticking. Bake 10–13 minutes or until cookies are set. Let cookies cool a little on cookie sheets before removing them to wire racks. Yields 3 dozen.

Lalee Backus, Buffalo, NY

Chocolate Streusel Bars

People who like chocolate will love this . . . the inside is so creamy and rich.

1¾ cups all-purpose flour
1¼ cups powdered sugar
½ cup cocoa powder
1 cup cold butter
1 (8-ounce) package cream
   cheese, softened
1 (14-ounce) can sweetened
   condensed milk
1 egg, beaten
2 teaspoons vanilla
½ cup chopped pecans

Preheat oven to 350°. In a large bowl, combine flour, sugar, and cocoa. Cut in butter until crumbly (mixture will be dry). Divide and set aside 2 cups of mixture. Press the remaining mixture onto bottom of greased 9x13-inch pan; bake 15 minutes.

In a bowl, beat cream cheese until fluffy. Gradually add condensed milk. Beat until smooth; add egg and vanilla. Mix well and pour over crust. Combine nuts with reserved 2 cups of dry mixture. Sprinkle on top of cheese layer. Bake 25 minutes until lightly browned. Cool and cut into bars. Store in refrigerator.

Brenda Harrison, Chattanooga, TN

Chewies

1 stick margarine
1 (1-pound) box light brown
   sugar
2 eggs
2 cups self-rising flour
½ teaspoon vanilla
1 cup chopped pecans
Powdered Sugar (for dusting)

Preheat oven to 350°. Grease a 9x13-inch pan with shortening. Melt margarine in microwave in a large microwave-safe bowl. Add brown sugar and mix until blended. Add eggs, flour, vanilla, and pecans. Spread mixture evenly in pan. Bake for 20–25 minutes. Cool completely in pan. Sprinkle with powdered sugar and cut into squares.

Note: Mixture will be very thick.

Cindy Connelly, Cope, SC

Editor's Extra: The addition of 1 cup finely chopped apples or ½ cup chocolate chips makes a nice variation.

Batter Up Brownies

½ cup oil
1½ cups sugar
½ teaspoon salt
3 eggs
½ cup peanut butter

1 teaspoon vanilla
1 cup flour
½ teaspoon baking powder
1 cup semisweet chocolate chips
1 cup chopped nuts (optional)

Starting with oil, mix ingredients in order given, mixing thoroughly. Spread into a well-greased 9x13x2-inch pan. Bake for 25–30 minutes in a preheated 350° oven. Cut into squares after brownies have cooled completely.

Patty Cotronea, Rome, NY

I first made these brownies as a class project when I was in the tenth grade. I had to make a product, give an oral report, and provide a demonstration. I actually made up the batter in class, and baked them in the home-ec oven. The class loved the results, and I made an A+. After all these years, they still get an A+ every time I make them!

—Patty Cotronea

Ooey Gooey Brownies

1 (20-ounce) package brownie
   mix (chewy fudge-type)
2 eggs
½ cup oil
¼ cup water

½ cup milk chocolate chips
½ cup white chocolate chips
½ cup peanut butter chips
1 cup miniature marshmallows

Heat oven to 350°. Prepare a 9x13-inch pan by spraying with cooking spray. Mix first 4 ingredients together in medium bowl with a wooden spoon. Stir in last 4 ingredients. Mix well. Pour into prepared baking pan. Bake in oven 25–30 minutes. Remove from oven. Let cool in pan at least 1 hour before cutting. Cut with a plastic knife to prevent tearing. Transfer to a serving plate and serve.

Norma Dyer, Cary, NC

Creamy White Brownie

1 (22.5-ounce) package brownie
   mix
1 (8-ounce) package cream
   cheese, softened
2 eggs

½ cup sugar
1 teaspoon vanilla
1 (12-ounce) package white
   chocolate chips, divided

Combine brownie mix as directed on package. Spray a 9x13-inch pan with cooking spray. Pour half the brownie mixture in pan. Mix cream cheese, eggs, sugar, and vanilla until creamy; pour over brownie mix. Add ½ the white chocolate chips, then remaining ½ of brownie mixture. Top with remaining white chocolate chips. Bake in 350° oven for 25–30 minutes. Cut into squares after cooling.

Becky Jolly, Marion, NC

Crème de Menthe Bars

LAYER 1:

½ cup margarine
½ cup cocoa
½ cup confectioners' sugar

2 cups (scant) graham cracker crumbs

Melt margarine in saucepan. Add cocoa, sugar, and crumbs. Mix well. Press into bottom of 9x13-inch pan.

LAYER 2:

½ cup margarine
⅓ cup crème de menthe

3 cups confectioners' sugar

Melt margarine in mixing bowl. Add crème de menthe and sugar. Mix on high speed until thoroughly mixed. Pour over first layer. Chill one hour.

LAYER 3:

1 (12-ounce) package chocolate chips

½ cup margarine

Melt margarine in saucepan. Add chips and stir until melted. Spread over crème de menthe layer. Chill at least one hour. Cut into small squares. Store in refrigerator.

Note: Use white crème de menthe and add red food coloring for a nice pink middle—great for Valentine's Day.

Julie A. Jenick, Amsterdam, NY

Marble Mallow Bars

**1 cup butter or margarine,
softened
⅔ cup brown sugar**

**1 teaspoon vanilla
2 cups flour
3 cups miniature marshmallows**

Preheat oven to 350º. Cream butter, sugar, and vanilla. Add flour gradually; mix well. Spread in greased 10x15-inch pan. Bake 15 minutes. Sprinkle top with marshmallows; bake 5 minutes more.

TOPPING:
**1 cup chocolate chips
3 tablespoons butter or margarine**

1 tablespoon water

Melt chocolate chips and butter; add water; stir until smooth. Drizzle over marshmallows. Cool; cut into bars.

Leanne Sedani, Cameron, WI

Chocolate Marshmallow Squares

**1 (16-ounce) package chocolate
chips
1 (16-ounce) package
butterscotch chips**

**¼ cup butter
½ cup peanut butter
1 (10-ounce) bag miniature
marshmallows**

In a double boiler, melt chocolate chips, butterscotch chips, butter, and peanut butter. Let cool for a few minutes, then add marshmallows and mix together. Put in a greased 9x9-inch pan, then refrigerate. Cut into squares.

Dorothy (Dottie) McFarland, Toledo, OH

Chocolate Marshmallow Sundae Bars

BARS:

1 cup butter or margarine
½ cup cocoa
2 cups sugar
1½ cups flour
4 eggs

1 cup chopped nuts
1 cup flaked coconut
1 (7-ounce) jar marshmallow
  crème

Melt butter or margarine and cocoa together. In a large bowl, combine sugar, flour, and eggs. Add cocoa mixture and mix well. Stir in nuts and coconut. Pour into buttered 9x13-inch baking pan and bake in preheated 350° oven for 30 minutes. Remove from oven and spread with marshmallow crème immediately. While cake is baking, prepare Frosting.

FROSTING:

½ cup butter or margarine
½ cup cocoa
½ cup evaporated milk

4 cups powdered sugar
1 teaspoon vanilla
1 cup chopped nuts

Melt butter or margarine; stir in cocoa. Stir in milk. Gradually add powdered sugar and beat until smooth. Add vanilla and nuts. The Frosting may be spooned onto cake as soon as the marshmallow crème has been spread. It will not spread evenly, but will produce a marbled effect. Cool and cut into bars or squares.

LeAnn Thom, Dickinson, ND

When my husband was a little boy back in the 1940s, his family would go to the Borden Ice Cream parlor to get a sundae. When he wanted one during the week, they asked, "Why do you think it's called a Sunday?" And they got away with that for a long time.

—Gwen

Yum-Yum Raspberry Almond Bars

1 stick margarine, softened	2 eggs
1 stick butter, softened	2 cups flour
8 ounces almond paste	2 cups sugar

Mix ingredients together. Pat mixture into a 9x13-inch pan. Bake at 350° for 35 minutes or until golden brown. Set aside.

1 (3-ounce) package cream cheese, softened	½ cup raspberry jam
	1 (6-ounce) package milk chocolate chips
¼ cup butter, softened	
1¾ cups powdered sugar	1 tablespoon shortening
1 teaspoon vanilla	

Beat cream cheese, butter, powdered sugar, and vanilla. Add raspberry jam; mix. Spread over top of cooled bars. Melt milk chocolate chips over low heat. Add shortening and mix well. Drizzle chocolate mixture over raspberry-cream cheese topping. Cut into bars.

Susan Harter, Blakesburg, IA

Crunchy, Chocolate-y Toffee Bars

2¼ cups flour	¾ cup dark brown sugar
1 teaspoon baking powder	2 eggs
½ teaspoon salt	1 teaspoon vanilla
1 cup butter, softened	2 cups toffee bits, crushed
¾ cup light brown sugar	1½ cups mini-chocolate chips

Preheat oven to 350°. In a large bowl, combine flour, baking powder and salt. In a mixer, beat butter and sugar until fluffy. Beat in eggs and vanilla. Add in flour mixture one half at a time. Stir in crushed toffee bars, and spread in greased baking pan. Sprinkle mini-chocolate chips on top and gently press into top of batter. Bake for 30 minutes. Cool and cut into bars.

Dawn Jaksons, North Pole, AK

It's a Snap! Peanut Brittle

½ pound (2 sticks) butter
  (no substitute)

1 cup sugar
1 cup peanuts (or any nuts)

In a cast-iron skillet, melt butter and sugar over medium-high heat. Cook, stirring, until caramel color (about 8 minutes); add nuts. Continue to cook about 2 minutes, stirring; do not let it burn. Pour into greased cookie sheet and spread thin with a spatula. When cool, blot with clean dish towel and break into pieces. Enjoy!

Margo Graupman, Grants Pass, OR

Editor's Extra: You can use any kind of nuts—we like dry roasted, unsalted peanuts.

Chocolate Bark

1½ sleeves saltine crackers
1 cup butter
1 cup sugar
1 tablespoon vanilla

1 (12-ounce) package semisweet
  chocolate chips
1 (8-ounce) bag flaked coconut
  (optional)

Preheat oven to 375°. Line lipped cookie sheet with aluminum foil. Place saltines salt-side-up, covering entire cookie sheet. Melt butter; add sugar and bring to a boil, then cook over medium heat for 3 minutes, stirring constantly. Mixture will become thick and bubbly. Remove from heat and add vanilla. Pour mixture over saltines, covering them entirely. Bake in oven 6–7 minutes. (Do not let them burn.) Remove from oven and pour chocolate chips on top. As they melt, spread over all crackers. (If you want the chips to be even easier to spread, place back in oven for a minute.) Sprinkle coconut on top. You can also use any other toppings you like. Place in refrigerator for 2 hours. Remove and break up into pieces. Can store in a airtight tin.

Nancy Cangialosi, Farmingdale, NY

QVC-hocolate Truffles

1 cup heavy cream
1 pound semisweet chocolate
1 cup chopped nuts for topping
1 cup coconut for topping
1 cup cocoa powder for topping
1 cup toffee candy bits for topping
24 paper candy cups

On low heat in medium saucepan, bring cream to a simmer. Add chocolate and stir until smooth. Refrigerate 2 hours until firm.

Shape dough into 1-inch balls and roll in desired toppings. Place in paper candy cups and serve. Best if kept in refrigerator. Makes 2 dozen candies.

Pamela Weiner, Arlington, TX

Micro-Minute Fudge

3 cups semisweet or milk chocolate chips
1 (14-ounce) can sweetened condensed milk
¼ cup butter
1 cup chopped nuts (optional)

Place all ingredients except nuts in micro-safe bowl. Microwave at MEDIUM-HIGH until chocolate chips are melted, usually about 3–5 minutes, stirring once or twice. Stir in nuts, if desired. Pour into well-greased 8x8-inch-square baking dish. Refrigerate until set.

Variation: Can substitute 1 cup peanut butter chips for chocolate chips.

April Ngo, Roanoke, VA

Vanilla Bun Candy Bars

1 (12-ounce) package chocolate
  chips
1 (12-ounce) package
  butterscotch chips
1 (18-ounce) jar peanut butter
2 (12-ounce) containers dry
  roasted peanuts

$\frac{1}{2}$ pound (1 cup) butter
$\frac{1}{2}$ cup milk
$\frac{1}{4}$ cup vanilla instant
  pudding (dry)
1 tablespoon vanilla
2 pounds powdered sugar

Melt together chips and peanut butter in double boiler (or microwave). Grease a 9x13-inch pan, then line with buttered foil. Pour $\frac{1}{2}$ mixture into pan, then add peanuts to remaining $\frac{1}{2}$ mixture; set aside. Chill layer in freezer while making filling.

In a saucepan, combine butter, milk, and pudding mix. Boil for one minute. Add vanilla; stir in powdered sugar. Spread mixture over chilled chocolate. Push mixture to edges of pan. Pour reserved chocolate mixture over top. Chill for one day. Turn chilled mixture out (upside down), remove foil, and cut.

Retta Monahan, Benton, WI

Caramel Corn Puffs

2 (5-ounce) bags puff corn curls,
  or 1 (8-ounce) bag
2 sticks butter (no substitute)

$\frac{1}{2}$ cup light corn syrup
1 cup brown sugar
1 teaspoon baking soda

Place puff corn curls in large roastng pan. In $2\frac{1}{2}$-quart saucepan, mix remaining ingredients. Cook 2 minutes over medium heat. Pour over corn curls. Stir until mixed. Place in 250° oven for 45 minutes. Stir every 10 minutes. Remove from oven. Pour on wax paper. Cool and break into pieces.

June Jensen, Melrose Park, IL

Pies and
Other Desserts

Old-Fashioned Egg Pie

1 cup sugar
1 tablespoon flour
4 eggs, separated
2½ cups milk
2 tablespoons margarine,
  softened

1 teaspoon vanilla
1 (9-inch) deep-dish pie crust,
  unbaked
Nutmeg

Combine sugar and flour. Add egg yolks, milk, margarine, and vanilla. In separate bowl beat egg whites until stiff. Fold whites into yolk mixture. Pour into unbaked pie crust; sprinkle with nutmeg. Bake in preheated 350° oven 30–40 minutes (oven temperatures vary) until set. It will shake when ready to take out. Do not overbake. Serves 6.

Joyce Martin, Florence, MS

Editor's Extra: On very old recipes that have been handed down from our ancestors, chances are the amount of eggs called for was larger than a similar recipe today. Great grandmother's eggs probably came from the hens in the backyard who didn't have enriched food, so they were generally much smaller than what we can now buy in the carton. A hen that laid an egg the size of today's extra large eggs would have no doubt won the blue ribbon at Granny's state fair!

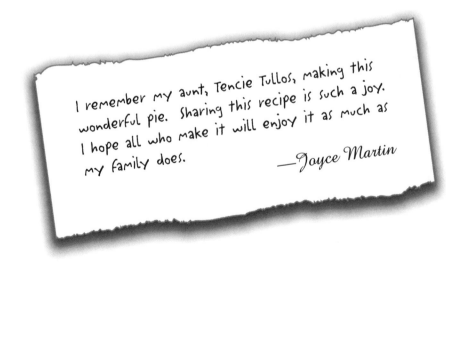

I remember my aunt, Tencie Tullos, making this wonderful pie. Sharing this recipe is such a joy. I hope all who make it will enjoy it as much as my family does.

—Joyce Martin

Pistachio Cream Pie

CRUST:

3 tablespoons sugar
3 tablespoons melted butter
1¼ cups cinnamon graham
   cracker crumbs (approximately
   20 squares)

2 tablespoons finely ground
   pistachio nuts

Combine sugar with butter and stir until dissolved. Add in crumbs and pistachios, mixing until coated. Press mixture on bottom and along sides of a 9-inch pie plate. Bake at 325° for 8–10 minutes or until lightly browned. Cool completely before adding Filling.

FILLING:

1 (3.4-ounce) box pistachio
   pudding
1¾ cups milk

1 (8-ounce) tub nondairy
   whipped topping, divided

Mix pudding and milk until it takes on a smooth consistency. Gently fold in half the whipped topping until fully combined. Pour into cooled Crust.

TOPPING:

1 teaspoon nutmeg
½ teaspoon vanilla extract

Chopped pistachios for garnish

Gently fold nutmeg and vanilla into remaining whipped topping until evenly mixed. Spread over top of pie and garnish with chopped pistachios. Chill or freeze to desired consistency, at least 2 hours.

Janine Gerads, St. Cloud, MN

Taffy Apple Cheese Cake Pie

FILLING:

2 tablespoons butter
1 cup brown sugar, divided
4 medium apples, peeled, cored,
    and thinly sliced
21 vanilla caramels, unwrapped
1/4 cup half-and-half
1 (8-ounce) package cream
    cheese, softened

1/2 teaspoon pumpkin pie spice
1 1/2 teaspoons vanilla
1 egg
1 (15-ounce) package refrigerator
    pie crust

In a large skillet, melt butter with 1/2 cup brown sugar. Stir constantly; add apple slices. Cook, stirring, 12–15 minutes or until apples are caramel in color and tender. Drain, if necessary. Set aside.

In top of double boiler or medium heavy saucepan, over low heat, melt caramels with half-and-half until mixture is smooth. Stir frequently; keep warm. In small bowl, beat cream cheese with remaining 1/2 cup brown sugar until light and fluffy. Add pumpkin pie spice, vanilla, and egg. Beat till blended.

Put pie crust in 10-inch deep pie dish. Pour apples into crust; pour cream cheese mixture over apples; drizzle caramel mixture over. Bake at 400° until pie crust is done and pie is set up.

TOPPING:

1/2 cup finely chopped milk
    chocolate chips
3/4 cup finely chopped pecans

1 (8-ounce) container frozen
    dairy whip, softened
1 teaspoon pumpkin pie spice

When done, put milk chocolate chips on while hot and swirl as they melt. Sprinkle with chopped pecans. Cool, then top with whipped topping and sprinkle with pumpkin pie spice. Refrigerate.

Karen Staker, Liscomb, IA

Family Favorite Lemon Chess Pie

1½ cups sugar
3 eggs, beaten
1 teaspoon vinegar
5 tablespoons butter, melted and
    slightly cooled

1 teaspoon vanilla
1 tablespoon cornmeal
Zest of 1 lemon
1 (9-inch) unbaked pie shell
Ground cinnamon

Preheat oven to 325°. Mix first 7 ingredients in order and pour into a 9-inch pie shell. Dust top with ground cinnamon. Place pie in preheated oven on a baking sheet (to catch drips), and bake 40–45 minutes (check for doneness after 40 minutes). Like many pies, it will rise and then settle as it cools.

Pamela Pollitt, Kiawah Island, SC

Tropical Mai Tai Pie

COCONUT CRUST:
2 cups flaked coconut   ¼ cup butter, melted

Preheat oven to 300°. In small bowl, combine coconut and melted butter. Mix well and press mixture onto bottom and sides of a 9-inch pie pan. Bake for 25 minutes. Cool crust before filling.

1 (8-ounce) package cream
    cheese, softened
1 (14-ounce) can sweetened
    condensed milk
1 (6-ounce) can frozen orange
    juice concentrate, thawed
⅓ cup light rum

2 teaspoons orange-flavored
    liqueur (optional)
1 (4½-ounce) container frozen
    nondairy whipped topping,
    thawed
Flaked coconut, toasted, for
    garnish

In large mixing bowl, beat cream cheese until light and fluffy. Add condensed milk and orange juice concentrate and beat until smooth. Stir in light rum and orange liqueur, if desired. Fold in nondairy whipped topping. Pour into Coconut Crust and refrigerate for 4–6 hours until firm. Garnish with toasted coconut.

Variation: For a lighter version, use ⅓ less fat cream cheese, light whipped topping, and nonfat sweetened condensed milk—just as delicious.

Rebecca A. Rogers, Lexington, KY

Hawaiian Strawberry Pie

1 (6-ounce) graham cracker
   crust
2 cups sliced fresh strawberries
1 (4-serving) package sugar-free
   strawberry gelatin
1 (4-serving) package sugar-free
   vanilla cook-and-serve
   pudding mix

1 (8-ounce) can crushed
   pineapple, packed in fruit
   juice, drained, and ¼ cup
   liquid reserved
1¼ cups water
1 teaspoon coconut extract
1 cup lite whipped topping
2 tablespoons flaked coconut

Place crust on a wire rack. Evenly arrange strawberries in crust.
In a medium saucepan, combine dry gelatin, dry pudding mix,
reserved pineapple liquid, and water. Cook over medium heat for
5 minutes or until mixture thickens and starts to boil, stirring
often with a wire whisk. Evenly spoon hot sauce mixture over
strawberries. Allow pie filling to cool for 5 minutes while on wire
rack. Refrigerate for at least 1 hour.

In a medium bowl, combine drained pineapple and coconut
extract. Add lite whipped topping. Mix gently to combine. Spread
topping mixture evenly over set strawberry filling. Evenly sprinkle coconut over top. Continue to refrigerate for at least 1 more
hour. Cut into 8 pieces.

Per serving: 187 Calories, 7gm Fat, 2gm Protein, 29gm Carbohydrate, 251mg Sodium, 2gm
Fiber; Diabetic Exchanges: 1 Starch, 1 Fruit, 1 Fat

JoAnna Lund, QVC Guest, DeWitt, IA

I created this recipe back in 1992 for my Healthy
Exchanges Food Newsletter, and it's remained my
favorite dessert through the creation of thousands of
recipes since. In fact, someday when I'm stirring up
angel food cake in "Cookbook Heaven," I want my
epitaph to read: "She shared HELP with the rest of
the world, and she created Hawaiian Strawberry Pie!"

—JoAnna Lund

Meet Cliff! This is JoAnna Lund's truck-drivin' husband she is always talking about when she demos her Healthy Exchanges cookbooks.

Coconut-Buttermilk Pie

½ (15-ounce) package
  refrigerator pie crusts
2 cups flaked coconut
½ cup butter, melted
1½ cups sugar
2 tablespoons all-purpose flour

4 eggs, well beaten
½ cup buttermilk
1 teaspoon vanilla extract
1 cup semisweet chocolate
  morsels

Fit one pie crust into a 9-inch pie plate according to package directions; fold edges under and crimp. Cover with plastic wrap and set aside.

Toast coconut on a baking sheet at 350° for 5 minutes or until golden brown, stirring twice. Set aside.

Beat butter, sugar, and flour at medium speed with an electric mixer until blended; add eggs, buttermilk, and vanilla, beating well. Stir in toasted coconut and chocolate morsels. Pour mixture into prepared pie crust.

Bake at 325° for 30 minutes; shield edges of pie crust with foil to prevent excessive browning. Bake 25–30 more minutes, or until set.

Rebecca A. Rogers, Lexington, KY

Silky Peanut Butter Pie

CRUST:

1¼ cups crushed chocolate
  cookies

3 tablespoons sugar
⅓ cup butter, melted

Mix together crushed chocolate cookies and sugar. Add melted butter till mixed together. Pack into bottom and sides of 9-inch springform pan. Bake for 8 minutes at 350°. Remove from oven and cool.

FILLING:

1 (8-ounce) package cream
  cheese, softened
1 cup sugar
1 cup creamy peanut butter

1 tablespoon melted butter
1 teaspoon vanilla
1 cup heavy cream, beaten
  until stiff

Beat cream cheese, sugar, peanut butter, melted butter, and vanilla until creamy. Gently fold in half the beaten cream until blended, then fold in remaining cream. Spread Filling on Crust; smooth top.

TOPPING:

1 cup semisweet chocolate chips   3 tablespoons brewed coffee

Combine chocolate chips and coffee in microwave-safe bowl. Cover with plastic. Microwave on HIGH 1½–2 minutes. Stir until smooth. Cool slightly, then pour over top of Filling.

Refrigerate pie one hour until chocolate is firm, then cover loosely and refrigerate overnight.

Karen Bootz, Sterling Heights, MI

Peanut Butter Crumb Pie

CRUST:

1½ cups graham cracker crumbs
   (about 20, crushed)

2 tablespoons sugar
⅓ cup peanut butter

Mix well; press into a 9-inch pie pan. Bake at 350° for 10 minutes.

FILLING:

1½ cups sugar
⅓ cup cornstarch
½ cup cocoa
½ teaspoon salt

4 egg yolks, slightly beaten
3 cups milk
3 tablespoons peanut butter

Stir together sugar, cornstarch, cocoa, and salt. Blend egg yolks and milk. Gradually add to cocoa mixture. Cook over medium heat, stirring constantly, until mixture thickens and boils. Boil and stir one minute. Remove from heat and add peanut butter. Add to Crust. Chill before serving. If desired, make a meringue from the egg whites.

Evie Reigh, Bellwood, PA

Lite and Easy Chocolate Éclair Pie

Graham crackers
2 (3.4-ounce) boxes French
   vanilla instant pudding
3 cups plus 2 tablespoons skim
   milk, divided

1 (8-ounce) container fat-free
   whipped topping
1 tub milk chocolate frosting

Spray a 9x13x2-inch pan with cooking spray. Layer bottom of pan with graham crackers. In large bowl, mix together pudding and 3 cups milk. Beat until mixture begins to thicken; fold in whipped topping. Spread evenly over graham crackers. Add another layer of graham crackers over pudding mixture. Mix remaining 2 tablespoons milk with chocolate frosting. Spread evenly over top layer of graham crackers. Refrigerate overnight.

Vickie Reed, Nashville, TN

Sky High Chocolate Pie

2 whole eggs and 4 egg yolks
  (save whites)
1½ cups sugar
⅓ cup cocoa
6 tablespoons all-purpose flour

1 (15-ounce) can evaporated milk
10 ounces whole milk
1 tablespoon vanilla
½ cup butter
2 pie shells, baked

Preheat oven to 325°. In a large saucepan, combine eggs and yolks, sugar, cocoa, flour, milks, vanilla, and butter. Cook on medium heat, stirring constantly, until mixture thickens. Pour into pie shells.

MERINGUE:
1 tablespoon cornstarch
⅓ cup cold water
¼ teaspoon cream of tartar

½ cup sugar
4 egg whites (from above)
½ teaspoon vanilla

In a small saucepan, bring cornstarch and water to a simmer. Set aside. Mix cream of tartar and sugar in a small cup, and set aside. Beat the egg whites till peaks form. Beat in sugar mixture one teaspoon at a time. Slowly add vanilla and cornstarch mixture, and beat until stiff peaks form. Spread Meringue on pies. Bake at 325° for 20 minutes; allow to cool. Serves 16.

Charleen Damron, Kodiak, AK

Microwave Easy Chocolate Pie

$\frac{1}{3}$ cup cocoa (or more, to taste)
1–1$\frac{1}{4}$ cups granulated sugar
$\frac{1}{4}$ teaspoon salt
$\frac{1}{3}$ cup cornstarch
3 cups milk (may use low fat
   or whole)

3 tablespoons butter
1$\frac{1}{2}$ teaspoons real vanilla
1 (9- or 10-inch) pie crust, baked
Whipped cream

Combine cocoa, sugar, salt and cornstarch in a medium to large microwave-safe dish. Gradually stir or whisk in milk, until smooth. Microwave on MEDIUM-HIGH (power number 8) for 9–11 minutes, or until desired thickness. Stop after every 3 minutes and stir, for a total of 9 minutes. Continue cooking the additional 2 minutes if needed, or until cooked to your liking. Be sure to stop and stir every 3 minutes (a whisk works great). Add butter and vanilla; stir well. Pour into baked crust. Put a piece of plastic wrap over filling, completely covering it to keep "skin" from forming on surface. Refrigerate until cool. Remove plastic wrap and top with whipped cream or whipped topping.

Deanna Bailey, Duncan, OK

When I developed this recipe for the microwave, I was so excited to not have to stand over a hot stove and stir for 30 minutes or longer. Also, for those who are allergic, it is eggless.

—Deanna Bailey

Creamy Chocolate Chip Pie

40 marshmallows
$^2/_3$ cup milk
1 pint whipping cream

2 squares semisweet chocolate
2 teaspoons vanilla
1 (9-inch) graham cracker crust

Melt marshmallows in milk in large pot over medium heat. Stir till smooth, then chill. Grate chocolate, saving a little to decorate top. Whip cream and fold into chilled marshmallow mixture. Add grated chocolate and vanilla. Pour mixture into crust. Garnish with whipped topping and grated chocolate, if desired. Refrigerate. This pie is better if made the day before serving.

H. Elaine Burns, Brownsburg, IN

Orange Pineapple Cobbler

2 (20-ounce) cans pineapple chunks, drained, reserve juice
1 (11-ounce) can Mandarin oranges, drained, discard juice
2 (3-ounce) boxes orange gelatin

1 (18$^1/_4$-ounce) package pineapple cake mix
1 stick ($^1/_2$ cup) butter or margarine, sliced
1$^1/_2$ cups water

In a greased 9x13-inch glass pan, add the following layer by layer (do not stir). In bottom of pan, empty pineapple chunks and Mandarin oranges. Add 1$^1/_2$ cups reserved pineapple juice. Sprinkle orange gelatin (dry) over pineapple, oranges, and juice. Empty cake mix (dry) over top; dot with sliced butter or margarine. Carefully pour water over top of all layers. DO NOT STIR. Bake at 350º for 1 hour. Cool and serve with whipped cream, cool whip, or ice cream. Serves 15.

Karen Burgess, Charlotte, NC

Crockpot Peach Cobbler

4 (15-ounce) cans sliced or
   diced peaches, undrained
1 stick butter
1½–2 cups sugar to taste

1½ teaspoons ground cinnamon
1 (10-count) can biscuits, baked
   and broken into bite-size pieces

Empty canned peaches into crockpot along with butter, sugar, and cinnamon. Turn on HIGH until butter melts, stirring often. Once butter has melted, add biscuits, stirring to mix well. Turn crockpot to LOW and stir occasionally. Let simmer for 2 hours while flavors blend and biscuits soften. Can be served with vanilla ice cream.

Nancy Cadden Seale, Live Oak, FL

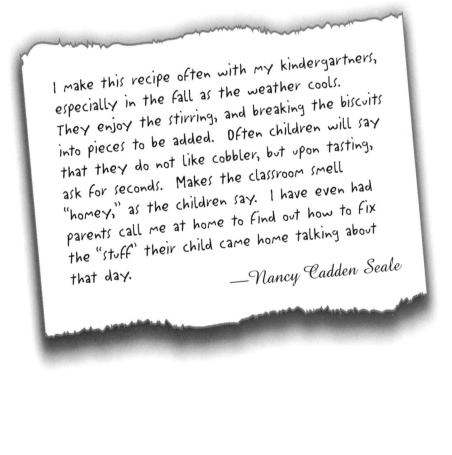

I make this recipe often with my kindergartners, especially in the fall as the weather cools. They enjoy the stirring, and breaking the biscuits into pieces to be added. Often children will say that they do not like cobbler, but upon tasting, ask for seconds. Makes the classroom smell "homey," as the children say. I have even had parents call me at home to find out how to fix the "stuff" their child came home talking about that day.

—Nancy Cadden Seale

Black Forest Cherry Cobbler

3 (15-ounce) cans dark sweet
  cherries (not pie filling)
2 (3-ounce) boxes cherry gelatin
1 (18¼-ounce) package German
  chocolate cake mix

½ cup mini-chocolate chips
1 stick butter or margarine,
  sliced and softened
1½ cups water

In a 9x13-inch pan, empty dark sweet cherries along with syrup from 2 cans. Sprinkle dry cherry gelatin over cherries and syrup; sprinkle dry German chocolate cake mix over top. Sprinkle with chocolate chips. Dot sliced margarine on top; carefully pour water over the top of all layers. DO NOT STIR. Bake at 350° for one hour. Cool and serve with whipped cream, whipped topping, or ice cream. Serves 15.

Karen Burgess, Charlotte, NC

The Berry Best Cobbler

2 cups berries (your choice of
  what is available)
1¾ cups sugar, divided
3 tablespoons butter, softened
1 cup flour, sifted
1 teaspoon baking powder

½ teaspoon salt, divided
½ cup milk
1 tablespoon cornstarch
1 cup boiling water
Whipped cream for topping

Line well-buttered 9x9-inch pan with berries. Cream ¾ cup sugar and butter together. Combine flour, baking powder, and ¼ teaspoon salt. Add milk and flour mixture alternately to butter mixture. Pour over berries. Combine remaining 1 cup sugar, cornstarch, and remaining ¼ teaspoon salt; sprinkle over mixture. Pour boiling water over all (do not mix) and bake at 350° for 1 hour. Serve warm topped with whipped cream.

Linda Skelding, Clearwater, FL

This was my mom's recipe. She was such a
wonderful cook!
—Linda Skelding

Big Sweet Potato Cobbler

BASIC PIE DOUGH:

2 cups all-purpose flour
1 teaspoon salt
1 teaspoon baking powder

²/₃ cup shortening
5 tablespoons ice water

Sift, then measure flour. Resift it with salt and baking powder. Cut shortening into flour mixture with a pastry blender, or work it in with tips of your fingers until grainy like cornmeal. Sprinkle water over dry ingredients and mix together to form a dough ball. (If needed, add additional water to hold ingredients together.) When you can make a ball, stop handling it. Divide dough into 2 slightly uneven parts, keeping smaller one for top crust. (A pastry cloth with roller stocking is highly recommended.)

FILLING:

2 pounds sweet potatoes
1 cup white sugar
¹/₄ cup flour
1 teaspoon nutmeg
1 teaspoon cinnamon
1 teaspoon salt
2 cups water (use water from
   the cooking of the sweet
   potatoes)

1 teaspoon vanilla
1 teaspoon rum extract
1 tablespoon lemon juice
¹/₄ pound butter (1 stick)

Peel potatoes, cut into uniform slices, cover with water, and cook until barely tender (reserve cooking water). Mix all dry ingredients together. Combine all liquid ingredients together. Roll out larger pie crust ball into a rectangle to fit a 9x13-inch pan or baking dish. Place potatoes on top of uncooked bottom crust.

Pour dry ingredients over potatoes and dot with butter. Gently pour liquid over all. Cover with remaining crust. Bake in 400° oven for one hour.

Marta Cofer, Ironton, OH

Apple Twisters

1½ cups flour
1 teaspoon salt
½ cup shortening
4–5 tablespoons plus ½ cup
   water, divided

2 large apples
½ cup butter, melted
¼ cup sugar
¼ cup brown sugar
1 tablespoon cinnamon

In mixing bowl, sift together flour and salt. Cut in shortening until particles are the size of small peas. Sprinkle 4–5 tablespoons water over mixture. Toss lightly with a fork, adding liquid to driest parts, until dough is moistened enough to hold together. Form into a ball and flatten to a ½-inch thickness. Roll out on a floured board to a 10x16-inch rectangle. Cut into 16 strips.

   Peel, core, and slice apples into 8 wedges each. Wrap one strip of dough around each apple wedge. Arrange, not touching, in a greased 9x13x2-inch pan with sides. Brush twisters with melted butter. Combine sugars and cinnamon; sprinkle over buttered twisters. Gently pour remaining ½ cup water evenly over all. Bake in 400° oven 25–30 minutes or until brown. Serve hot or cold. Great with ice cream. Makes 16 twisters.

Tricia Costa, Great Mills, MD

Toasty Angel Dessert

1 loaf angel food cake
½ stick butter, softened
½ cup packed light brown sugar

6 pineapple slices
1 cup dairy sour cream

Preheat broiler to high. Slice angel cake into 6 slices. In a bowl, mix butter with brown sugar. Spread butter/sugar mixture on one side of cake slices and toast under broiler for 1–2 minutes—be careful not to burn. Turn slices over and spread butter/sugar mixture on other side, and again broil. Put on individual serving plates and top each cake slice with a pineapple slice. Cut in half. (I like to cut the round parts of slices to look like angel wings.) Add a dollop of sour cream in the middle and serve.

Carol Olson, Madison, WI

Fresh Fruit Pizza

⅔ cup butter
1 cup flour
3 tablespoons sugar
1 (8-ounce) package cream
  cheese, softened

1 cup powdered sugar
2 cups whipped topping
½ cup slivered almonds
Fresh fruit of choice

Melt butter; add flour and sugar. Spread on lightly greased pizza pan and bake 10 minutes in a 400° oven.

Mix together cream cheese, powdered sugar, and whipped topping. Spread on cooled crust. Sprinkle almonds on top. Finish with a single layer of your favorite fresh fruit. (I use peaches and blueberries.) Cut into slices and serve.

Amiee Bretz, Brighton, MI

Brownie Fruit Pizza

1 (19.8-ounce) box brownie mix
  with nuts
1 egg
¼ cup oil
⅓ cup boiling water
1 (8-ounce) package cream
  cheese, softened
4 tablespoons sugar
1 (8-ounce) container whipped
  topping

2 cups sliced fresh strawberries
2 bananas, sliced
1 (8-ounce) can pineapple
  chunks, drained
1 (11-ounce) can Mandarin
  oranges, drained
1 square chocolate, melted
  (optional)

To brownie mix, add egg, oil, and water, and mix well. Place in 12-inch pizza pan and bake for 15 minutes at 350°. Cool on wire rack.

Mix softened cream cheese and sugar together till smooth; add whipped topping, and mix well. Spread over top of cooled baked brownie. Refrigerate.

Add fruit right before ready to eat. Place strawberries around pizza in a circle, then add bananas in the same way, and pineapple chunks, and Mandarin oranges, till entire brownie is covered with fruit. If desired, drizzle melted chocolate square over fruit. Slice and eat! Yields 10–12 servings.

Carol Caton, Carlisle, OH

Quickie Apple Crunch

1 (21-ounce) can apple pie filling
1 cup sugar
1 cup self-rising flour
1 egg, beaten
Squeeze margarine
Ground cinnamon

Empty pie filling into lightly greased pie plate. In separate bowl, combine sugar, flour, and egg. Mix until crumbly. Sprinkle mixture over top of pie filling. Drizzle with margarine and sprinkle with cinnamon. Bake in 350° oven 35 minutes or until brown.

Pamela Hasibar, Bishopville, SC

All American Trifle

Patriotically delicious!

2 (12-ounce) prepared pound cakes
2 pints strawberries
2 pints blueberries
1 (28-ounce) jar strawberry glaze
½ cup mini-chocolate chips, divided
1 (16- to 24-ounce) container frozen whipped topping, thawed

Cut pound cake into approximately 1-inch cubes. Rinse and dry berries. Put glaze in medium-size bowl; slice strawberries into glaze and stir gently to combine. Save one really nice looking berry to decorate top.

In clear glass trifle dish, put a layer of strawberries, just enough to cover bottom of dish. Add ⅓ of cake pieces (push down slightly), a layer of whipped topping, layer of blueberries, and another layer of strawberries. Then sprinkle with about half the mini-chips (reserve 2 tablespoons to decorate top). Repeat layers, packing slightly. Repeat again if you have room. Finish off top with whipped topping to cover. Add reserved strawberry and sprinkle reserved chips around outside edge. You can even drizzle some of the glaze (without strawberries) on the top. Serves a large group.

Josie Tomars, Scottsdale, AZ

Colossal Caramel Apple Trifle

A very impressive dessert. Delicious and pretty, too!

1 (18¼-ounce) yellow cake mix
4 cups cold milk
2 (3.4-ounce) packages vanilla
    instant pudding mix
½ teaspoon apple pie spice, or
    ½ teaspoon cinnamon and a
    little nutmeg
1 (8-ounce) jar caramel ice
    cream topping, divided

¾ cup chopped pecans, toasted,
    divided
1 (21-ounce) can apple pie filling,
    divided
2 (8-ounce) cartons frozen
    whipped topping, thawed,
    divided

Prepare and bake cake according to package directions, using 2 (8-inch) round pans. Cool cake in pans 8 minutes, then remove to wire racks and cool completely. In a large bowl, whisk milk, pudding, and apple pie spice for 2 minutes. Let stand for 2 minutes.

Cut one cake layer, if necessary, to fit in bottom of punch bowl or large glass bowl. Poke holes in cake with a straw; gradually pour ⅓ caramel over cake. Sprinkle ⅓ pecans on, then ½ pudding. Spoon ½ can pie filling over pudding; spread with 1 carton topping. Top with remaining cake, then repeat layers. After second carton of topping, drizzle with remaining caramel and sprinkle with remaining pecans. Refrigerate until serving.

Susan Ulrich, North Canton, OH

Cookie Trifle Delight

1 (8-ounce) package cream
  cheese, softened
3 (3.4-ounce) packages vanilla
  instant pudding
1 quart whole milk

1 (12-ounce) container whipped
  topping, thawed
1 (20-ounce) package cream-
  filled chocolate sandwich
  cookies, crushed

Combine cream cheese, pudding mix, and milk in large mixing bowl. When mixture begins to set up, fold in whipped topping. In large glass or trifle bowl, place a layer of cookie crumbs then a layer of pudding mix; repeat until all is used, ending with crumbs. Save a dollop of cream mixture and one whole cookie for garnish.

Variation: Add any flavor cookie and food coloring to the cream mixture according to the holiday or occasion.

Chris Pryme, QVC Guest, Dolgeville, NY

In just a snap, Chris Pryme can tell you how to handle your storage problems!

Strawberry Shortcake Trifle

2 cups milk
1 (5-ounce) package vanilla
    instant pudding
1 (14-ounce) can sweetened
    condensed milk
1 (16-ounce) carton whipped
    topping
5 pints strawberries, sliced
1 angel food cake, torn into
    pieces

Mix together milk, pudding, and condensed milk. Refrigerate 30 minutes. Mix in whipped topping. Just before serving, layer or combine with strawberries and angel food cake.

Tonya Harford, Phoenix, AZ

Southern Red Velvet Trifle

1 ($18^1/_4$-ounce) red velvet cake
    mix (substitute buttermilk for
    water)
2 (8-ounce) packages cream
    cheese, softened
4 cups powdered sugar
2 tablespoons heavy cream
1 tablespoon vanilla
2 (12-ounce) containers whipped
    topping
$3/_4$ cup coffee liqueur

Bake and cool cake per box directions, using buttermilk instead of water. Cut cake into cubes. When ready to assemble, beat together cream cheese with the powdered sugar, heavy cream, and vanilla. Fold in whipped topping with spatula. Layer in trifle bowl or pretty cut glass bowl as follows: red velvet cake cubes, drizzles of coffee liqueur, and whipped frosting mixture. Repeat layers. Store in refrigerator. Serves 12.

Susan Cathey, Grapevine, TX

Butter Pecan Trifle

1 (18¼-ounce) box butter
 pecan cake mix
2 (8-ounce) packages cream
 cheese, softened
4 cups powdered sugar

2 tablespoons heavy cream
1 tablespoon vanilla
2 (12-ounce) containers whipped
 topping, thawed
¾ cup rum

Prepare and bake cake mix as directed on box. Cool cake and cut into cubes. When ready to assemble, beat together cream cheese, powdered sugar, heavy cream, and vanilla. Fold in whipped topping with a spatula. In a trifle bowl or pretty cut glass bowl, layer cake cubes, which have been drizzled with rum, and whipped frosting mixture. Repeat Layers. Store in refrigerator. Serves 12.

Susan Cathey, Grapevine, TX

Raspberry Chocolate Chip Mocha Trifle

This recipe is a keeper. A bought pound cake, angel food cake, or ladyfingers works well, too.

2 rounded teaspoons instant
 coffee granules
2 cups hot water
1 white sheet cake
1 (8-ounce) package cream
 cheese, softened

1 (12-ounce) tub whipped
 topping
¾ cup chocolate raspberry
 chips, divided
A few tablespoons milk

Dissolve coffee granules in water and set aside. Cube cake and layer half in a trifle bowl. Pour half the coffee on top of cake pieces to saturate. Mix cream cheese and whipped topping. Fold in ½ cup raspberry chips. Spread half cream cheese mixture over first layer of cake. Repeat layers. Melt remaining ¼ cup chips in microwave. Add milk, stir, and heat up just a little to make a nice glaze. Pour on top. Chill and enjoy!

Jan Marie Albert, Carson City, NV

Strawberry Brownie Dessert

BROWNIE:

¾ cup all-purpose flour
¾ cup cocoa
¼ teaspoon salt
½ cup butter, room temperature

½ cup sugar
½ cup brown sugar, packed
3 eggs
2 teaspoons pure vanilla extract

Combine flour, cocoa, and salt and set aside. In another bowl, beat butter, sugar, and brown sugar until creamy. Add eggs, one at a time, and mix well. Add vanilla. Gradually add flour mixture. Bake 30–35 minutes in a greased pie pan at 350° until center is set. Cool completely.

TOPPING:

¼ cup strawberry-flavored
  yogurt
1 (8-ounce) container frozen
  whipped topping, thawed,
  divided

1 pint strawberries, sliced
  (reserve 8 slices)

In a bowl, mix strawberry yogurt and 6 ounces whipped topping. Fold in sliced strawberries.

   Spread mixture over brownies. Top edge of pie with 8 dollops of whipped topping. Add a strawberry slice to each dollop. Slice in wedges to serve.

Susan Harter, Blakesburg, IA

Dessert Everybody Loves

1 cup flour
1 cup chopped pecans
1 cup sweet butter, softened
1 (8-ounce) package cream
  cheese, softened
1 cup confectioners' sugar

1 (12-ounce) container whipped
  topping, divided
2 (3.4-ounce) packages chocolate
  instant pudding
3 cups milk

Mix flour, nuts, and butter. Press into a 9x13x2-inch pan. Bake at
300° for 15 minutes. Cool.

Mix cream cheese, sugar, and half the whipped topping. Spread
over cooled crust. Mix pudding and milk until thick and creamy.
Spread over cream cheese layer. Top with remaining whipped topping. Garnish with chocolate curls or toasted nuts. Chill.

Merritta Dane, Naples, FL

Editor's Extra: Fun to sprinkle chopped candy bars on top.

Banana Suicide

This is soooo good!

1 (18¼-ounce) box banana
  cake mix
1 (8-ounce) container whipped
  topping
1 (3-ounce) box banana instant
  pudding

1 banana, sliced
1 cup crushed vanilla wafer
  cookies, divided

Bake cake according to package directions in 2 greased and floured
9-inch-round cake pans; let cool. Mix whipped topping with powered banana pudding. Frost bottom layer of cake with whipped
topping mixture, then cover with sliced banana; sprinkle with ½
cup crushed vanilla wafers. Add top layer of cake, then spread
remaining whipped topping mixture over entire cake; sprinkle top
with remaining vanilla wafer crumbs.

Amy Middleton, Flint, MI

Nita's Best Ever Nana Puddin'

1 quart milk
6 tablespoons flour
1½ cups sugar
1½ teaspoons vanilla extract

6 egg yolks, lightly beaten
 (save whites)
6 ripe bananas, sliced, divided
1 box vanilla wafers, divided

Mix first 5 ingredients in a large heavy saucepan, whisking to mix well. Cook over medium heat until just thickened, stirring constantly to prevent sticking to pan. Layer half the bananas, half the vanilla wafers, and half the pudding in a 9x13-inch glass baking dish; repeat layers.

TOPPING:
6 egg whites
Pinch of salt

1 teaspoon vanilla extract
1 cup sugar

Beat egg whites on high speed until soft peaks form. Add salt and vanilla flavoring. Add sugar, 1–2 tablespoons at a time, and cream until very fluffy. Spread over pudding, completely covering it. Broil in oven until golden brown, being very careful not to burn.

Stephanie Hixon, Birmingham, AL

This is a recipe for THE most wonderful banana pudding in the world! According to my step-grandmother, Juanita Chambers, "Mamma was of German descent, but most of her cooking was good old southern cooking." All four of her girls are good cooks. This is the only recipe that we have of hers, and it is treasured.

—Stephanie Hixon

Easy Baklava

1 box phyllo pastry
1 cup butter, melted
1 cup sugar

1 cup chopped walnuts
³/₄ teaspoons cinnamon

Preheat oven to 325°. Cut phyllo pastry in half and trim sides to fit into a 9x13-inch pan. Lay half the pastry on bottom of pan. Mix sugar, nuts, and cinnamon, and spread over bottom layer of phyllo. Cover with remaining half of pastry. Cut into squares or diamonds. Pour butter over top of pastry. Bake at 325° for 50–55 minutes.

GLAZE:
³/₄ cup sugar
¹/₂ cup water

1 teaspoon lemon juice

While baklava is baking, combine in a small saucepan the Glaze ingredients, and bring to a boil. Reduce to consistency of honey and let cool. Drizzle cool Glaze over hot baklava.

Variations: Canned apple or peach pie filling can be substituted for the sugar, nuts, and cinnamon.

Bev Moe, Gwinn, MI

Low-Fat Raisin Bread Custard Pudding

2²/₃ cups skim milk
¹/₄ cup light margarine
Egg substitute (equivalent of
 3 eggs)

¹/₂ cup sugar
1 teaspoon vanilla
¹/₄ teaspoon salt
3 cups raisin bread cubes

Scald milk; add margarine, and allow to cool. Combine eggs and sugar; beat well. Add cooled milk, vanilla, and salt. Place bread cubes in 1¹/₂-quart casserole dish sprayed with cooking spray. Pour egg-milk mixture over bread. Bake at 350° for 45–60 minutes. Let cool a bit. Eat warm or cold.

Deborah Deschenes, Westport, MA

Cappuccino Custards with Buttered Pecan Rum Sauce

CAPPUCCINO CUSTARDS:

4 large eggs
$\frac{1}{2}$ cup granulated sugar
$\frac{1}{2}$ teaspoon salt
$1\frac{1}{2}$ cups evaporated milk
1 tablespoon instant coffee
  crystals

1 cup warm water
1 tablespoon Tahitian or
  Mexican vanilla

Preheat oven to 300°. Combine eggs, sugar, and salt in large mixer bowl. Add evaporated milk. Dissolve coffee into warm water and add vanilla. Pour into the egg/milk mixture; beat until mixed. Pour into 6 (6-ounce) custard cups, sprayed with cooking spray. Place cups in a 9x13-inch baking pan; fill pan with hot water to 1-inch depth.

Bake for 35–40 minutes or until knife inserted near center comes out clean. Remove cups to wire rack to cool completely. Refrigerate until ready to serve.

BUTTERED PECAN RUM SAUCE:

2 tablespoons rum flavor/extract
4 teaspoons butter
1 cup pecan and syrup ice cream
  topping

2 tablespoons corn syrup
$\frac{1}{2}$ cup brown sugar
Whipped cream for garnish

Combine ingredients in a small saucepan and slowly bring to a simmer. Stir 2 minutes, or until brown sugar is dissolved. Set aside.

Run a knife slowly around edge of each custard dish and turn onto a dessert plate. Drizzle with Buttered Pecan Rum Sauce. Garnish with whipped cream, if desired.

Note: These may be served in the ramekins as well.

Leah Lyon, Ada, OK

Easy Mocha Mousse

2 cups heavy whipping cream
1 (3.5-ounce) box chocolate
  instant pudding

1 tablespoon mocha instant
  coffee granules

With an electric mixer, begin whipping cream on medium speed. When it begins to thicken, stop the mixer. Stir in pudding mix and mocha coffee granules with a spatula. When they are sufficiently incorporated, turn mixer back on high and whip all ingredients together. The mousse is finished when it resembles thick chocolate whipped cream. Yields 4–6 servings.

Colleen Lamberty, Syracuse, IN

Chocolate Gelato to Die For

1½ cups milk
½ cup heavy cream
5 ounces good milk chocolate,
  chopped small

½ cup sugar
4 egg yolks
2 teaspoons vanilla

In a saucepan, heat milk and cream to scalding; remove from heat. Add chopped chocolate and stir until completely melted. In a large bowl, whisk sugar with egg yolks until mixture is light and fluffy. Gradually pour hot chocolate mixture into egg mixture, whisking constantly.

Heat mixture in a double boiler over simmering water, stirring constantly with a whisk or wooden spoon, until it thickens enough to coat the back of a spoon. Add vanilla extract and let cool to room temperature. Refrigerate, covered, until completely cold, preferably overnight. Process mixture in an ice cream freezer following manufacturer's instructions. Serve immediately. Yields approximately 3½ cups.

Richard Fiore, Dayton, OH

Island Napoleons

A delightfully light tropical taste . . . it makes a beautiful presentation.

6 ounces cream cheese, softened
1 cup sweetened condensed milk
¼ cup cream of coconut
½ cup Key lime juice, fresh or
 bottled
¼ cup sour cream
1 (17.25 ounce) package frozen
 puff paste, thawed

¾ cup raspberries
¾ cup chopped fresh mango
 (optional)
¼ cup powdered sugar for
 garnish

In a medium bowl, combine cream cheese, condensed milk, and cream of coconut. Beat until mixture is smooth and well combined. Fold in lime juice and sour cream. Cover bowl with plastic wrap and refrigerate until needed.

Line a large baking sheet with a baking mat or parchment paper. On a lightly floured surface, roll each pastry sheet to a 10-inch square. Cut each pastry into 4 (5x5-inch) squares. Transfer to prepared baking sheet. Pierce each pastry all over with tines of a fork. Freeze pastries 10 minutes.

Preheat oven to 375°. Bake until pastries are crisp and golden brown, 17–20 minutes. Remove baking sheet from oven, transfer pastries to a rack, and cool completely.

Place 1 pastry square on each of 8 dessert plates. Make a pocket in each pastry and fill with ⅛ of filling. Spread each portion with 2 tablespoons raspberries and some chopped mango, if desired. Sift powdered sugar over the top of each Napoleon.

Carole Resnick, Cleveland, OH

Pineapple Tarts with Strawberry Fans

1 (1-pound) box frozen puffed
　pastry shells
1 (3-ounce) package cream
　cheese, softened
1 (8-ounce) container whipped
　topping, thawed

1 (8-ounce) can crushed
　pineapple, drained
Powdered sugar

Bake shells according to package directions. Cool and set aside. Whip cream cheese and whipped topping together. Add pineapple. Fill shells with mixture. Sprinkle shells with powdered sugar and, place a Strawberry Fan on top of each. Serve on dessert plates that have been dusted with powdered sugar.

STRAWBERRY FANS:
6 medium-size strawberries

Wash strawberries and dry with a paper towel, leaving stem intact. Lay strawberry on its side on a cutting board and, with a sharp knife, make ⅛-inch slices across the strawberry about ⅔ of the way up to the stem. Gently press until the strawberry "fans" out. Serves 6.

Janet Venditti, Pittsburgh, PA

Mystery Strawberry Shortcake

Nobody can guess what's in it! Best made with fresh strawberries.

2 sleeves saltine crackers
2 quarts sugared strawberries

Whipped topping

Start by layering crackers in a 12x12-inch pan. Make one layer of crackers, then one layer of strawberries; continue layering until you finish with a layer of strawberries. Let soak overnight in refrigerator. Serve with whipped topping.

Lois Ann Rodenbaugh, Collinsville, IL

Editor's Extra: We were skeptical when we read this . . . till we tried it. This is a truly tasty "make-do" recipe.

This is Heaven!

1 (8-ounce) package thin
  chocolate wafers
¼ cup margarine, melted
½ cup chopped walnuts
1 cup milk

1 (10½-ounce) package
  mini-marshmallows
1 pint whipping cream
1 teaspoon vanilla

Crush chocolate wafers finely. Mix wafers with melted margarine and walnuts. Spread ½ of mixture in a 9x13-inch dish. Scald milk; remove from heat, dump marshmallows in milk, and stir until melted. Cool 10 minutes.

Whip cream. Fold whipped cream into cooled marshmallow mixture, add vanilla, then pour over cookie layer. Top this with other ½ of cookie mixture. Cover with plastic wrap and put in fridge overnight. This is definitely heaven!

Debbie Douglas, Prescott, AZ

Black Forest Dessert

Don't let the lite ingredients fool you—this dessert is out-of-this-world fabulous!

½ cup margarine
1 cup water
1 cup flour
4 eggs, slightly beaten
1 (3-ounce) package sugar-free
  white chocolate instant pudding
1¾ cups skim milk
1 (8-ounce) package fat-free
  cream cheese, softened

1 (8-ounce) container fat-free
  whipped topping
25 reduced-fat cream-filled
  chocolate cookies, crushed
½ (21-ounce) can lite cherry
  pie filling

Melt margarine in pan. Add water and bring to full boil. Remove from heat and stir in flour. Cool slightly. Beat in eggs. Mix until it forms a ball. Spread in a greased 9x13-inch pan, and bake 30 minutes at 400°. Allow to cool. (It will puff up and fall.)

Mix pudding and milk according to directions. Beat cream cheese; slowly mix in pudding until smooth. Fold in whipped topping. Sprinkle cookie crumbs over crust. Pour pudding mixture on top. Drop pie filling over top of pudding. Refrigerate. Serves 12–15.

Susan L. Anderson, Fort Madison, IA

Black Forest Moo Cow Sundae Bar Dessert

12 ice cream sandwiches
   (vanilla/chocolate)
1 (21-ounce) can cherry pie filling
1 (8- or 12-ounce) tub whipped
   topping, divided

1 (7-ounce) bottle quick-
   hardening ice cream topping

Lay sandwiches (about 6) in a 9x13-inch glass pan to fit one layer. Spoon pie filling over sandwiches (save 3 tablespoons for garnish). Spoon half of whipped topping over pie filling to cover. Lay remaining sandwiches over topping. Cover sandwiches with remaining whipped topping (adjust amount to suit your taste). Drizzle ice cream shell topping over all. Freeze for one hour. Garnish with whipped cream and reserved cherries. Mmmmm!

M. Conrad, Fort Smith, AR

Crusty Fried Ice Cream

Ice cream, any flavor
Thin-sliced white bread
Vegetable oil for frying

Cinnamon (optional)
Fudge sauce

Scoop large balls of ice cream onto wax-paper-lined pan. Refreeze at least an hour. Cut crust from bread; wrap two slices around ice cream balls with corners meeting, and seal with hands so that ice cream is completely covered. Wipe away any excess ice cream. Re-freeze overnight on same pan.

   In large deep pan, heat oil (deep enough to cover entire ball) to 365° (use thermometer). Dip frozen balls into hot grease and deep-fry quickly (about 15 seconds), turning often with a big slotted spoon. Roll in cinnamon, if desired. Serve immediately with hot fudge sauce on top.

Heather Creel, Franklin, TN

Mom's Chocolate Malted Milk Candy Bar Ice Cream

5 chocolate malted milk
  candy bars
½ gallon whole milk
5–6 eggs
1¼ cups sugar
2 tablespoons cornstarch

½ teaspoon salt
1 (14-ounce) can sweetened
  condensed milk
1 (12-ounce) can evaporated
  milk
1 tablespoon real vanilla extract

Cut up candy bars. Heat milk, stirring constantly; add candy bars to hot milk and simmer until melted, stirring constantly. Beat eggs until fluffy; add sugar mixed with cornstarch and salt, to eggs and beat again. Add egg mixture to milk/candy bar mixture, and cook, stirring constantly, until cream coats spoon. Add condensed milk, evaporated milk, and vanilla. Let cool. Pour into ice cream freezer and add milk, if necessary. Crank (or plug it in) until frozen.

Bruce Kolb, New York, NY

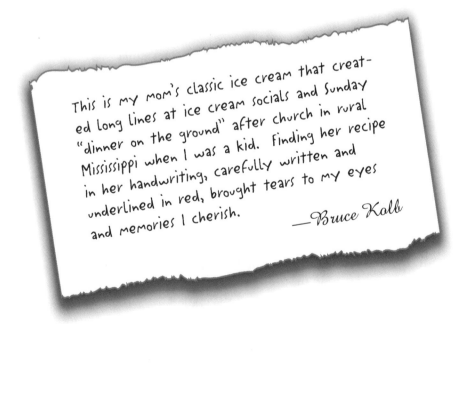

This is my mom's classic ice cream that created long lines at ice cream socials and Sunday "dinner on the ground" after church in rural Mississippi when I was a kid. Finding her recipe in her handwriting, carefully written and underlined in red, brought tears to my eyes and memories I cherish.

—Bruce Kolb

Mmmmm Hot Fudge Sauce

1 (12-ounce) package semisweet chocolate chips
2 sticks butter or margarine
1 (1-pound) box powdered sugar, divided

1 (12-ounce) can evaporated milk, divided
1 teaspoon vanilla

In a large bowl, melt butter or margarine and chocolate chips in the microwave. Add half the powdered sugar, and beat with mixer to get rid of lumps. Mix in half the evaporated milk, then add remaining powdered sugar and evaporated milk alternately, mixing thoroughly. Microwave 4–6 minutes, or until mixture starts to boil. Stir in vanilla. Let cool slightly (it thickens) before serving.

Cora Ennis, Columbia, MO

Coffee Ice Cream Cookie Freeze

This is insanely delicious!

½ gallon coffee ice cream, softened
1 cup chopped pecans, toasted, divided
28 chocolate sandwich cookies
¼ cup butter, melted
1 cup sugar

1 (5-ounce) can evaporated milk
1 teaspoon vanilla
4 (1-ounce) squares semisweet chocolate
6 tablespoons butter
1 (12-ounce) container frozen whipped topping, softened

While ice cream is softening, toast pecans sprayed with small amount of butter in a 350° oven about 5 minutes. Set aside. Crush cookies fine and mix with melted butter. Spread in bottom of a 9x13-inch pan and put in freezer to set, about 20 minutes.

Spread softened ice cream on top of cookie mixture. Put back in freezer to harden. Mix together sugar, milk, vanilla, chocolate, and 6 tablespoons butter. Boil 1 minute; cool. When cool, pour over ice cream layer and refreeze.

Mix whipped topping with half the cooled toasted pecans; spread over chocolate layer and refreeze. Top with remaining chopped pecans. Keep frozen at all times. Cut into squares to serve.

Judy Wilson, Seneca Falls, NY

List of
Contributors

A

Abernathy, Pat
Adcock, Anita
Adriaansen, Carolyn
Albert, Jan Marie
Alexander, Lucinda
Alexander, Shawn
Anderson, Susan L.
Anderton, Dannie
Anderton, Scott
Angerman, Nan
Ash, Kristina

B

Backus, Lalee
Bailey, Brenda
Bailey, Deanna
Barndt, Diane
Barnette, Leslie
Batty, Colleen
Baxter, Rosanne
Beaney, Wendy
Bell, Linda
Bell, Wendy
Bendinelli, Krista
Birtic, Carol
Bock, Dorothy
Boman, Ilene
Bootz, Karen
Born, Jean
Bower, Paula
Boyd, Robin
Brackett, Sarah
Bradshaw, Gail
Brady, Jim
Branch, Kelly Ann
Brenneman, Sharon
Bretz, Amiee
Brewster, Bob
Brumbaugh, Annette
Burgess, Karen
Burnham, Melinda
Burns, Billie
Burns, H. Elaine

C

Calkins, Tammy
Campbell, Christy
Campbell, Queenie
Cangialosi, Nancy
Cantrell, Virginia
Carter, Susan
Casto, Linda
Cathey, Susan
Caton, Carol
Caylor, Nita
Churchill, Jill
Cipollone, Yvonne
Clapp, Jane F.
Clark, Brenda
Cofer, Marta
Collins, Stephen
Compton, Kathy
Connelly, Cindy
Conrad, M
Cornelison, Kimberly
Costa, Tricia
Cotronea, Patty
Courtney, Jackie
Creel, Heather
Crocetto, Debbie
Cuffel, Mckall

D

Dafoe, Cynthia
Damron, Charleen
Dane, Merritta
Daniel, Cindy
Davis, Bonnie
Dawkins, Carroll
Dean, Debbie
DeFeo, Janet
Delduce, Karen
DeMyer-Nemser, Sharon
Deschenes, Deborah
Diehl, Jan
Dodge, Kimberly
Doshier, Karen
Douglas, Debbie
Downs-Ash, Linda
Dulovich, Ruthann
Dunagin, La Rue
Duynslager, Gretchen
Dyer, Norma

E

Early, Connie
Early, Val
East, Pamela
Eby, Jennifer
Edwards, Jen
Ennis, Cora
Etzler, Carolyn
Evans, Lori

F

Farrell, Kim
Ferguson, Vivian
Fiore, Richard
Fixx, Alice Kasman
Flynn, Doris
Flynt, Lisa
Fondren, Paula
Ford, Karen
Friday, Sara
Fuselier, Mable

G

Gadsby, Edwina
Gaskill, Allison "Judy"
Gerads, Janine
Gerber, Tracy
Gibson, Melanie
Gioia, Jill
Girard, Sherry
Glass, Rhonda
Golankiewicz, Natalie Leon
Goodson, Marilyn
Grant, Carol
Granthum, Theresa
Grassie, Linda
Graupman, Margo
Graville, Gina

H

Hammond, Terri
Hamric, Julie
Harbour, Jennifer
Harden, Lisa
Harford, Tonya
Harmon, Patricia
Harris, Kitty
Harrison, Brenda
Harrison, Kathy
Harter, Susan
Hasibar, Pamela
Haywood, Karen
Heck, Dorothy
Heckman, Linda
Hendley, Joyce
Hess-Layne, Linda
Hill, Valerie Parr
Hixon, Stephanie

Holovka, Suzanne
Hooker-Leep, Kari
Houghton, June
Howell, Donna
Hutcherson, Donna

I

Ignatius, Mary Ellen
Ives, Jean

J

Jablon, Moira
Jaksons, Dawn
Jefferson, Barbara
Jenick, Julie A.
Jensen, June
Johnson, Pat
Jolly, Becky
Jones, Cynthia
Jordan, Cynthia
Juratovac, Arlene
Juris, Glenda

K

Kaiser, Alberta Lee
Kasle, Donna
Kasman, Helen
Keating, Laura
Kelly, Dana
Kenning, Merilee
Kier, Marie Louise
Kitterman, Cheryl
Knowles, Diane L.
Kolb, Bruce
Korthals, Carrie
Kortjohn, Sandra
Kratochwil, Penny
Krolikowski, Dianne
Kvetkosky, Carol

L

LaBrake, Lisa
LaFon, Sarah
Laino, Judith
Lamas, Sandy
Lamb, James
Lamberty, Colleen
Landrum, Kathie
Lariscy, Janet
Lehman, Linda

Lemieur, Lisa
Lichtenberg, John
Lloyd, Doris M.
Logan, Belinda
Lollar, Larry
Lund, Joanna
Lyon, Leah

M

Maldonado, Tammy
Marano, Irene
Marcotte, Lisa
Markowitz, Hayden
Marsh, Sally
Martin, Bethany
Martin, Joyce
Maslowski, Linda
Mason, Barbara Ann
Massey, Heather
Maulding, Meg
McAlvey, Jan
McFarland, Dorothy (Dottie)
McGhee, Connie
McGovern, Margaret
McKinney, Tina
McLean, Nona
McRae, Cheryl
McRoy, Leigh Ann
Mendoza, Christina
Menzel, Shelley Joy
Meredith, Katie Sue
Michael, Todd
Middleton, Amy
Miller, Amy
Minchew, Katy B.
Minnetti, Robyn
Mirando, Sandra
Misilli, MarkCharles
Missel, Kathy
Mitchell, Diane
Mitchell, Marie
Mize, Amanda
Moe, Bev
Molczyk, Karin
Monahan, Retta
Montgomery, Margret
Moretzsohn, Chris
Morgan, Tab
Morreale, Debbie
Morris, June
Morrow, Rosemary
Moseley, Trey

Murray, Betty

N

Naron, Sherry
Negro, Frank
Ngo, April

O

Oakley, Faith
Oestreicher, Marilyn
Olson, Carol
Olson, Charlene
Organ, Misty
Orr, Gloria
Ortiguerra, Michele

P

Palmer-Poirier, Cynthia
Parslow, Janet
Parsons, Sharon
Peek, JoAnn
Pettee, Debbie
Pidgeon, Sandie
Pieczonka, Judy
Pin, Mary
Pittman, Brenda
Plitt, Margaret
Plowman, Kay
Pollitt, Pamela
Pope, Melanie
Porter, Beverly
Powell, Darlene
Pryme, Chris

R

Rauzin, Allicin
Ray, Clarence
Reed, Diane
Reed, Vickie
Rees, June
Reigh, Evie
Resnick, Carole
Reynolds, Kay
Reynolds, Noreen
Richardson, Becki
Robertson, Debbie
Rodenbaugh, Lois Ann
Roetzel, Janet
Rogers, Rebecca A.

S

Saracusa, Karen
Schmidt, Paula
Schneider, Dean
Schwartz, Howard
Seale, Nancy
Seaman, Linda
Seay, Carol
Sedani, Leanne
Segneri, Nicole
Sheeley, Nedra
Shepherd, Hilda
Sherman, Barbara
Shigekawa, Marietta
Sickel, Denise
Siefert, Jan
Sikorski, Chris
Skelding, Linda
Sliwoski, Joni
Smith, Norma
Smith, Peggy
Snyder, Chris
Soteriou, Sue
Sowards, Cheryl
Spencer, Kristin
Staker, Karen
Steinman, Jeanie
Stevens, Robin
Stewart, Kristin
Stohr, Victoria
Strasser, Lisa
Strecker, Jody
Stringer, Sonja
Stroschin, Jane

Stuhr, Connie
Svasek, Marlene
Swaffield, Kathleen
Swanson, Rita
Swilling, Judi

T

Taylor, Lottie
Teraberry, Amy
Thibodeaux, Tonia
Thom, LeAnn
Thomas, Barbara
Thompson, Eileen
Tieman, Teresa
Timmons, Joel
Todd, Deirdre
Tomars, Josie
Tosten, Karen
Trackey, Janet
Tredici, Anne
Tylus, Sheila

U

Ulrich, Susan
Umbriac, Marie

V

Varnell, Terri
Venditti, Janet
Voorhees, Sharon

W

Wagner, Faith-Anne
Wagner, Lori

Ward, LaVern
Warth, Terri
Watkins, Nicole
Weber, Thomasine
Wedgeworth, Debbie
Weiner, Pamela
Wetmore, Ruth
Williams, Elizabeth
Williams, Kay
Williams, Kelly
Williams, Mika
Williams, Reece
Wilson, Judy
Wimer, Sarah
Wobby, Paula
Wood, Glenda
Wright, Betty Lou
Wright, Norma
Wuestman, Penny

X

Xanthakis, Denise

Y

Yablon, Deborah
Yanagisako, Wilma
Younkins, Sharon A.

Z

Zonio, Donna

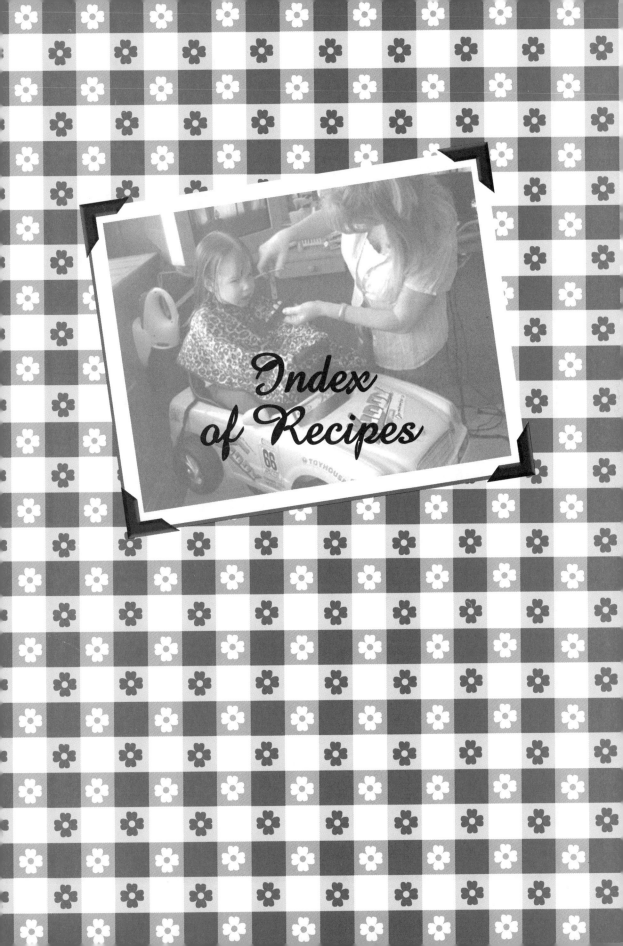

Index
of Recipes